Democratic Drain

Democratic Drain links two of the most compelling topics of our time: immigration and democracy. With a blend of in-depth interviews and data analysis across 149 countries, Justin Gest explores how global migration filters people with liberal democratic values out of authoritarian spaces, enabling democratic backsliding around the world. At a global scale, the correlation between migratory choices and political values introduces a new reason why authoritarian countries may have struggled to democratize in the decades since the end of the Cold War – a period when flows of international migrants have grown so significantly, populism has spread, and authoritarians' resolve has steadily hardened. At a time when the world is increasingly sorting into democratic and undemocratic spaces, Gest's timely and innovative analysis raises important political and policy questions about how democracies might compensate for the inadvertent effects of global human mobility.

Justin Gest is Professor of Policy and Government and Director of the Public Policy Program at George Mason University's Schar School of Policy and Government. He is the award-winning author of seven books and a regular news commentator on immigration and the politics of demographic change.

Democratic Drain

Global Migration and the Struggle for Democracy

JUSTIN GEST

George Mason University

CAMBRIDGE
UNIVERSITY PRESS

CAMBRIDGE
UNIVERSITY PRESS

Shaftesbury Road, Cambridge CB2 8EA, United Kingdom

One Liberty Plaza, 20th Floor, New York, NY 10006, USA

477 Williamstown Road, Port Melbourne, VIC 3207, Australia

314–321, 3rd Floor, Plot 3, Splendor Forum, Jasola District Centre,
New Delhi – 110025, India

Cambridge University Press is part of Cambridge University Press & Assessment,
a department of the University of Cambridge.

We share the University's mission to contribute to society through the pursuit of
education, learning and research at the highest international levels of excellence.

www.cambridge.org
Information on this title: www.cambridge.org/9781009726917
DOI: 10.1017/9781009726924

First published 2026

A catalogue record for this publication is available from the British Library

Library of Congress Cataloging-in-Publication Data
NAMES: Gest, Justin author
TITLE: Democratic drain : global migration and the struggle for democracy /
Justin Gest, George Mason University, Virginia.
DESCRIPTION: Cambridge ; New York, NY : Cambridge University Press, 2026. |
Includes bibliographical references.
IDENTIFIERS: LCCN 2025034654 | ISBN 9781009726917 hardback |
ISBN 9781009726924 ebook
SUBJECTS: LCSH: Emigration and immigration – Political aspects | Democracy
Classification: LCC JV6255 .G476 2026
LC record available at https://lccn.loc.gov/2025034654

ISBN 978-1-009-72691-7 Hardback

Contents

Figures

Tables

Preface

"Do you have a spare bedroom in Madrid?"

"Probably a good time to have left the country."

"Maybe I'll come join you over there."

As I awoke in the bedroom of my Spanish sabbatical flat the morning of November 6, 2024, the text messages from American friends and colleagues had already accumulated.

Donald Trump just won the 2024 presidential election. He would return to the White House despite his refusal to accept the results of the 2020 presidential election and his public promises to pardon insurgents who attacked the US Capitol, to prosecute his rivals, to use regulatory powers to force political loyalty, and to deploy the military to quash dissent.

These were messages sent by established professionals – people with families, people with a promising future in the United States. Surely, they were jokes, an extension of the refrain that wealthier Americans had uttered many times before: "If Trump wins again, I'm moving to Canada." Privileged people kidding around.

But according to Google,[1] internet searches for "move to Canada" surged twelvefold in the twenty-four hours after polls closed on election day. Similar searches about moving to New Zealand climbed nearly twentyfold, while those for Australia jumped eightfold. In the post-election period, more than one in five US residents, 22 percent, said they were more likely to move out of their home. Of those who said they were suddenly more likely to move, 36 percent said the election results inspired them to consider a different country.[2] After broad research funding cuts in the opening days of the second Trump administration,

American scientists submitted 32 percent more job applications to foreign institutions in the first quarter of 2025 than during the same period the year before.[3] According to the UK Home Office, a record number of Americans applied for British citizenship during the same period.[4] Visa services firms reported heightened interest in countries such as Germany, Ireland, and Scandinavian countries – all stable, liberal democracies, much like Spain.

Some of the people behind the searches were merely curious. However, according to the research I present in this book, many were likely to be as serious as the implications of Trump's reelection for the future of American democracy.

As I will show, the consequences associated with their departures would be grave. When people with liberal democratic values depart, it depletes the society they leave behind of precisely the individuals required to advocate for the protection of liberal democratic institutions in the future – a sorting effect that enables authoritarian politics thereafter. Much like "brain drain," where the departure of emigrants from the Global South depletes those countries of skilled and entrepreneurial workers, "Democratic Drain" depletes societies of citizens with liberal democratic values.

In the pages that follow, I explore the mechanics behind this phenomenon with interviews, fieldwork, and public opinion data in 149 countries worldwide. Across different regions and political environments, I find that prospective migrants hold less authoritarian and more democratic political preferences than their countrymen. While the differences between prospective migrants and their countrymen are sometimes marginal, the effect is exponentially amplified when every year about nine million people move to a country that is substantially more democratic than their country of origin.

I also discover that prospective migrants are latently drawn to democracies that reflect the political and civic values they embrace. Far beyond the United States, I find that people's interest in emigrating spikes in the immediate aftermath of elections, particularly those which have the effect of weakening democratic institutions in the years thereafter – an effect that is concentrated among people who report expectations of democratic institutional integrity.

The concept of Democratic Drain is a versatile one and may also be used to describe sorting effects according to social and political values anywhere. Indeed, North America and Europe have likely experienced a pervasive Democratic Drain at the regional level as liberals and progressives have been observed to gravitate toward more tolerant, cosmopolitan, and higher-educated urban centers, while people with more authoritarian values remain in the hinterlands.[5] In more federalist countries like the United States, where power is devolved to regional governments, it is also reasonable to expect Democratic Drain to take place across states and provinces.[6] However, this book is squarely concerned with such sorting as it takes place across borders, and the way international mobility alters, and is altered by, national political development.

Unlike countries like Hungary or Ecuador, Serbia or the Philippines, the threats associated with authoritarianism are relatively new to the United States, which possesses an independent judiciary and robust civil society organizations better positioned to constrain authoritarian power grabs than the institutions of weaker, less established democracies. And so America's liberal democratic infrastructure may be just as likely to stiffen as it is likely to crumble in the face of this test.

My findings raise the stakes by identifying a lurking demographic phenomenon that, if triggered, would enable further authoritarian developments in the world's longest standing democracy – and in many other countries subject to democratic backsliding, too.

Acknowledgments

From its conception to publication, this book required a decade to prepare, and I could not have completed my work without a lot of help and goodwill from friends, colleagues, and several institutions.

In all, this book assembles information about the perspectives, plans, and political behavior as reported by nearly one million people to thousands of pollsters and, in numerous cases, to me personally. So first let me thank my respondents for taking the time to speak with all of us. In particular, I especially appreciate the courage of the democratic dissidents, activists, and public officials that I interviewed while they were in exile. Thank you for your trust at a time when you had reasons to fear for your life and the lives of your families. Even at your weakest, you displayed such strength.

Once my various data sets were assembled, I leaned on several dear colleagues for help with data analysis. My deepest thanks to Jeremy Ferwerda, Lucas Núñez, and Tyler Reny – my longtime co-authors and longtime friends. This book is theirs, too.

At the very beginning of this study, I was aided by guidance and support from my colleagues Heba El-Shazli and Rich Nielsen, and mentors like Jack Goldstone, David Held, Peter Mandaville, and Henrietta Moore. Early on, I also received valuable advice from scholars like Fiona Adamson, Katrina Burgess, Daphne Halikiopoulou, Maria Koinova, and Gerasimos Tsourapas.

Once I developed the concept, my research was made possible thanks to a series of polling partnerships with the International Republican Institute (IRI). Thank you, Scott Mastic, for your vision, leadership, and friendship. Among IRI's executives and directors, I am thankful for the support of Kimber Shearer, Jan Surotchak, Paul McCarthy, Sonja Gloeckle, and Judy Van Rest. In the field, I was aided by members of IRI's professional staff and their collaborators, including Jenna Consigli, Lisa Cresce, Ramsey Day, Pavol Holec, Daniel Kaddik, Andrea Keerbs, Owen Kirby, Jacob Moroza-Rasmussen, Thibault Muzergues, Annika Parks, Alex Tarascio, Ilja Vojnovic, Luke Waggoner, and Ipsos' Mathieu Gallard. Lamentably, before this book was completed, IRI became the victim of the very democratic backsliding this book examines. I hope my work can serve as one of many testaments to the profound impact and virtue of democracy promotion in all its forms.

The book's global scope is thanks to a partnership with Gallup, Inc., which has long valued academic scholarship and remains an exemplar of evidence-based analysis. At Gallup, I thank Gale Muller, Rachel Penrod, Emily Miller, and Mohamed Younis, but particularly Jon Clifton for his insatiable curiosity, his open mind, and his friendship.

In the Middle East, I'd like to thank Bassam Al-Kuwatli, Nader Said, Samer Said, and Mayss Al Zoubi for their hard work to facilitate my research in very unstable conditions. Thank you to Hangyoung Lee for his assistance with my studies of social networks.

In the field, my interviews would not have been possible without the impeccable facilitation of Blanka Szilasi in Budapest, and Nemanja Stanimirovic and Zhanel Sabit in Belgrade. Thank you for your diligence, hard work, and versatility as translators, fixers, and research assistants. During my fieldwork, I was also supported by Szabolcs Pogonyi in Budapest and Belgrade, Irem Güney and Ole Frahm in Istanbul, and György, Tatjana, George, and Ádám Hargitai in Budapest.

At George Mason University, I was backed by a group of top academic professionals who offered excellent administrative support. Mark Rozell generously approved my study leave application and has championed my scholarship since my first day on campus. Holly Park, Naoru Koizumi, Eileen Gallagher, Julie Hudson, Andrea Taylor, and Syed Azam Salauddin meticulously managed my research finances and contracts. And sincere thanks to my extraordinary team of George Mason University research assistants: Tim O'Shea, Sally Kishi, Jena Musmar, and Nathan Stolzenfeld.

Down the home stretch, I received support from the Institute for Humane Studies (IHS) and the Aspen Institute España that was indispensable. At IHS, my deep thanks to Jeanne Hoffman, Stephen McAndrew, Ashley Nikkel, Maria Rogacheva, and Emily Chamlee-Wright for supporting my study leave and for an immensely valuable book manuscript workshop. At Aspen, thank you to José María De Areilza, Santiago Liniers, Irene Olombrada, and Gabriela Aznar for welcoming me as a fellow and facilitating a separate and equally impactful book manuscript workshop. During these workshops, I received brilliant feedback from Berta Álvarez Miranda, Sheri Berman, Michael Clemens, Katharine Donato, Anna Grzymala-Busse, Christian Joppke, Dana Moss, Eva Østergaard Nielsen, Ignacio Sánchez-Cuenca, Niloufer Sidiqui, Murat Somer, and Vicente Valentim.

In bringing this book to market, I'd like to thank Robert Dreesen and Rachel Blaifeder at Cambridge University Press for recognizing the promise of my research and ensuring its successful publication so deftly. I also thank Swati Kumari, Claire Sissen, and Edward Street for their careful editing and preparation of the manuscript in the production process. In promoting and publicizing my research and ideas, I would also like to thank Megan Posco, Nancy Aaronson, Alex Reeves, and Kristie De Peña. And special thanks to the family of Marc Chagall for the honor of placing his enchanting artwork on the book cover. In conveying his own journey, he commemorated the journeys of millions of others – including my ancestors – who emigrated thereafter in search of freedom, opportunity, and peace.

Finally, I am sincerely thankful for the love of my parents, Max and Gail, my wife Monika, and our children Valentina and Hugo. I suppose the phenomenon of Democratic Drain indirectly brought us all together. If the world really is one big sort, I feel so blessed to have somehow wound up with you.

I

Democratic Drain

Nikolai Kirilov is not the face of global democratic activism. His passion is music.

Slender, with thin blonde hair and serious gray eyes, the forty-year-old Russian is a professional violinist who plays for St. Petersburg's Capella Orchestra. During the day, he works for the Symphony Orchestra of the State Academy of St. Petersburg. He believes in the virtues of democratic governance and political freedom, but has never considered himself a "politically active" citizen.

"I don't want to be interested in politics," he says. "But it's impossible in Russia. We have to dig around to look for the truth; propaganda is everywhere."

Russia's lack of transparency and freedom of speech irks him and he had wild daydreams of leaving the country when the Russian government, under false pretenses, launched a full-scale military invasion of Georgia in 2008 and forcibly seized Crimea and the Donbas region from Ukraine in 2014. But he could not leave his friends and family behind.

Once, Nikolai traveled to Nizhny Novgorod in Central Russia to protest when Russian Orthodox clergy confiscated land from a local university to build a new cathedral – part of the Church's nationwide push to acquire public spaces in Russia since around 2010.[1] He was not injured during the demonstrations, but he witnessed police officers brutally beating a nonviolent woman who was marching alongside him.

Nikolai has stayed off the streets since then, even after Russian President Vladimir Putin invaded Ukraine on February 24, 2022. His mother was born in Ukraine and her side of the family still lives there, but he has learned to avoid public defiance. The day after the outbreak of war, however, Nikolai was chatting privately with colleagues during their lunch break at the Academy, when he shared that he was against the war. It was a casual chat and everyone returned to their work shortly after.

But three days later, on March 1, he was summoned to the director's office.

"The Academy is a state organization," Nikolai said he was told, "and if you are against the special operation, then you are against the state. We don't have any laws under which we can fire you. But if you don't leave, I'll turn your life into a nightmare."

After being coerced into writing a letter of resignation, Nikolai returned to his apartment, placed his violin and some clothes into a bag, and boarded a flight to Belgrade, Serbia – the only major European city accepting Russian flights after the invasion of Ukraine.

When I interviewed Nikolai over coffee at the Kafe Moskva in Central Belgrade, he recounted his dream to play in an orchestra again and study classical music in Vienna.

His face gaunt, he peered longingly toward the entrance where a suited pianist slowly, reverently played Tchaikovsky's *Swan Lake* under a brushed gold chandelier. Each note resonated against the large glass windows and art deco molding, above the din of the salon's guests in their red velvet chairs. Many of them had politics on their minds.

BELGRADE

Outside Kafe Moskva (Figure 1.1), the unfolding, undulating melody escaped the revolving door to its sunlit patio, where Ivana Dumanić sat overlooking the Terazijska Fountain – a rare moment of solace in what had been a turbulent week for her.

Ivana is not an icon of democratic activism either. A mother of three, the forty-year-old freelance forestry engineer with curly orange hair had packed the family's belongings into bags and boxes that now filled her living room in the Vračar municipality of Belgrade. She was moving to Rijeka, Croatia, to reunite with her husband after Serbia's president, Aleksandar Vučić, had been reelected eight days before.

A former prime minister who served as information minister in 1998 under the genocidal strongman Slobodan Milosevic, Vučić has nudged Serbia toward increasingly autocratic rule. International watchdogs and opposition parties regularly accuse his government of extensive

FIGURE I.I Hotel Moskva, Belgrade, Serbia.

corruption, nepotism, media control, attacks on political opponents, and ties with organized crime.[2] Still, he won a second term and his party won a parliamentary majority by a landslide on April 3, 2022 in what Ivana calls "a diagnosis" of her country's state.

"There will be no amelioration," she said, unzipping her vermillion coat. "I love my country but I have no more reasons [to stay]. I do not want my children to live like me, to grow up at protests … I want a better life, where you don't need personal connections to go to the doctor's office or to get a job in one's own field of expertise … I had hoped earlier, hoped that it would get better, hoped for a change, for an enlightenment. But it didn't happen," she said with finality. "And that's it."

Ivana's husband previously ran a company that provided emergency plumbing repairs to public institutions. He was hired by the city of Belgrade while Dragan Đilas, now the country's liberal opposition leader, was mayor. Her husband won the contract without being a member of Đilas' party, without even voting for him.

"It wasn't much money but it was all clean, transparent," Ivana explained. "Then came [Vučić and] the Serbian Progressive Party [SNS], and it wasn't like that anymore. [Our municipality] now has its own contractor who is politically appointed and who chooses people close to him [for subcontracting]. It is just a terrible grabbing of money, constant blackmail."

"'If you don't give us a cut, you're not getting any,'" she impersonated. "It is humiliating. There was constant nudging to join the party in order to get a better deal. They asked us to get them a list of 50 'secure' votes for SNS. 'You are working for *us!*,'" she mimicked them again, pointing at her chest emphatically. "We were not working for Vračar municipality anymore, but for SNS."

Ivana and her husband decided to cancel their subcontract.

"We went to live with my parents. It wasn't suitable housing, but we didn't have money to rent an apartment because we lost [all our business]. Then, we decided that we are starting over. The children may eat slightly lower quality food, but we will not be humiliated."

At that moment, Ivana and her husband resolved that he would go abroad until Serbian politics changed. He eventually found work with an energy company in Hungary and has resided there ever since. Ivana has shuttled between Belgrade and Budapest for years, but the family ultimately resolved to move to Croatia.

"Hungary was a bit fascist toward foreigners," she said.

As in Serbia that week, it was suddenly clear that Hungary was not going to change either.

BUDAPEST

The day that Serbian voters returned Vučić to power, Hungarians reelected their Prime Minister Viktor Orbán and his Fidesz Party to a fourth consecutive four-year term in government.

Like Vučić, Orbán had been criticized for democratic backsliding due to reforms that undercut the integrity of Hungary's elections, judiciary, universities, and press. For related reasons, Orbán's Fidesz Party defiantly left the European Parliament's center-right European People's Party (EPP) in March 2021 after fellow EPP members suspended them two years before. Many Hungarians were wary of Orbán's proximity to the Kremlin after the Russian invasion of Ukraine, just beyond Hungary's eastern border. But Orbán capitalized on his control of Hungary's media and political institutions to persuade voters that the coalition of Hungarian political parties that united to oppose him were too close to Brussels and would bring Hungary into the war. Thanks to strategic gerrymandering, Orbán and Fidesz won 135 of 199 parliamentary seats – a legislative supermajority large enough to amend the constitution.

This dismayed Bogi Bakos, a twenty-three-year-old recent university graduate. But she wasn't waiting around for her country to democratize anyway.

We met at Auróra, a counterculture courtyard bar with an alternative, intelligentsia crowd. Confident and fluent in English, she wore a black leather jacket over a mesh sports bra, with silver hoop earrings under her straight-cut, blonde hair. Sipping beer with six other friends, neither Bogi nor almost anyone else in her party was planning to stay in Hungary long.

"I think the people from my bubble – the people from the upper-middle class who have a kind of Western way of thinking, are well traveled, well-educated – they are raised in a way that the opportunities [abroad] are in their mind," she said. "They have the trajectory to leave. Also, it is easier to leave when you are young, because then you don't have a career yet, you don't have to leave so many things behind. ... Most of my friends already left or plan to leave anyway, so we don't really have a choice. That's probably why I was willing to study something I cannot pursue in Hungary. I am studying to become a marine biologist, so I'll need to live somewhere near the sea," she added, laughing. She'll likely head to Spain.

What happens to the people who are left behind?

"I think that change will come in Hungary," she said distantly. "It's like going to therapy. Before making the decision that you need to change, something tragic must happen. And I think it's true for Hungary too. We are not yet at the point of change, but it is really soon. People have been suppressed for a really long time now. The people in the countryside know that they suffer from Fidesz. People in smaller villages, a third of Hungarians don't have enough money to put aside at the end of the month. They live month by month.

"But the problem with Fidesz's power is that the system keeps itself alive. People who don't agree with Fidesz leave and the people who stay are influenced by the government. And their children will be taught to believe what Fidesz tells them, so the system reinforces itself even if the old Fidesz voters die or leave too."

With this frustration, Bogi was detecting a sorting phenomenon among her countrymen that sustained its increasingly authoritarian government – a phenomenon that reaches well beyond Central and Eastern Europe to the rest of the world (see Figure 1.2). And while it is substantially driven by millions of educated liberals like Bogi, emigrating for reasons other than the political circumstances in their country of origin,

FIGURE 1.2 Keleti Train Station, Budapest, Hungary.

it is deepened by the departure of millions more like Ivana and Nikolai, who have to different degrees been exposed to the adverse effects of democratic decline without being persecuted.

BRAIN DRAIN

Politics aside, thousands of educated professionals like Bogi, Ivana, and Nikolai leave their countries of origin every day. And when they do, they often move to more developed and stable economies with better employment and income prospects. And so rich markets get richer. And because the emigrants deplete their homeland of resources they would otherwise apply – their talent and intellect, but also their purchasing power and ingenuity – poor markets become poorer. This phenomenon is called "brain drain."

Brain drain has been extensively studied,[3] and it is the principal lens through which governments, researchers, and business actors understand the April 2022 departures of Bogi, Ivana, and Nikolai.

Nikolai is one of hundreds of thousands of Russians, many of them young professionals, who emigrated in the weeks after the invasion of Ukraine. One survey estimated that around 300,000 Russian workers had departed in the first three weeks after the war started – approximating

Russia's yearly total in 2014, 2015, and 2016.[4] (Previously, Russia's highest recent outflow took place in 2020, when 500,000 people emigrated.) Another 400,000 Russians are estimated to have departed when the Kremlin decided to enlist young men off the streets to bolster its flagging military in September 2022. The exodus was the largest since the 1917 Revolution, when millions of members of Russia's nobility and educated bourgeoisie fled the emerging communist state. Several million Russians left after the Soviet Union's demise in 1991 too, but did so over several years.[5] In a March 26, 2023 speech in Warsaw, US President Joe Biden said the exodus from Russia was "a remarkable brain drain in such a short period of time."[6]

"The people who are either leaving or planning to leave are highly educated and generally young," Elina Ribakova, deputy chief economist at the Institute of International Finance, told the *Wall Street Journal* at the time. "This is your most productive part of the labor force that is disappearing."[7]

In the first month after war began, the tech industry – one of Russia's fastest growing sectors – lost between 50,000 and 70,000 workers, according to data presented by the Russian Association for Electronic Communications during a March 22, 2022 committee hearing at the State Duma, the lower house of Russia's parliament; the group anticipated as many as 100,000 more would leave in the following month.[8] While some have trickled back to Russia, many will never return.[9]

DEMOCRATIC DRAIN

While much attention has been paid to the skillset of those leaving, there has been less focus on their values.

In this book, I call attention to the fact that many people who choose to depart their countries of origin – whether for economic opportunities abroad or otherwise – are likely to hold more liberal democratic values than those who remain in the country of origin. Emigration thus depletes a country not only of its economic capital but also its political capital.

Just as brain drain leaves countries poorer and less productive, Democratic Drain enables authoritarian political developments – often at the same time. It is unlikely to *cause* authoritarian turns by itself because there are many other variables present and, as I show, many emigrants leave only once an authoritarian-leaning party or candidate gains power. But any time a disproportionate number of people with liberal and democratic values leave a society, a principal barrier to democratic backsliding is removed.

Some democratically inclined emigrants – or "demigrants" – may be catalyzed to depart by geopolitical events like Russia's February 2022 invasion of Ukraine, or democratic deconsolidation like Vučić's reelection in Serbia shortly thereafter. For this subset, their departure may entail significant professional costs. In Ivana's case, she is seeking economic opportunities outside of Serbia, but she is leaving principally because of political developments in Belgrade. Ivana's husband had already been abroad for several years before she made the decision to look for employment in Croatia, too. She is disillusioned by the corruption of the Progressive Party and, with its reelection, lost confidence that any change would come. Any economic implications of Ivana's departure are an externality, a residual effect of Serbian political trends.

However, the departure of highly educated professionals like Bogi and her aspirant contemporaries in Hungary is a far more ordinary, and therefore pervasive, demographic development. Indeed, Bogi is not leaving Hungary because she is concerned about the authoritarian tendencies of the Orbán government and the ruling Fidesz Party, though she *is* concerned. She is leaving because she is pursuing employment and educational opportunities abroad. And when she departs, she will – passively, not necessarily deliberately – take her political values, preferences, and votes with her. Statistically, she will be less likely to cast ballots in upcoming elections and she will no longer march the streets of Budapest, as she has before, to protest Fidesz policies such as its recent ban on marriages and adoptions by same-sex couples. Here, the political effects are the externality, a residual consequence of Bogi's departure.

The phenomenon of Democratic Drain has been less recognized by social scientists because most migrants keep their politics hidden from view and their decisions to depart are uncoordinated, independent from one another. When researchers have queried immigrants about the original motivations for their departures, respondents like Ivana often cite the family members they rejoined or, in the case of Bogi, the career they ultimately pursued. Unless they are refugees or asylum seekers, they tend to omit their latent discontent with the status of the political institutions in their countries of origin – a form of recency bias that can mask their underlying sentiments.

As a result, most social scientists who study human mobility argue that immigration is driven by social network ties and opportunities for economic advancement. Other researchers have focused on psychological or demographic predispositions, like the disproportionate number of men in labor migrant flows,[10] migrants' comfort with taking risks,[11] or migrants' higher level of civic engagement.[12] Acknowledging the phenomenon of

Democratic Drain does not invalidate these findings. Rather, I am calling attention to a pattern that has gone almost entirely unnoticed underneath these more established dynamics.

To the extent this pattern has been previously observed, it is in a limited number of domestic or regional studies.[13] In this book, I consider trends in 149 countries and self-governing territories. I examine the trend from the perspectives of prospective migrants, migrants, nonmigrants, and democracy advocates both in the countries of origin and the diaspora. I also examine the mechanics of this trend by scrutinizing migrants' destination preferences, social networks, and the timing of their decision-making.

Drawing on this body of research, I find that democratic values are an independent and powerful predictor of people's desire to emigrate. In other words, demigrants make up a substantial share of emigrants. More specifically, I find that people who want to migrate out of nondemocratic states tend to be disproportionately younger, educated, and middle-income, and have more democratic proclivities and less authoritarian personalities. When offered a discrete choice between equally prosperous destination countries with different governments, these prospective emigrants strongly prefer places that feature democratic – as opposed to authoritarian – institutions. I also find that, while emigrants may depart at any time, people with democratic proclivities are especially motivated to leave after election outcomes in which an authoritarian party or ruler is elected or reelected to power, particularly after an earlier period of democratic progress.

GLOBAL IMPLICATIONS

At a global scale, the correlation between migration choices and democratic values implies that people around the world are self-sorting into more and less democratic spaces. This introduces a novel condition that may have enabled authoritarian countries to persist in the decades since the end of the Cold War spurred the so-called Third Wave of democratization – a period when the stock of international migrants has grown so significantly worldwide.[14]

In Europe, Democratic Drain would enable the authoritarian-leaning governments in countries like Hungary, Poland, Serbia, and Turkey, which emerged after periods of more liberal democracy.[15] Together, these countries have sent millions of immigrants to Western Europe since the end of the Cold War and they have experienced gradual democratic backsliding since 2015, with the election and endurance of Fidesz in Hungary, the Law and Justice Party in Poland, the SNS in Serbia, and the Justice and Development

Party in Turkey.[16] As many Eastern European states are inside the European Union's (EU's) free mobility zone, migrants are able to leave and return at will, unlike most people aspiring to depart their countries of origin for political reasons or any other. It is thus reasonable to expect that this legal environment would produce Democratic Drain in a more pronounced fashion. In this book, I focus closely on the dynamics in this region.

I also consider countries like Egypt and Tunisia, where Arab Spring revolts deposed authoritarian regimes, only for the countries to return to authoritarian rule as democratic opposition groups could not consolidate sufficient support in the years thereafter. After deposing their governments, pro-democratic voices have been similarly overshadowed by violent civil conflict in Libya and Yemen. Pro-democracy groups also struggled in Arab Spring venues like Morocco, Jordan, and Bahrain, where autocrats were able to stay in power through patronage and public accommodations. Of course, numerous forces interacted to produce this authoritarian stability, but the sheer scale of Democratic Drain, at a minimum, suggests the depletion of the ranks of people who might otherwise espouse liberal and democratic values – those positioned to support institutional change. The Middle East and North Africa have comprised the principal origin of overseas migrants – regular and irregular – to the European continent for decades. And many countries in the region possess postcolonial family and linguistic ties to European states, which has facilitated persistent mobility and likely Democratic Drain. As a result, I also closely examine this region in the chapters that follow.

Still, comparable conditions are present elsewhere among the regions that send millions of migrants to the world's democracies. A number of Latin American states have struggled to consolidate their democracies despite the end of Cold War-era communist pressures and significant economic development in some regions. Institutional instability plagues many Latin American countries like Peru, Bolivia, and Ecuador; corruption, violence, and rule of law deficits pervade Mexico and Central America; autocrats have governed Venezuela for two decades; and though Brazil voted out its authoritarian president Jair Bolsonaro in 2022, it did so only narrowly. Though Argentina, Brazil, Paraguay, and Uruguay formed a free mobility zone, much of Latin America's migration remains northbound toward the United States and to Spain.

In Southeast Asia, democratic institutions and norms are declining in the region's principal countries of emigration. In India, long a robust multi-party democracy, the Hindu nationalist Bharatiya Janata Party has presided over discriminatory policies against the country's large Muslim minority and undermined freedom of speech. In Pakistan, the military's grip on political power has allowed it to selectively constrain civil liberties and apply the extralegal use of force against civilians. The Philippines suffers from persistent corruption and political violence, and in the last decade China has clawed back rights and freedoms in Hong Kong. While large numbers of Hong Kongers were able to emigrate to the United Kingdom following a 2020 crackdown, there are fewer legal pathways for Asian migrants to democracies. Large numbers of temporary migrants flow to the Arabian Gulf's kingdoms and emirates, but there are tighter admissions policies in regional democracies like Australia, Japan, New Zealand, and South Korea.

INDIVIDUAL BY INDIVIDUAL

The phenomenon of Democratic Drain is therefore not merely a thought-provoking quirk of immigration demography; it shines light on an individual-by-individual dynamic that could limit the spread of democracy to new spaces and facilitate backsliding in some previously established democracies.

This account can be overlaid onto a rich literature about the more structural causes and constraints of democratic consolidation since the end of the Cold War. In 1991, many political observers believed that democratization was simply inevitable everywhere.[17] However, as the Third Wave's momentum faded without transitions in the Middle East, much of Africa, and parts of Asia, scholars turned increasingly to the question of why authoritarian regimes have persisted, producing one of political science's largest literatures.[18]

Modernization theorists predicted that democracy was less likely to take hold without economic development.[19] Political scientists like Harvard University's Samuel Huntington argued that economic development played a central role in Third Wave democratizations by helping create a well-educated middle class that was open to democracy.[20] But in the wake of the failure of the Middle East and China to democratize in the 1990s and 2000s, economic explanations largely fell out of favor. These regions had higher per capita incomes than many other countries, but far less democracy.[21]

Some scholars attribute this struggle to democratize to the way that natural resource wealth allows authoritarian governments to persist. In particular, oil revenues have allowed regimes to build up powerful militaries and effectively bribe citizens (and political opponents) with social benefits and even direct payments for their acquiescence to autocratic rule. While this account offers one of the most persuasive explanations of authoritarian persistence in some states with great natural resources, other nondemocratic regimes have endured without them.

Another prominent account of Third Wave democratization has considered the importance of external forces. In 1991, Huntington noted that the end of the Cold War caused United States foreign policymakers to shift from opposing communism to promoting democracy and human rights. But external actors have been more successful at propping up authoritarian regimes than promoting democracy since the initial post-1991 transitions in Latin America and Europe. A number of authoritarian regimes have continued to receive US support even after the end of the Cold War as America has sought to protect the world's oil supply and prevent the spread of Islamism.[22] Other authoritarian governments have found a new friend in China, which has bolstered weak states to capitalize on access to their markets or natural resources.[23]

If anything, the post-2010 global wave of populism has actually produced democratic deficits in a number of previously consolidated democracies. Observers have sought to explain this backlash in different ways. One set argues that populist voting is the product of economic grievances related to inequality and diminished socioeconomic stability.[24] Others point to a sense of cultural threat derived from increasing ethnic and religious diversity.[25] In seminal research, political scientist Daniel Ziblatt has shown the way conservative parties have designed campaigns that strategically divided their societies along lines of race, nationality, ethnicity, or religion to remain competitive amid the expansion of the electorate to immigrants and minorities.[26] But this strategy has ended up reinforcing social divisions, emboldening nationalist ideologies, and whetting popular appetite for ever more muscular assertions of the national character and democratic backsliding.

With the notable exceptions of political sociologists Seymour Martin Lipset and Barrington Moore, who have noted the importance of the democratically inclined middle classes, a focus on the role of non-elite individual actors is largely absent from the canon of explanations for democratic political development. In this alternative and complementary perspective, I refocus the lens on personal and household decision-making – the value-based differences of those who leave and remain – and apply it to make sense of broader trends.

My approach follows in the tradition of social theorist Joseph Schumpeter's "methodological individualism."[27] Sociologist Max Weber later captured its essence when he argued that social trends should be examined as the result of "the particular acts of individual persons," since they alone can be treated as comprehensible agents.[28] Seizing upon this logic later in the twentieth century, Friedrich von Hayek explored how broad economic phenomena can emerge as the unintended consequences of local individual's actions.[29] In other words, the phenomenal outcomes that people together achieve may bear no resemblance to the ones that they intended. Still, he contended, it is critical that we understand their calculations if we are to appreciate the results they produce and why they their behavior persists.

In focusing on individual attitudes and preferences, my findings paint a much fuller picture of the emigrant politics interplaying with global political development. Emigrants' departures instantiate their acquisition of civil and democratic rights and reflect people's evaluation of the prospects for liberal democratic institutions in their countries of origin in the context of the transition costs associated with emigrating. Depending on individuals' circumstances, this calculus will be conditioned by an individual's perception of their social and economic outlook in another country, the opportunity structures that may facilitate their departure and arrival abroad, and their sense of political efficacy in their country of origin.

Related research has already shown that the emigration of disgruntled citizens may act as a "pressure release valve" and reduce the likelihood of uprisings and revolutions for regime change – under authoritarians or otherwise.[30] Political sociologist Jack Goldstone has written that several kinds of demographic change increase the risks of uprisings and revolutions.[31] These include the rapid growth of the labor force in weak economies, particularly a rapid increase in educated youths aspiring to elite positions when such positions are scarce; and also unequal population growth rates between different ethnic groups owing to fertility differences or immigration dynamics.[32] Emigrants' departure has been shown to have mitigated pressure on authoritarian regimes in the island nations of the Pacific,[33] the Philippines under President Ferdinand Marcos,[34] and in Egypt in the late twentieth century.[35]

But the scale of annual flows from authoritarian-leaning countries to democratic countries worldwide is immense, suggesting the potential scope of a Democratic Drain phenomenon. Between 2015 and 2019, the most recent period for which complete global data is available, over 45 million people moved to a country that was substantially more democratic than their country of origin – more than two in every five global migrants.[36] As shown in Table 1.1, since 1990, the average number of people who made such a move is over 37 million per five-year period. Measured more conservatively, Table 1.2 presents estimates of migrants moving from less

TABLE 1.1 *Estimated total migrants from an origin country to a destination with a V-Dem Liberal Democracy Index score that is 0.10 higher than their own on a 0–1 scale.*

Year	Total migrants moving to a more democratic destination, by five-year period	Share of total migrant flows by five-year period (%)
2015–2019	45,318,266	41.2
2010–2014	43,942,730	42.8
2005–2009	37,595,945	40.9
2000–2004	34,498,270	41.9
1995–1999	33,086,481	46.5
1990–1994	28,448,630	39.2
Five-year average	37,148,386	42.0

TABLE 1.2 *Estimated total migrants from an origin country that scores under 0.70 on the V-Dem Liberal Democracy Index on a 0–1 scale to a country that scores over 0.70.*[37]

Year	Total migrants moving from less democratic countries to the world's most democratic countries, by five-year period	Share of total migrant flows by five-year period (%)
2015–2019	29,512,134	26.8
2010–2014	25,234,592	24.6
2005–2009	25,599,509	27.9
2000–2004	23,069,250	28.0
1995–1999	19,682,813	27.7
1990–1994	17,728,674	24.4
Five-year average	23,471,162	26.5

Source: Migration flow estimates are derived from Guy Abel and Joel Cohen, "Bilateral International Migration Flow Estimates for 200 Countries," *Scientific Data* 6, no. 82 (2019). The authors estimate bilateral migration flows disaggregated by sex over a thirty-year period from 1990 through 2020 based on stock data. Bilateral migrant stock data are thought to have greater spatial coverage and fewer problems of comparability than bilateral flow data. Total worldwide migrant flows for each five-year period to calculate share of world migrant flows are: 72,564,433 (1990–1994); 71,108,818 (1995–1999); 82,362,188 (2000–2004); 91,925,175 (2005–2009); 102,757,487 (2010–2014); 110,027,413 (2015–2019).

democratic environments to the world's most democratic environments annually. I find there were nearly 30 million such people between 2015 and 2019 alone, and an average of 23 million per five-year period since 1990 – about a 27 percent share of global flows. While a portion of these annual flows are humanitarian migrants, the vast majority are voluntary. In this book, I examine the different dynamics of this voluntary emigration, but particularly those among dissidents and demigrants.

DISSIDENTS

When casual observers of world politics think of liberal democrats leaving their countries of origin for destinations that align with their political values, they conventionally envision dissidents – activists, often elites, who oppose the current regime or government of their countries. Authoritarians are bolstered when dissidents emigrate and, in some cases, the regimes actively facilitate or force their emigration and exile by making dissidents uncomfortable.[38] Depending on the country and its leadership, dissidents are subject to harassment and intimidation by authorities, imprisonment, death threats against them and their loved ones, and generally difficult operating conditions. Their work is complicated by ever-changing rules, scrutiny by law enforcement, and political institutions designed to advantage those already in power. Research shows that a lack of political rights generates asylum applications.[39]

Less commonly, dissidents can also be pulled and pushed abroad, ironically, by the supranational organizations that promote their activism. Organizations like the National Endowment for Democracy, Amnesty International, and United States Agency for International Development advise local democratic activists and often extract them from their context to offer further training and connect them with peers in other countries. Despite their virtuous intentions, many of the selected fellows and trainees become acculturated to Western, liberal environments and a substantial number of leaders stay abroad to pursue broader advocacy directions in those environments, which distract their attention from their original agendas. Others may return to their countries of origin equipped with new vernaculars, political demands, and cosmopolitan ideas that fail to resonate with fellow citizens. A further consequence is that activists' contact with other émigrés abroad may build a network that facilitates their own future emigration.[40]

To be clear, dissidents are distinct from humanitarian migrants. Refugees and asylum seekers are classes of migrants formally designated by international law, who leave their countries of origin to escape political persecution and oppression at the hands of governments or some other authority. Many refugees and asylum seekers are fleeing political systems that discriminate against them for their race, ethnicity, religion, sexuality, political beliefs, or ideology. So, yes, many seek the kind of freedom, rights, and self-governance that democracies offer. And when large numbers of them leave, it is reasonable to expect the countrymen they leave behind to comprise a more concentrated assembly of people who tolerate or even support the authoritarians in power – the dynamics behind Democratic Drain.[41]

However, humanitarian migrants do not necessarily hold more liberal and democratic values than their countrymen. They may oppose certain modes of authoritarianism because they and members of their faction have been its targets. And the traumas of this experience may inspire many to support liberal democracy consequently. But had they been given the opportunity to govern before the trauma of persecution and forced migration, opposition parties in such settings may have been equally likely to govern in such a way that oppresses political opponents and discriminates against other factions too. Some of those that emigrate even support authoritarian parties in destination countries, if those parties reflect their values. And so the effect of humanitarian migrants' departure on the prospects for democracy in their countries of origin depend on the extent to which those oppressed by authoritarians in power hold liberal democratic values. Alternatively, when democratic activists depart, their organizations and movements are weakened.

Nikolai's circumstances reveal the growing complexity surrounding conventional legal classifications. On the one hand, the Russian violinist was not imprisoned or physically harmed for his political views. In fact, he never really made his views public; he shared them in a private lunchtime conversation. On the other hand, he lost his beloved job because his views were revealed and his concern with further penalties were enough to depart. His situation reveals the widening continuum between refugee migration and voluntary migration, but more pertinently here, the continuum between dissidents – those who, like Nikolai, experience the effects of democratic backsliding more personally – and demigrants – who experience the effects more sociotropically or indirectly.

DEMIGRANTS

Demigrants ("DEM-ə-grənts") – a term I am introducing – depart under far more conventional circumstances. In a first set of circumstances, people leave voluntarily in response to illiberal or undemocratic political developments – much like Ivana from Serbia. Their emigration may be catalyzed by new government policies that they oppose or by the election of parties and candidates they have contested. Because of the universal foundations of liberalism and democracy, it is more likely that people with liberal democratic values would depart their countries of origin than conservatives whose ideologies are typically more rooted in the primacy of the local nation and its heritage, however these are constructed. To emphasize, these emigrants are not forced to depart according to the legal definition of forced migration related to persecution or violence. Though they may be pressurized by political circumstances, they ultimately *choose* to leave in search of environments that are more likely to accommodate their values and preferences, or at least protect their freedom to live uninhibited by the authoritarian regimes they flee.

In a second set of circumstances for demigrants, people depart voluntarily in response to a career opportunity or a chance to reunite with family members abroad. They may pursue a better or more specialized education, an investment opportunity, a job, a higher income, or simply the greater economic stability provided by countries with higher standards of living, greater labor protections, and welfare programs. Like Bogi from Hungary, many demigrants are educated and middle-class professionals who are likely to be attracted to the freedom, rights, and strong economies of liberal democratic countries;[42] they may even be recruited by companies and agencies in those countries.

Most wealthy economies today design their immigration regimes to facilitate the admission of highly skilled migrants like scientists, engineers, doctors, nurses, and software developers.[43] Since around 2005, European states have modified their labor visa standards to almost exclusively admit those with marketable skills. Concurrently, states like Australia, Canada, and the United Kingdom have pursued points-based policies which evaluate migrants on a range of criteria and favor applicants who possess technical skills, higher education credentials, and language fluency. As I show, because these emigrants happen to hold more liberal democratic values than the countrymen they leave behind, these admissions policies simultaneously limit the international mobility of people with lower skills and inadvertently deplete countries of origin of democratic political capital.

And so while Nikolai, Ivana, and Bogi are not the faces of global democratic activism today, their uncoordinated departures from Russia, Serbia, and Hungary – when combined with those of other people with liberal democratic values – enable democratic backsliding in their countries of origin. They should neither be blamed for their decision to depart, nor the democratic backsliding their departure may facilitate. As I have emphasized, decisions to depart are deeply personal and often apolitical. When they are sensitive to political developments, they are often pressurized by state actions designed to discomfort those who might otherwise resist authoritarian power grabs and rights suppression. Democratic Drain is thus a byproduct of voluntary migration flows, but otherwise attributable to the choices that authoritarian-leaning governments deliberately present to dissidents and demigrants.

DEMOCRATIC GAIN?

In recent years, a widespread acknowledgment of brain drain has been complicated by observations of a potentially offsetting, counterphenomenon: brain *gain*. Brain gain refers to the benefits that countries of origin enjoy when successful emigrants remit large sums of financial and intellectual capital to their friends and family in countries of origin.[44] Financial remittances now comprise over 20 percent of the national economy in countries such as Kyrgyzstan, Nepal, Moldova, Samoa, Lesotho, Armenia, and Haiti. In Tajikistan, such contributions make up a remarkable 51 percent of GDP.[45] Less measurably, brain gain also takes place when migrant business owners outsource labor to their homelands or when business ideas and innovation are shared with family and childhood friends to implement at home.[46] Or circular migration may occur, when individuals who have had success abroad return home to start a business, bringing with them capital, experience, and more democratic ideas born of living in a democratic county.[47]

Accordingly, those initially learning of a Democratic Drain phenomenon may point to an analogous "democratic gain" that could take place after emigration. And it is true that some emigrants seek to sustain their engagement with their previous political agendas, or even more actively reinsert themselves into homeland debates with their newfound freedom abroad.[48] Researchers have noted the impact that diaspora activists have made on elections, wars, and other political disputes in places of origin like Sri Lanka, Nagorno-Karabakh, and states in the Balkans.[49] Elite emigration has been found to invigorate India's democracy when elites emigrate for opportunities abroad and leave space for countrymen from historically disadvantaged groups to grow.[50] In theory, foreign-educated individuals can promote democracy in their home country after being educated in democratic destination states.[51] Migration could be a counterbalance to ethnic strife in countries of origin and reduce homeland corruption.[52] Indeed, social scientists have found that hermit autocracies endure longer than those that permit exposure to international influences.[53]

However, the influence of authoritarian states' diaspora activists has not been especially democratic, as migrants frequently support one warring faction over another. Indeed, where diasporas have influenced homelands in the past, they have been more successful in supporting paramilitary groups, not democratization. For example, the Tamil Tigers of Sri Lanka and the Kosovar Liberation Army – both of which benefited from substantial foreign donations and support in the 1990s and 2000s – were engaged in bloody battles of ethnic conflict. Such examples demonstrate how prospects for "democratic gain" require a country of origin that is in fact receptive to the liberal democratic ideas and political capital that expatriates may seek to remit. Authoritarian states are typically not interested in the transfer of democratic perspectives from their diasporas.[54] And often, emigrants find governments in their countries of origin to be inaccessible to their lobbying.[55]

There are notable exceptions where democrats return to office in their homelands, but they are not examples of people who advocated for liberal reforms from abroad. Ayad Allawi was the prime minister of postwar Iraq in 2004 and 2005, but was effectively installed by the United States military. Mohammed Nur returned to Somalia from London to be the mayor of Mogadishu, but he was appointed by unelected officials. A stronger example comes from the exiled members of Tunisia's Islamist Ennahda Party, who returned to stand for election after the country's 2011 Jasmine Revolution deposed the regime of longtime dictator Zine El Abidine Ben Ali and stimulated a series of uprisings around the Arab world. However, the party's leadership had previously advocated for an Islamic state and justified political violence.

Given the amount of consultation, deliberation, and organization required to build and sustain successful democracies, examples of democratization from abroad are therefore rare. Emigrants are typically consumed by the adjustments they must make to resettle in destination countries. Once abroad, many emigrants have limited capacity for activism. While 141 countries now offer some form of non-resident citizen voting,[56] voting rates among diaspora communities are generally very low.[57] Some emigrants left to deliberately remove themselves from a dangerous political climate. The vast majority never repatriate. Moreover, many governments slander departed democratic leaders as "treasonous" once they leave their countries of origin. This tarnishes activists' reputations and debilitates their influence and mobilization efforts.

This maps well onto Albert O. Hirschman's versatile 1970 classification of "exit, voice, and loyalty,"[58] from which many studies of diaspora political engagement also draw. Here, "exit" reflects the choice to emigrate and thereby divest from a government or state – what many scholars have called "voting with your feet." Meanwhile, "voice" is embodied by those who stay in their country of origin to communicate their dissent to the government and rehabilitate its institutions. But contrary to any suggestion that those who stay are more committed to changing the state where they continue to reside, my research finds that those who wish to emigrate are disproportionately more democratic in their proclivities. In a globalized world where access to and information about other societies is more readily available to people who are democratically inclined, exit supersedes voice.[59]

BOOK OUTLINE

With a blend of rigorous statistical analysis and detailed narratives from immersive, interview-based field research around the world, the chapters that follow examine the dynamics and mechanics behind the departure of both demigrants and dissidents – respectively, the mass and elite components of the Democratic Drain phenomenon.

Democracy's Carriers

Chapter 2 profiles prospective migrants around the world. Based on global polling, I answer three related questions: What are the demographic and psychological attributes of prospective migrants? Do prospective migrants hold more liberal democratic values than their countrymen? Do prospective migrants prefer democratic destinations?

Demographically, I find that prospective migrants are likely to be younger, educated, socially connected, and open-minded adults. And crucially, they hold less authoritarian and more democratic political values than their countrymen. This means that if they leave, the society they leave behind will not only become older, less educated, and more insular; it means that their society will also become less democratic and more authoritarian in its orientation. Taken in the context of what we already know about the extensive consequences of brain drain, these findings show how authoritarian-leaning countries are being depleted of precisely the people who are best placed to contribute to their economic modernization *and* their political liberalization.

I then ask whether prospective migrants would prefer destinations that align with their democratic political preferences rather than their material motivations. Broadly, the conventional wisdom among both experts and nonexperts is that emigrants prefer destinations that, above all, offer well-paid and stable jobs and perhaps access to welfare benefits. But based on a conjoint survey design in five countries in the Middle East and North Africa, I find that demigrants' initial destination preferences draw them to democracies that reflect the political and civic values they hold, even if this means sacrificing their material well-being to some extent. This discovery adds a new dimension to Democratic Drain. Not only are many authoritarian countries being depleted of people with democratic values; these individuals are inclined to self-sort into a dichotomized world of free, democratic destinations and increasingly authoritarian holdouts.

Outvoted, Voting Out

Chapter 3 takes a closer look at the mechanics of Democratic Drain. More specifically, I ask *when* demigrants are likely to depart. There have been numerous historic examples of an exodus following a major turn of political events, such as a brutal crackdown on dissent or freedom, the nationalization of private industry, or the outbreak of civil or international conflict. But elections are far more mundane political events that nonetheless inspire all citizens to consider their country's future.

Focusing on 127 countries worldwide, I find that people's interest in emigrating spikes in the immediate aftermath of national elections when an authoritarian-leaning party or ruler is elected to public office. Importantly, this effect is limited only to people who hold expectations of democratic norms and institutional integrity. Those who question the honesty of the election, suspect corruption among public officials, or feel that freedom of speech is constrained are significantly more likely to say they would like to leave when faced with the future deconsolidation of their country's democratic institutions.

Elections are therefore precipitating events for individuals disappointed by the results and concerned about the political future. Previously unnoticed over the ebb and flow of electoral cycles, Democratic Drain removes the people who are most likely to voice their dissatisfaction and most likely to demand institutional integrity in less democratic spaces.

The Sliding Scale

Chapter 4 engages the average people behind these trends. In particular, I tell the stories of Hungarians compelled to leave after the reelection of Prime Minister Viktor Orbán to a fourth consecutive term with a parliamentary supermajority, and I chronicle the experiences of Serbs crestfallen after the reelection of President Aleksandar Vučić to a second term. Some mundane, some extraordinary, their first-person narratives display the household considerations behind a mass population phenomenon.

I then leverage a unique study of European public opinion to reveal the way that Eastern Europeans who move West under the EU's free mobility rules likely hold more liberal democratic proclivities than those in their countries of origin who wish to migrate, and how those prospective migrants hold more liberal democratic proclivities than their countrymen who don't wish to move at all – a sliding scale of liberal democratic views among people with the same origins.

Of course, not all Eastern European countries have elected authoritarian-leaning governments; some have avoided even a flirtation. But elections are not the only political impetus for departure. It was not the 2018 reelection of President Vladimir Putin that drove an exodus from Russia; it was his megalomaniacal invasion of Ukraine in February 2022. I conclude this chapter with the personal accounts of Russians fleeing the Kremlin's foreign adventures and domestic crackdown, and show how their motivations reflect those of demigrants mobilized by elections or upgrades to their quality of life.

Democratic Gain

Chapter 5 considers the possibility that, while people with liberal and democratic proclivities may leave their countries of origin, they may influence the democratization of their homelands from abroad – the possible "democratic gain" I note earlier. Could emigrants' advocacy from abroad offset the effects of their departure on prospects for democracy? I study the case of Syria.

Syria is precisely the kind of country where emigrants might be expected to have had far more freedom and capacity to advocate for liberal democratic norms abroad than those who remained under the despotic rule of Bashar al-Assad until December 2024. After the oppressive Assad dictatorship was challenged by opposition groups in 2011, many activists in Syria's massive diaspora mobilized to support and influence people living in rebel-held territory – a test of would-be "democratic gain."

However, in a social network analysis of Syrians in regions governed by the Free Syrian Army in 2015, I find almost no evidence of their impact. Despite their presumed prominence in the West, a majority of Syrians could not even name a single pro-democratic leader from abroad – let alone identify their influence. And perhaps most damningly, the departure of former Syrian citizens for other countries was viewed by most respondents as an abandonment of their cause – an offense worse than being previously complicit with the oppressive Assad regime. Taken together with other research showing the limits of democratic diaspora activism, I conclude that the potential for "democratic gain" is severely constrained.

A Human Base

Chapter 6 concludes the book by turning the lens to exiled dissidents to contextualize the impact of demigrants' departures. Unlike demigrants, who may hold opposing views but depart voluntarily without government involvement, dissidents are often pressured or coerced to leave their countries of origin because of their opposition to the government and its policies. As organizers of democratic movements, they offer a unique perspective about the cumulative effect of people's emigration over time.

Based on two dozen interviews with activists from across the Middle East several years after the Arab uprisings, I tell their stories and demonstrate what their loss has meant to the pro-democratic movements they left behind. Through their narratives, I discern the extent to which their political agendas rely on rank-and-file supporters who are also positioned to leave as demigrants.

Looking back on this sobering collection of information, I consider the political and policy implications of Democratic Drain. This emergent phenomenon raises questions about how democracies might compensate for the inadvertent effects of global human mobility before the world further sorts into democratic and undemocratic spaces.

2

Democracy's Carriers

On Tuesday, April 1, 1980, a Havana municipal bus was commandeered by Hector Sanyustiz and four others on Avenida Quinta in the once fashionable Miramar neighborhood and, under fire from ministry guards, rammed through the iron gates of the Peruvian Embassy to seek asylum.

When the Peruvian mission ultimately offered humanitarian protection to the perpetrators that Friday, the Cuban government under President Fidel Castro publicly declared it would refuse to protect the Embassy any longer.

The guards had not been gone long before the first group of young men seeking asylum arrived. After furtively checking for soldiers, they hastily climbed over the Embassy fence. Glancing over their shoulders, they hurried across the broad lawn toward the white marble buildings of the Embassy. Stopped and searched by cautious Peruvian security officers, the young men were questioned, documented by consular staff, and released to wander in the gardens.

More people passed cautiously through the Embassy gates and freely roamed about the carefully maintained terraces. Some sat in the shade of mango and papaya trees, talking quietly. Many of the earliest arrivals were young men seeking freedom, opportunity, and looking to avoid military service. But soon families with small children, young married couples, and seniors arrived too. By Saturday morning, 500 people were scattered throughout the grounds, sleeping on benches and between flower beds.

By that Easter Monday, the Embassy grounds had filled with over 10,000 people. The gardens had been trampled and all the fruit from the trees had been eaten. Inside, people chanted, *"¡Perú! ¡Perú!"* while hundreds of Castro supporters outside replied, *"¡Fidel! ¡Fidel!"* and called them worms, *"¡Gusanos!"*

After another week passed, Castro proclaimed that the port of Mariel – fifty kilometers to the West – would be opened to anyone wishing to leave Cuba. Exiles in the United States rushed to hire boats in Miami and Key West to rescue their relatives. In all, 125,000 Cubans – the vast majority of them blue-collar, working-class people – fled to the United States in about 1,700 boats that overwhelmed the US Coast Guard.

In an article weeks later, the state-backed newspaper *Granma* wrote, "As everybody knows, it is in the United States, their natural habitat, that the great majority of the common criminals, lumpen, and other antisocial elements, for whom there is no place in our land of revolution, want to live."[1]

Despite the diplomatic embarrassment of his miscalculation, Castro intuitively understood the concept of Democratic Drain – that it wasn't just the exile of political opponents and dissidents that would relieve political pressure from his revolutionary regime; it was the emigration of average people, those inclined to depart for family and economic reasons.[2] He understood that every discontent – independently of whether they were actually political activists – carried the latent political capital that could one day be organized to topple or otherwise challenge his rule.[3]

To be sure, the initial wave of Cuban exiles who came to Miami in 1959 were supporters of the overthrown Batista government, later joined by the Cuban executives of US satellite offices and *los ricos* whose property had been confiscated by the new regime. But many apolitical professionals joined them, too, especially physicians. With the economic hardship and severe authoritarianism Cuba experienced in the 1960s, many laborers and people from the middle classes turned against the revolution, too. In response, on September 28, 1965, Castro opened the port of Camarioca – 100 kilometers to Havana's east – and US President Lyndon Johnson chartered "freedom flights," which, together with commissioned boats, would carry over 250,000 Cubans across the Florida Straits by 1974. By 1994, after the collapse of the Soviet Union cut the Cuban economy by almost half, there were riots in the streets and Castro would again exempt from emigration restrictions any Cubans wanting to leave by their own means.

Though most of the emigrants over the decades were treated as asylum seekers upon their arrival, many were really economic migrants and family migrants.[4] They were more opposed to poverty and immobility than communism.

The US government understood this – it was long referred to as the "Cuban contradiction" to US refugee policy.[5] American officials also knew that, by accepting hundreds of thousands of Cuban asylum seekers, they sustained Castro's tyranny. But they were trying to avoid the disorder associated with thousands of undocumented immigrants and they were under enormous pressure from the families of Cuban immigrants already in the United States. Meanwhile, they were surely tempted by the opportunity to acquire Cuba's best and brightest human capital – new arrivals who would treasure America's freedoms and rights as much as anyone.

Since the end of the Cold War, emigration is far less restricted by authoritarian-leaning regimes worldwide. Exceptions like Cuba and North Korea are exceedingly rare. And as transportation and communications innovations have facilitated human mobility, a growing number of people are moving. Is it possible that, even without Castro's intentionality, emigrants' departures are producing the same effect?

Average People

In the context of a variety of structural factors thought to promote or constrain democracy, Democratic Drain emphasizes the role of average people – *gusanos* (worms), *escoria* (trash) according to Castro – to exercise democratic norms and demand democratic political institutions.

Correspondingly, I view democracy as not only reliant upon favorable conditions, like economic development and geopolitics, but on the people it governs to sustain it. In this sense, I think of even the most average individuals as democracy's "carriers" – a person who reinforces fair, liberal, transparent self-governance through their tacit consent and fortifies it through their participation and their resistance, should it be threatened. To extend this genetic metaphor, the carrier inherits and carries on democratic traits but may not necessarily show visible markers or symptoms of it.

Who are these carriers?

To answer this question, we need to study prospective voluntary migrants – demographically, ideologically, and in their migratory preferences. In this chapter, I discuss the results of worldwide polling of prospective voluntary migrants to answer three related questions:

1. What are the demographic and psychological attributes of prospective migrants?
2. Do prospective migrants hold more liberal democratic values than other countrymen and countrywomen?
3. Does democratic governance factor into prospective migrants' choice of destination?

Worldwide, the data show that prospective voluntary migrants tend to be people under forty-five, with moderate levels of formal education and relatively strong social networks, who hail from predominantly developing countries in regions featuring a number of authoritarian regimes. Psychologically, I find a correlation between people who wish to emigrate from their countries of origin and lower scores on the authoritarian personality scale. This liberal orientation – relative to countrymen and countrywomen who do not wish to emigrate – complements earlier studies that have associated migrants with psychological openness and adaptability to new environments and norms.

In my research on prospective migrants' political values, I find that prospective emigrants hold political views and preferences that are marginally more liberal and/or democratic than their countrymen and countrywomen. Across a number of metrics, prospective emigrants report relatively more support for free and fair elections, minority rights, freedom of speech, and the separation of church and state. They are also more likely to complain about a lack of transparency or corruption in their countries of origin. Moreover, when considering a hypothetical opportunity to depart, they are more likely to favor potential destinations that align with these political and institutional preferences.

These results constitute the demographic basis for Democratic Drain. If prospective migrants are disproportionately citizens with democratic proclivities, their departure (independent of the destination) necessarily depletes their countries of origin of democratic political capital – democracy's carriers. My findings complicate conventional wisdom and decades of scholarly research about the push and pull factors that motivate emigrants' destination preferences and they reveal a fundamental bias of global human mobility: Migration sorts people with more authoritarian leanings into authoritarian spaces and concentrates people who are inherently more liberal in democratic destinations.

ATTRIBUTES OF PROSPECTIVE MIGRANTS

Demographic Attributes

If the scale of annual migrants from authoritarian-leaning countries moving to democratic countries worldwide is large, the number of *prospective* migrants is staggering.[6] In Chapter 1, I estimate that over 45 million people moved to a country that is substantially more democratic than their country of origin between 2015 and 2019, the most recent five-year period for which complete data is available. But according to a 2021 study by Gallup, 16 percent of adults worldwide – which projects to almost 900 million people – said they would like to leave their country of origin permanently, if they could.[7] Separately, researchers have found that about 10 percent of prospective migrants plan to make their move in the next year.[8] (For further details, see Appendix A.) This still comprises a significant share of the world – about 63 million people in 2011 and 90 million people in 2021.[9]

Prospective migrants are concentrated in regions with a larger share of authoritarian regimes or democracies teetering on the edges of authoritarian rule, including Latin America and the Caribbean, sub-Saharan Africa, the Middle East, and North Africa (see Table 2.1). The desire to migrate rose to decade-high levels in each of these regions in 2021, but also substantially in other regions like Southeast Asia, South Asia, and among the Commonwealth of Independent States – a group of former Soviet republics in Eurasia. Gallup and others have also shown that migrants, particularly those seeking temporary labor, are disproportionately male.[10]

TABLE 2.1 *The share of prospective emigrants by region (Gallup 2021).*

Country	2011	2021
Latin America and the Caribbean	18	37
Sub-Saharan Africa	29	37
Middle East and North Africa	19	27
Commonwealth of Independent States	15	21
European Union	20	17
World	12	16
Southeast Asia	6	15
Northern America	10	15
South Asia	8	11
Australia/New Zealand	8	10
East Asia	7	4

Beyond this gender skew, prospective migrants are more likely to be younger and better educated and socially connected on average:

Younger: In 2011, the most recent year for which data is available, 24 percent of people between fifteen and twenty-four years old world-wide and 15 percent of people between twenty-five and forty-four years old worldwide wished to emigrate. Those between twenty-five and forty-four years of age were more likely to have prepared for such a move – by applying for employment or for a visa, pur-chasing transport, or looking for lodging – than people of other ages.

Educated: People who hold a secondary school degree or a university degree are twice as likely to want to emigrate from their countries of origin than people who do not. Further, people with university degrees are almost twice as likely as people with only an elementary education to have actively prepared for a move. Worldwide, those whose work is "professional" are more likely to want to emigrate and be prepared to emigrate than those who are unemployed or not employed in professional roles.

Socially Connected: Cross-border social networks also matter, sug-gesting that those who wish to leave are also more connected with foreign trends and ideas. Adults who say they can rely on help from friends and family in other countries when they need it are nearly three times more likely to say they would like to migrate than those who don't have such networks. Adults who receive remittances from friends and family abroad are also more likely to want to move away too.[11] These patterns persist among those who say their departure is imminent and those who have actively prepared to depart.

While most interactions between friends and relatives are about family matters and social affairs, research has demonstrated the ways in which ideas also circulate – business ideas, market trends, but also political ideas too.[12] Culture and political preferences from the country of origin have been found to diffuse into the political and partisan preferences of coun-trymen and countrywomen in the diaspora.[13] It is reasonable to expect these currents may also flow in the opposite direction too. Additionally, researchers have found that the more individuals rely on the family as a provider of services, insurance, and transfer of resources, the lower their civic engagement and political participation.[14] Inversely, when family members depart, this may lead those who remain to be more attentive to political dynamics.

Psychological Attributes

Personality and psychological traits are influential in the study of many economic decisions and social behaviors but have been largely overlooked in models of migration.[15] While migrants' propensity to start businesses has been attributed to discrimination by employers and the power of ethnic networks, research suggests that prospective migrants also tend to be more entrepreneurial and potentially open to new experiences.[16] People who prepare to emigrate are also more likely to prepare to start a new business and, when followed over a longer period, they often do so.

This may translate to liberal attitudes more broadly, as a voluntary migrant's departure certainly requires an openness to new social norms and political systems. And indeed, researchers have found that immigrants are disproportionately more psychologically "open," "extroverted," and "adaptable," and less "conscientious" and "neurotic."[17] Some researchers also find evidence that migrants are disproportionately adaptable and have higher IQs.[18] Extrapolating, these may constitute psychological precursors for resistance to authoritarian political governance.

Ultimately, however, psychological openness and adaptability are merely proxies for the relative liberalism I expect to characterize prospective migrants and the relative authoritarianism I expect to characterize people who do not wish to emigrate. Alas, there is very limited research on the extent of authoritarian personality attributes among prospective migrants vis-à-vis their fellow countrymen and countrywomen.

In part to examine this more closely, I oversaw an August 2020 poll of 19,296 people across 19 European countries, each interviewed in their native language. These include Bulgaria, the Czech Republic, Estonia, Hungary, Latvia, Lithuania, Poland, Romania, Slovakia, and Slovenia in Eastern Europe; and Austria, Denmark, France, Germany, Italy, the Netherlands, Spain, Sweden, and the United Kingdom in Western Europe. Initial samples of 1,000–1,200 European adults aged 18 and older were contacted in each country, drawing from an Ipsos online panel. After the final sample was obtained, respondent characteristics were weighted to be representative based on each country's population distribution with respect to gender, age, occupation, region, and population density.[19] Respondents were asked a variety of questions comprising a widely validated scale of authoritarian personality orientation.[20]

Focusing on the ten Eastern European countries, prospective migrants are 6.7 percent less authoritarian in their psychological orientation than their countrymen and countrywomen with no intention to depart.[21]

The relationship was statistically significant in each country, except Slovakia. And it was strongest in Hungary and Poland, countries with authoritarian-leaning parties in power at the time the survey was fielded.

In sum, prospective migrants tend to be under forty-five years old, with moderate levels of formal education and relatively strong social networks. They tend to come from developing countries in regions featuring a number of authoritarian regimes. Psychologically, I find a correlation between people who wish to emigrate from their countries of origin and less authoritarian personalities – an orientation that may be connected to a greater number of social ties abroad. As global migration persists, countries of origin will only become older, less educated, more authoritarian in their orientation, and possibly less socially connected with other countries.

POLITICAL VALUES

The political values of prospective emigrants are largely unknown. Studies that examine prospective emigrants' politics often do so in a manner specific to prospective emigrants' local partisan preferences or their perspectives on matters of local importance. But these preferences do not neatly align into universal ideological categories such that I may discern global trends that distinguish the views of prospective emigrants from those of their countrymen and countrywomen across regions of the world.

Still, a review of earlier work in different regions suggests that dissatisfaction with national political conditions often motivates people to emigrate, and many of the reported grievances relate to institutional integrity and transparency. Emigration has been correlated with citizens' experience with the political system and attitudes about its performance in a number of countries in Latin America and the Caribbean;[22] with a poor evaluation of the public sphere in the Netherlands;[23] with the perception of unfair elections in Georgia and Azerbaijan;[24] opposition to the ruling party and endorsements of democracy in Singapore;[25] exposure to news of military activity during the Nicaraguan Contra War;[26] and concern with corruption and low institutional trust in Romania and Spain.[27] In European countries, researchers have found a correlation between populist far-right party vote shares and net migration losses at the subnational level. They argue that emigration and the frustrations and grievances it generates are important sources of populist success.[28]

More broadly, authoritarianism and weak democratic institutions are associated with less transparency and more corruption. And as corruption increases, so does the number of citizens who report an interest in emigrating.[29] Corruption and weak democratic institutions are associated with unpredictable economic conditions, more insecurity, and a lower quality of life. Also, researchers have identified frustrations with public services and security among prospective migrants across a variety of developing nations in sub-Saharan Africa, Asia, and Latin America.[30]

Liberal and Democratic Proclivities

These findings introduce the possibility that emigrants more broadly hold political views and preferences that are marginally more liberal and/or democratic than their countrymen and countrywomen. To examine this possibility more closely, I contacted 8,591 people in 5 principal origin countries in the Middle East and North Africa[31] – Jordan, Lebanon, Libya, the Palestinian Territories,[32] and Tunisia.[33] According to 2020 United Nations data, there were 6.8 million expatriates in these countries' worldwide diasporas, 17 percent of their current populations – significantly higher than the world average (3 percent).[34]

Within the pooled group of people interviewed, 26.5 percent indicated that they were considering migrating to another state within the next twelve months[35] – almost identical to the 27 percent share Gallup identified in their 2021 study of the whole region (Table 2.1).[36] About nine out of ten prospective migrants were able to name a specific country to which they were considering migrating, and nearly one out of four indicated that they had already taken concrete steps to prepare for a move abroad.[37]

To ascertain respondents' democratic proclivities, I asked four questions that provide respondents with a choice between the relative freedom and disorder of liberal democratic governance or the control and security of autocratic or theocratic governance. This is what Lebanese respondents viewed:

> *I am going to read you a series of statements. Please let me know whether you strongly agree, agree, disagree, or strongly disagree with each of them.*
>
> 1. Before making decisions, the Lebanese government should consult religious law and seek approval from religious leaders.
> 2. It is better to have a strong and decisive leader who is unelected than a weak leader who is elected by the people.
> 3. The Lebanese government should comply with the interests of the majority, even if this comes at the expense of minority groups' civil rights.

4. The Lebanese government should be empowered to prosecute people who spread lies, blasphemy, or make unpatriotic statements.

Because these questions each force a more realistic tradeoff between the more and less desirable attributes of liberal democracy, this approach is a more valid – albeit harder – test of liberal democratic values than directly querying whether respondents "like" or "support" democratic governance nominally.

Pooling respondents across the five countries in Figure 2.1, I find that prospective migrants are marginally but significantly less likely to support the suppression of free speech, less likely to support unelected leaders independent of their virtue, and less likely to favor government consultation of religious law or religious bodies in the formation of policy. There were no significant differences between prospective migrants and nonmigrants in their views about the suppression of minority rights.

It is worth acknowledging that the actual levels of support for liberal democratic values is rather low. Most respondents – prospective migrants and nonmigrants alike – agreed with statements that are illiberal or undemocratic in nature. However, this is a "hard" test of true principles that may underestimate the extent of liberal democratic values among respondents. Because the questions consider hypothetical tradeoffs unrelated to a specific political question, they are rather abstract and absolute, which might incline respondents to be more cautious with their choices in countries without a tradition of liberal democracy in the first place. For this reason, the results represent a "floor" of liberal democratic values in

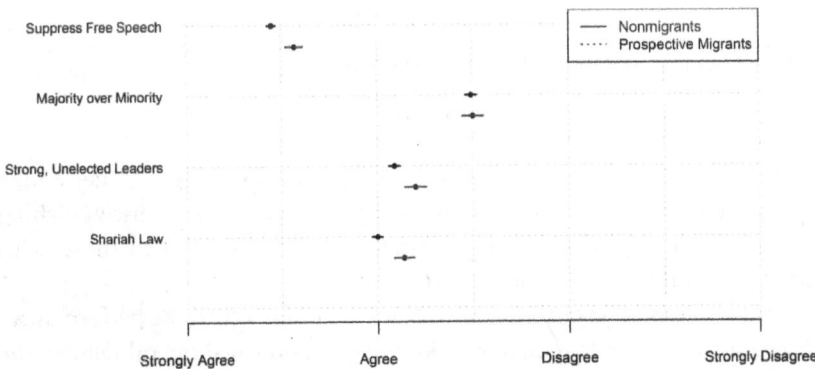

FIGURE 2.1 Democratic proclivities among prospective migrants and nonmigrants.

the selected countries, measured in the most conservative way possible to render confidence in my findings' validity.

For the purposes of evaluating the Democratic Drain phenomenon, the key is that those Middle Eastern and North African respondents who expressed their intent to migrate are those with relatively stronger liberal democratic proclivities. This average difference applies the same logic that has underpinned pervasive observations of brain drain. Here, beyond observing marginal differences in educational attainment, age, and gender, I observe marginal differences in political values.

Satisfaction with Liberal Democratic Institutions

We can corroborate and consider the extent of this phenomenon in far more countries if we broaden how liberal democratic values are measured. In results from 2004 to 2021, the Gallup World Poll asks respondents in 149 countries worldwide about the extent to which they are satisfied with a variety of liberal democratic protections and public institutions in their countries.[38] Administered to over 900,000 respondents worldwide,[39] here are 5 as they would have been viewed by someone from India:

Is corruption widespread throughout the government in India, or not? [Yes/No]

Do the media in this country have a lot of freedom, or not? [Yes/No]

In your opinion, how many people in your country, if any, are afraid to openly express their political views? [4 point scale][40]

In India, do you have confidence in each of the following, or not?

How about the honesty of elections? [Yes/No]

How about the national government? [Yes/No]

In Figure 2.2, I aggregate these five indicators into a single, scaled index of dissatisfaction with institutions ranging from −1 to 1, distinguishing people holding predominantly positive views (−1 to 0) and those with predominantly negative views (0 to 1).

As measures of dissatisfaction and lack of confidence, these performance-based indicators only indirectly ask about respondents' liberal democratic values. But it is a safe assumption that only someone who is concerned about institutional integrity, media freedom, freedom of speech, and fair

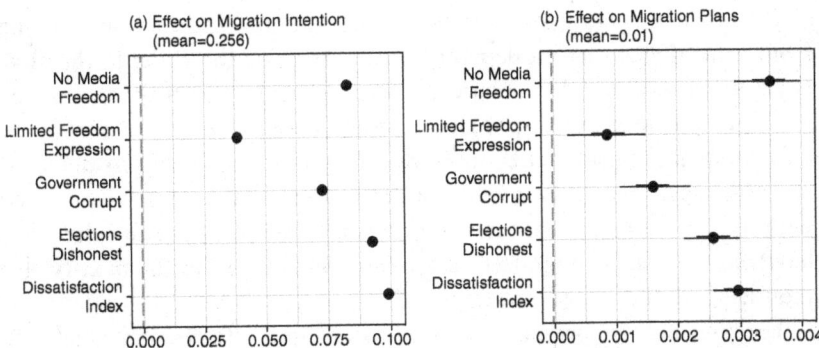

FIGURE 2.2 Dissatisfaction with democratic quality and migration intentions (panel a) and plans (panel b).

elections would be dissatisfied by their shortcomings. To be clear, just because respondents perceive a lack of liberal democratic norms does not confirm a democratic deficit; feelings are not facts. But I am here specifically concerned about the characteristics of people who hold liberal democratic values such that they might feel dissatisfied when these values go unfulfilled. And it would be quite rare for someone who supports the suppression of news media to lament a shortage of press freedom. Later I will show that these measures of public sentiments are also corroborated by standardized measures of liberal democracy, too.

After controlling for respondents' self-reported personal economic situation and exposure to crime and violence (which may also motivate them to emigrate),[41] I find that people with more negative views about the democratic quality of their country are more likely to want to emigrate (Figure 2.2(a)) and to have made plans to do so within the next twelve months (Figure 2.2(b)) – results that confirm the phenomenon I see in the Middle East and North Africa more specifically. (For country-by-country results, disaggregated by indicator, please see the tables in Appendix B. For analyses with alternative specifications and a list of countries and election years, please see Appendix C.)

Across over 900,000 people and 149 countries worldwide between 2004 and 2021, people without confidence in their national government are 11.9 percent more likely to want to emigrate. People who think elections are dishonest are 9.3 percent more likely to want to emigrate. Those who think there is limited media freedom are 8.3 percent more likely to want to emigrate. People who think their government is corrupt are 7.3 percent more likely to want to emigrate and those who think that free speech is limited are 3.9 percent more likely to want to emigrate.[42]

Based on this summative index of institutional satisfaction, moving from neutral views about democratic quality (o on the scale) to the most negative views about democratic quality is associated with approximately a 41 percent increase in people's average *desire* to migrate across the 149 countries considered.[43] Similarly, moving from neutral to the most negative views about the quality of democratic institutions is associated with a 29 percent increase in the number of people reporting that they have *made plans* to migrate to a foreign country within the next twelve months – another substantial jump.[44]

Looking only at people who wish to emigrate offers another lens. In 2021, 87.5 percent of people worldwide who report wanting to emigrate think there is limited freedom of expression in their country; 84.3 percent think their government is corrupt; 66.7 percent believe that elections in their respective countries are dishonest; 65.4 percent have no confidence in their national government; and 46.5 percent think there is limited media freedom.

Overall, prospective migrants tend to hold quite grim perceptions of their countries' democratic outlook. Employing the scaled measure of satisfaction with liberal democratic institutions in Figure 2.3, across 121 countries in 2021, 34.2 percent of the prospective migrants polled were very dissatisfied (greater than 0.5), while an additional 33.7 percent of the prospective migrants polled were moderately dissatisfied (between 0 and 0.5) with their country's liberal democratic institutions. Only 32.1 percent of prospective migrants were – on average – satisfied with their country's liberal democratic institutions.

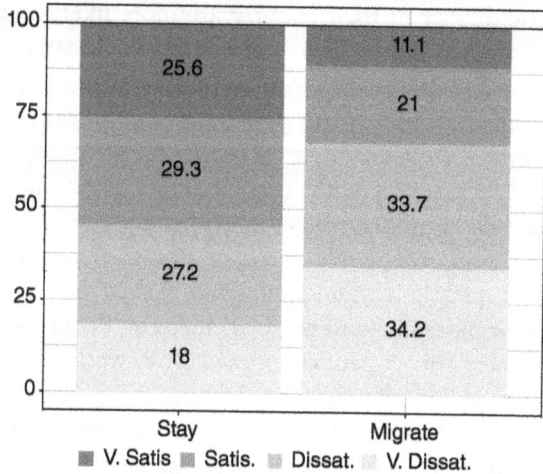

FIGURE 2.3 Level of satisfaction with democracy quality in 2021, by migration intention.

In comparison, among citizens of these countries who do *not* have a desire to migrate, 54.9 percentage are generally satisfied with their country's liberal democratic institutions and only 18 percent are very dissatisfied with those institutions. While this distribution demonstrates the clear relationship between interest in emigration and dissatisfaction with the state of public institutions, it also reveals that there is also a smaller share of the dissatisfied who prefer to stay in their countries of origin. Migration ultimately involves an evaluation of the tradeoff between one's prospects in the country of origin and the destination – politically, the certainty of one's efficacy internally and the certainty of one's rights and freedoms abroad.

Whatever the status of these institutions, they will only weaken should prospective migrants ultimately depart. Despite their lack of faith in liberal democratic norms in their respective countries, prospective migrants are marginally but significantly more likely to be civically engaged, as measured by their self-reported volunteer activity, donations to charity, and community service.[45]

In sum, extensive evidence suggests that, on average, prospective migrants hold more liberal democratic views, are more critical of their countries' respective institutions, yet would have been more likely to participate in them were they to stay.

DESTINATION PREFERENCES

With such political proclivities, it is possible that – all things equal, and separate from the family ties that underpin chain migration – prospective migrants would select destinations that align with their institutional preferences. If so, this would complicate conventional wisdom and decades of scholarly research about the push and pull factors that motivate emigrants' destination preferences.[46] Broadly, this research field can be partitioned into studies that stress economic motivations – the vast majority – and those that emphasize nonmaterial factors.

Economic Factors

The traditional understanding of migration preferences argues that economic considerations, specifically employment opportunities, dominate migrants' decision-making. Some of the most influential economists have argued that migration preferences were directly related to wage differences between origin and destination countries.[47] Subsequent arguments have also accounted for labor market conditions in the origin country and insurance and credit market failures.[48] The resulting meta-argument, which has – with some finality – been called the "new economics of labor migration," remains the dominant approach for explaining variation in migrant destination choice.[49]

Although most economic accounts use wage differences between sending and receiving states to predict migrant flows, a parallel literature has focused on the availability of welfare benefits within the destination state. This controversial "welfare magnet" hypothesis – most famously asserted by Harvard economist George Borjas – contends that migrants seek destinations with generous welfare provisions based on migratory flows inside the United States and Europe.[50] But it is highly contested. Using more detailed samples, scholars have found no substantial evidence of internal welfare migration across state borders in the United States.[51] And in Europe, most related studies have also documented a weak correlation between immigration and social expenditures.[52] As a result, the question of whether welfare benefits function as a meaningful pull factor in shaping international migration flows remains unsettled.

Social Ties and Democracy

The other prominent strand of scholarship discounts the role of economic considerations in shaping migrants' destination choice in favor of nonmaterial concerns, especially the role of social ties. This view was popularized by Princeton demographer Doug Massey, who argued that migration strengthens and expands bilateral social networks and makes future migration more likely.[53]

While acknowledging the role played by direct ties, more recent work has demonstrated how the presence of co-ethnic communities within destination countries may provide advantages in the absence of familial or social connections. For instance, established co-ethnic communities may provide new arrivals with information about how to find jobs and public services,[54] and may diminish the costs of migration and integration more broadly.[55] These studies predict that migration flows will be self-sustaining, with migrants most likely to select destinations with established co-ethnic communities.

Only recently, and in the context of increased migration across the developing world, have scholars argued that international migrants prioritize moving to societies where they can be assured a baseline of liberal democratic rights and freedoms. In particular, the importance of political speech, labor-market access, social service provisions, and legal protection has been found to play a role in bilateral migrant flows from 178 origin countries to 18 destinations between 1980 and 2006.[56] This work builds upon earlier studies that documented migrants' prioritization of political rights,[57]

democratic political institutions,[58] and an absence of corruption and discrimination.[59] By incorporating political factors, these perspectives further
nuance a debate previously defined by social or economic considerations.

Moving Targets

The uncertainty around what really drives prospective migrants' destination
preferences can be traced to two challenges researchers face. First, nearly
all conclusions have been drawn from surveys of immigrants who have
already settled in their country of destination and do not reflect the pool of
future migrants; rather, they represent the subset of people who previously
had the ability to complete a move.[60] This ability is actually a function
of admissions policies, migration costs, and informational flows.[61] When
asked about original destination preferences, these settled migrants also
likely engage in backward-looking – and therefore unreliable – reasoning.[62]

Second, the various pull factors believed to attract migrants are multidimensional and they tend to covary.[63] In other words, destination states
with higher wages often have generous welfare programs, stronger democratic institutions, *and* earlier generations of immigrants[64] – making it
harder to determine which of these attributes is truly driving prospective
migrants' preferences.[65] According to the polling displayed in Table 2.2,
the top nine most preferred destinations in the world are all democracies – but they also boast strong economies. To address these challenges, I
isolate the independent draw of the different pull factors before prospective migrants' choices are informed by realities on the ground.

TABLE 2.2 *The world's most preferred*
destination countries (Gallup 2021).

Country	2011	2021
United States	22%	18%
Canada	5%	8%
Germany	5%	7%
Spain	3%	4%
France	5%	4%
United Kingdom	7%	4%
Australia	4%	4%
Japan	1%	3%
Italy	3%	3%
Saudi Arabia	5%	2%

I employ a conjoint survey design – an approach widely used to model instances in which people decide between options that vary across a range of characteristics.[66] In contrast to direct questioning, conjoint designs give respondents the freedom to share their preferences more freely,[67] and they map more closely to respondents' actual behavior.[68] Conjoints were originally developed by marketing researchers who were trying to determine what drove consumers to select chocolate bars or laundry detergent. Within the field of migration studies, conjoint designs have recently been leveraged to understand citizens' preferences about immigrant admissions,[69] asylum seekers and refugees,[70] and immigration policies more generally.[71] To date, however, a conjoint design has not been leveraged to understand migrants' destination preferences.

The same group of respondents from Jordan, Lebanon, Libya, Palestine, and Tunisia was presented with two hypothetical country profiles, composed of a series of characteristics. Although everyone considered the same set of characteristics, the attributes within each profile vary randomly across each conjoint comparison, creating different tradeoffs in each comparison. After viewing the comparison, respondents were asked to select the country they prefer and to provide a rating on a 7-point scale reflecting their level of interest in moving to the hypothetical destination.[72] Based on these responses, I can determine the degree to which each characteristic shaped respondents' choices.[73]

Assume that you decided to move to another country for some reason, and you had the opportunity to move only to one of two hypothetical countries. Listen closely as I read their full descriptions to you:

Country A
- Close to Tunisia
- Economy is declining; few opportunities to find work
- Democratic government that protects human rights and offers full freedom
- Immigrants have immediate access to welfare benefits and health care
- Many Tunisians currently live there

Country B
- Far from Tunisia
- Economy is growing; opportunities to find work
- Autocratic government; does not protect human rights or offer full freedom

- Immigrants do *not* have immediate access to welfare benefits and health care
- Very few Tunisians currently live there

Questions

1. If you had to choose, which country would you move to?
   a. Country A
   b. Country B
2. On a scale of 1–7 (1 = not at all interested, 7 = very interested), how would you rate each country?
   a. Country A
   b. Country B

The national characteristics within the conjoint align with the contours of debates about what really drives emigrants' destination preferences:

- job availability;
- welfare accessibility;
- regime type;
- the presence of countrymen and countrywomen; and
- geographic distance from the origin country.[74]

While these factors often vary together across destination states, there remain plenty of differences and exceptions. For instance, Arab Gulf states like Qatar or Bahrain may provide immigrants with strong job opportunities in the absence of liberal democracy. Likewise, liberal democratic countries like the United Kingdom and the United States offer access to labor markets while fencing off public benefits from third country nationals. So the choice I present to prospective migrants represents reflects real-world variation in abstract destination characteristics.[75]

A Quest for Democracy and Prosperity

Given that the five countries I study differ in so many ways – their government, their economy, their social stability – it is remarkable that the rank order of priorities for emigrant destinations are so similar.

Holding other characteristics constant, prospective migrants consistently selected liberal democratic countries and those with high job availability. Prospective immigrants were 26.9 percent more likely to select a country profile if it was a democracy than if it was not. And they were 25.2 percent more likely to select a country profile if the economy was growing than if it was not.

While the appeal of growing economies with ample job opportunities has been well documented, the draw of democracies – to a slightly greater degree even – is a stunning finding. And the results also hold true among the subset of people who had already made plans to depart and despite the differences in the country destinations to which respondents' said they ideally want to move.

I also find that, in the context of other considerations, respondents are not likely to select destinations based on their geographic proximity or the presence of more countrymen and countrywomen. For some, this result will be quite surprising.[76] It challenges the persistent relationship that scholars have documented between flows and adjacent countries with established populations of immigrants[77] – what has been called "chain migration." Despite all the examples of chain migration from Mexico to the US, Morocco to Spain, and China to Japan, it is possible that geographic distance and the presence of countrymen and countrywomen may not shape migrants' priorities absent the actual opportunities they facilitate. In other words, Mexican people do not migrate to the United States because they independently want to be with other Mexicans; they migrate to the United States because their cousin tipped them off about a new round of hiring at her company or because their son has sponsored them for a visa.

The Welfare Magnet Reconsidered

My findings about the controversial "welfare magnet" theory are mixed. Respondents were 17 percent more likely to select a country with welfare programs available upon arrival. On the one hand, this validates the idea that prospective migrants prefer destinations where they have access to government benefits. On the other hand, the appeal of welfare access is substantially less than the appeal of job availability, perhaps reflecting the intention of the "social safety net" as a secondary, backup plan to employment.

Holding democratic governance constant, I calculate the share of respondents who were more likely to select a state with a robust labor market but no immediate access to welfare benefits, and those who were less likely to select a state with a weaker labor market and immediate benefit access. The results show that the majority of respondents within the sample preferred employment opportunities to welfare. However, this tendency is not statistically detectable in conflict regions like Libya and the Palestinian Territories, suggesting a more contentious decision-making process. I also find that men and individuals with higher education levels are less likely to optimize on welfare benefits.

These results suggest that welfare-seeking preferences are a risk hedge among individuals living in unstable situations. And indeed, demand for welfare strongly depended on employment prospects for people living in potentially precarious situations, including younger people, respondents with below-median incomes, and those with less formal education.

Among those who might select destinations based on welfare access, it is unclear to what extent prospective immigrants hold accurate information about welfare generosity across destinations.[78] To check this, I asked Lebanese respondents to select countries that provided the most and least generous benefits; few individuals gave correct answers.[79] While a sizable minority of respondents were able to identify Sweden as a country with a generous safety net (29.2 percent), recognition of other policy regimes was limited. In total, 49.7 percent of prospective migrants selected one of the three countries with the most generous benefit regimes – a rate similar to a coin flip.

Indeed, the United States, which imposes a five-year ban on initial welfare access,[80] was identified by prospective migrants as the second most generous state listed. The most educated respondents were more likely to hold accurate information about the availability of benefits. And of course, this is the population subgroup least likely to consume them.

In sum, while my findings suggest that prospective migrants do indeed consider welfare accessibility when evaluating destinations, my results are inconsistent with the logic advanced by those who have argued that welfare-seeking behavior emerges due to migrants' tendency to rationally maximize their income. Rather, my results suggest that demand for welfare is largely a function of risk aversion and that this demand is relatively weaker among people considering migrating to high-income democracies.

THE BIG SORT

Taken together, this research paints a vivid illustration of demigrants, democracy's carriers. Demographically, they are more likely to be young adults who have completed high school and possibly university. They disproportionately hail from developing countries that have weaker democratic norms and institutions, if any. They have networks of friends and family abroad and are themselves open-minded, adaptable, and less oriented toward authoritarian ideals.

Crucially though, they hold more liberal democratic political values than their countrymen and countrywomen. This means that when they leave, the population they leave behind will not only skew older, less educated, and more insular; it means that the population will also become less democratic and more authoritarian in its orientation. And when they depart, demigrants' initial destination preferences will draw them to democracies that reflect the political and civic values they hold – depleting the developing and less democratic world of precisely the people poised to contribute to its modernization *and* liberalization.

These findings crystallize the dynamics of what is ultimately a big sort – an uncoordinated phenomenon dependent on the effects of millions of individuals self-selecting into a mobile future. Still, they do not tell us about its mechanics. What stimulates demigrants' departure? What can trigger and intensify Democratic Drain? Chapter 3 addresses these questions.

3

Outvoted, Voting Out

Hong Kong has long been a tropical harbor of free commerce and free speech off the southeast coast of the Chinese mainland. For many decades, the shining towers wedged between the docks of Kowloon Bay and the forest-draped face of Victoria Peak were icons of its precarious, exceptional status in an authoritarian region.

After 156 years under the British Empire, Westminster returned the former colony to Chinese control in 1997. And even then, the city was ruled by a "one country, two systems" principle and a Basic Law that promised Hong Kong's "way of life shall remain unchanged for 50 years."[1] While many Hong Kong residents had been wary of the mainland, people retained their ability to elect some representatives and pro-democracy advocates were able to operate and express themselves freely in a number of independent news outlets.

But in 2019, China proposed an extradition bill that would have allowed Hong Kong defendants to be sent for trial in China. Anger erupted into some of the largest protests the city had ever seen and turned into a broader anti-China and pro-democracy movement.[2] Even some supporters of the reforms criticized the speed at which Hong Kong Chief Executive Carrie Lam sought their passage.

According to organizers, more than a million people marched in protest at one point, a chorus of predominantly young people carrying umbrellas – a symbol of Hong Kong's pro-democracy activism – joined by business groups, human rights nongovernmental organizations, and an international community concerned with maintaining Hong Kong's historic autonomy.[3]

"[This] boils down to a display of people power in Hong Kong, a display in particular of young people power," opposition lawmaker Claudia Mo told tens of thousands who had gathered outside the Legislative Council building on Sunday, June 9, 2019.[4]

Referring to 2014 protests when 100,000 protestors immobilized the city's financial districts for 79 days demanding free and open elections, she added, "At the end of the Umbrella Movement, didn't we say, 'We will be back'? And now, we are back!"

But three weeks later, an hour before the twenty-third anniversary of the city's handover by the British government, Beijing responded by introducing a new National Security Law.

The wide-ranging rules – which tightened Beijing's control over law enforcement, the judiciary, and foreign and domestic news agencies – gave the Chinese government the power to shape life in Hong Kong like never before.[5] In addition to institutional changes, the law criminalized any act that was deemed to undermine the power or authority of the Chinese officials and any collusion with foreign or external forces, making it easier to prosecute protesters and silence political opponents. Individuals suspected of related offenses could be surveilled and tried in mainland China, and those convicted faced up to life in prison and were barred from seeking public office. After the rules entered into force, thousands of citizens, activists, and opposition officials protested in the streets anew and 10,000 were arrested or imprisoned by the state.[6] The opposition lawmaker Claudia Mo and human rights advocate Jimmy Sham Tsz-kit were both convicted for organizing a conspiracy to commit subversion and imprisoned with hundreds of other activists.

An exodus followed.

Amid the Chinese government's campaign to cleanse the city of any dissent, the Census and Statistics Department reported that more than 113,000 residents left the territory between 2020 and 2021. While Chinese officials attributed the trend to a "natural" decrease – Hong Kong has the lowest territorial fertility rate in the world – the withdrawal marked Hong Kong's biggest annual population drop since recordkeeping began in 1961.[7] After the British government opened a special visa scheme for Hong Kong residents holding British Overseas National Passports,[8] more than 130,000 Hong Kongers moved to the UK in eighteen months. The number of people between twenty and twenty-nine years old shrunk from 12 percent of the city's population in 2019 to 10 percent in 2022 – part of three consecutive years of overall population decline.[9]

Many of those who left Hong Kong were English-speaking professionals with attractive credentials – the skilled workers that so many developed economies covet. This is one reason that British Prime Minister Boris Johnson – who had just run two election campaigns centered on anti-immigration rhetoric – was keen to recruit Hong Kong citizens displaced or concerned by Beijing's oppressive turn. In fact, in 2022, shortly after Singapore overtook Hong Kong in a ranking of global financial centers, the Chinese government introduced a new class of visas that allows skilled, high-earning foreign talent to work in Hong Kong for more than one employer at a time.[10] Enacted unilaterally by Beijing, the changes did not address the true driver of Hong Kong's lost talent: the brutal imposition of authoritarian rule.[11]

Talented Hong Kongers were equally sought-after in the years before the 2020 instability. And had their exodus been just a matter of their aversion to instability – and not authoritarianism – it is reasonable to have expected a similar number of departures in 2014 during the Umbrella Movement demonstrations. And yet, emigration numbers did not spike then, ostensibly because Hong Kong preserved people's right to protest and voice their political preferences. In 2020, nonviolent protestors and leaders of the opposition were imprisoned,[12] independent news sources were forcibly closed, advocates were intimidated, and elections were suspended – only to be held under a new system in 2021 that made it easier for a pro-Beijing candidate to be appointed as chief executive and others as Legislative Council members.

As the *New York Times* reported at the time of the 2021 ballot, it felt like earlier elections in Hong Kong. Just one thing was missing: "Any uncertainty about the outcome."[13] In November 2024, in the largest single prosecution to date, forty-five defendants – including former high-profile lawmakers, activists, unionists, and journalists – received prison sentences ranging from fifty months to ten years. In the words of CNN reporters Chris Lau and Nectar Gan, the 2020 National Security Law transformed Hong Kong into a "mirror of the authoritarian Chinese mainland."

In this chapter, I seek to better understand the mechanics of Democratic Drain. More specifically, *when* do demigrants depart?

Beijing's crackdown was a violent turning point, scrutinized by the world's media. But such momentous events – like Turkish President Recep Erdoğan's 2016 state of emergency and the 2025 arrest of his principal political opponent, or Prime Minister Binyamin Netanyahu's 2023 suspension of judicial independence in Israel – do not take place as frequently as decisions to emigrate.

Examining the more subtle, mundane indicators that signal democratic backsliding and drive millions of people to leave would allow us to better understand Democratic Drain – not only as a demographic trend grounded in a correlation between people's politics and their desire to emigrate (Chapter 2), but as a phenomenon that can be explained and therefore anticipated.

In this chapter, I extend this vignette about Hong Kong – plus another about contemporary Russia – to show that historians and social scientists have previously explained certain cases of emigration without expulsion as nevertheless politically driven. But like Beijing's 2020 crackdown and Russia's post-2022 suppression of dissent, these are extreme and rare events. It is harder to discern Democratic Drain as a broader phenomenon, particularly in contemporary times without the benefits of hindsight.

To do so, I focus on 127 countries worldwide and find that people's interest in emigrating increases in the immediate aftermath of elections when a relatively less-democratic party or candidate is elected or reelected to public office. This effect is pronounced among people who hold democratic values and expectations of institutional integrity. Those who question the honesty of the election, suspect corruption among public officials, or feel that freedom of speech is constrained are significantly more likely to say they would like to leave.

This shows the way that elections are precipitating events for individuals disappointed by the results and concerned about the future of their political institutions. Previously unnoticed over the ebb and flow of electoral cycles, emigration removes people most likely to voice democratic preferences and demand institutional integrity in less democratic spaces.

HONG KONG, 1989

A number of cases in recent history display the mechanics of Democratic Drain, much as Hong Kong did after Beijing's introduction of the National Security Law in 2020. In fact, Hong Kong exemplified the phenomenon earlier in its recent history.

One might even go so far as to say that Hong Kong grew to prominence as a beneficiary of Democratic Drain. Many of its citizens sought refuge after the Chinese Civil War that produced the communist state in 1949. Hong Kong's industrialization was driven in no small part by the capitalist creed of entrepreneurs who had fled Shanghai.[14] This enterprising, individualistic class of people came to define Hong Kong's values of personal independence, self-help, and autonomy. It was a place where poverty was not a collective failure but a product of individuals' inadequacies.[15] These were people who had no interest in living under an autocratic regime and a centrally controlled economy.

After the 1984 Sino-British Agreement on the future of Hong Kong, its residents were not sanguine about the city's prospects once it was integrated into China as a "special administrative region" in 1997. In a 1988 poll, about three quarters of Hong Kongers anticipated the curtailment of their civil rights and individual liberty. About two thirds expected the decline of Hong Kong's unique legal system and a deterioration in living standards. Asked if life would be better and happier after 1997, more than half said it was unlikely. One in four believed that public order would collapse in the near future.[16] Still, while the number of emigrants rose steadily after 1984 – from about 20,000 people per year in the early 1980s to 30,000 after 1984 – they remained a small fraction of the population.

The events of 1989 dispelled any doubt.

On June 4, the Chinese government massacred several thousand peaceful demonstrators calling for, among other things, greater transparency, constitutional due process, democracy, and freedom of speech in Tiananmen Square – the central Beijing plaza where Mao Zedong proclaimed the founding of the People's Republic of China forty years before. Precipitated by the death of pro-reform Communist Party General Secretary Hu Yaobang in April 1989 and a period of great economic change, up to 1 million protestors – many students – had occupied the square daily for six weeks. The movement spread to 400 Chinese cities before the government declared martial law and deployed 300,000 troops to crush what it called a "riot" and a "counter-revolutionary rebellion."

It was a statement heard clearly in Hong Kong.

In January 1989, 75 percent of people in Hong Kong said that they had confidence in the future of Hong Kong. When martial law was declared across the border in May, only 52 percent of Hong Kongers felt the same way.[17]

In January 1989, 29 percent of people in Hong Kong said they were actively preparing to emigrate or that they had family members in another country who would secure their permanent residence. After the Beijing massacre, the share of prospective emigrants grew to 37 percent – more than double the share I observed in far less developed places like

Lebanon, Palestine, and Tunisia in the surveys I reported in Chapter 2. In the same poll, one third of Hong Kong's 1.55 million households said they were planning to emigrate. Among executives, professionals, and entrepreneurs, 64 percent planned to leave Hong Kong, 18 percent more than in January 1989.[18]

These were not empty yearnings; even with the handover eight years away, Hong Kongers made preparations. Applications for official certificates of clean criminal records, which are required by most countries' visa applications, doubled after June 1989. The number of visa petitions to the United States consulate in August 1989 was 85 percent higher than for the same month in the previous year while the number of petitions for September was up by 233 percent.[19] Many Hong Kongers or their families had emigrated once in their lives and they were prepared to do so again.

According to official estimates, departures spiked. One percent of the population – over 60,000 people – voluntarily left every year from 1990 to 1993, before economic decline in the West and a boom in the greater Chinese region moderated outflows.[20] While Hong Kong emigrants had predominantly moved to the United States in the early 1980s, Canada and Australia became more prominent destinations in the late 1980s and 1990s. The British government was so concerned by the outflows, they increased university tuition subsidies and introduced the British Nationality Selection Scheme, which provided up to 50,000 heads of household with British nationality and the right of housing.[21]

In describing the hundreds of thousands who prepared to depart after 1989, University of Hong Kong sociologist Wong Siu-lun referred to them as "elites who are pushed to leave by the perception of political threats, not pulled away by economic opportunities."[22] They felt powerless over government policies and preferred to express their dissatisfaction by leaving.[23]

They were torn between their attachment to China as their original motherland and their disgust with the communist state. Independent and cosmopolitan, many came to regard themselves primarily as "Hong Kong people" before 1989 – but more as a way of life and a place of residence – rather than as "Chinese." Accordingly, they were unsentimental and transactional about their departures. "Passports are regarded mainly as travel and insurance documents," Wong wrote in 1992. "They are not endowed with much emotional significance such as national commitment and loyalty."[24]

RUSSIA, 2022

After Vladimir Putin's invasion of Ukraine in February 2022, national commitment and loyalty were tested across Russia – the most recent and prominent case of Democratic Drain worldwide.

With his military's struggle to conquer Kyiv several weeks into the conflict, the Russian President called for a Stalin-like purge in a nationally televised address on March 16, 2022.[25] In particular, he condemned the "slave-like" Russians who supported the "Nazi" West and said the country should "distinguish true patriots from scum and traitors and simply spit them out like a fly that accidentally flew into their mouths." He went on, "I am convinced that such a natural and necessary self-purification of society will only strengthen our country, our solidarity, cohesion and readiness to respond to any challenges."[26]

Prominent opponents were never welcomed inside Putin's Russia, but subtle dissent among low-profile people had been broadly tolerated. With its invasion of Ukraine, however, the Kremlin criminalized all dissent and citizens were urged to report the names and contact details of "provocateurs" and "pests" in connection with the country's "special operation."[27] There were reports of students turning in teachers and people reporting their neighbors and even nearby diners in restaurants.[28]

Some fearing their prosecution, others fearing the descent of Russia into poverty or chaos, many liberal Russians fled. And while most emigrants left upon the suppression of dissent or with the September 2022 declaration of a military draft, a significant number left immediately with the outbreak of war.

Within 18 months of the war beginning, between 817,000 and 922,000 people left.[29] These Russians moved all over the world, but the largest recipient countries were Kazakhstan and Serbia, each with 150,000 emigrants.

Serbia – which shares Slavic cultural roots and ties to the Eastern Orthodox Church – has stayed neutral during the invasion of Ukraine and so its flag carrier Air Serbia is the only airline that could shuttle between Russia and Europe after the invasion.[30] With all other air traffic barred by airspace bans, seat capacity between Russia and Serbia surged by about 50 percent in the first week of March 2022 compared with pre-war levels.[31] The carrier at least doubled its capacity to Moscow and St. Petersburg after war began, even adding a widebody Airbus SE A330 aircraft previously used for flights to New York City.[32] After being criticized for widening this loophole, the Serbian government reduced seat availability and, after the announcement of a military draft in September 2022, ticket prices soared.[33]

Hotel Moskva

It was not the first time the Hotel Moskva in central Belgrade had received large numbers of liberal Russian dissidents.

Opened as the Rossiya Palace (Palata Rosija) in 1908, the Russian-backed complex overlooking the Sava River was once the largest building in the city – an opulent landmark that attracted Russian artists and offered international newspapers and Viennese classical music.[34] And after the Russian Civil War in 1923, the hotel brimmed with White Russians who had opposed the communist Bolsheviks and continued operating as militarized associations in exile. A mix of republican-minded liberals, social democrats, monarchists, and supporters of a united multinational Russia, many sought refuge in Belgrade before the outbreak of the Second World War.[35]

A century later, yet again a variety of Russian emigrants passed between the smooth, shiny, crimson tiles lining the entryway of the Vienna Secessionist building with its green accents and ancient Greek ornaments. But unlike their 1920s predecessors, my interviewees were not gathering themselves to resist the Russian autocracy; they were just trying to survive in an unstable time and build a new life.

Nikita is a thirty-three-year-old from St. Petersburg, who works remotely for a Cypriot company. He walked into the Hotel Moskva's café in a plain white T-shirt, his hair neatly combed, light stubble over his full lips. The pianist played an assertive rendition of Carlos Gardel's "Por Una Cabeza."

"Actually, there are two types of migrants from Russia," he said. "There are ideologically driven migrants and 'sausage migrants.' Ideological migrants are those who do not agree with what was happening in [Russia] or were against the war and migrated to where there is freedom of speech, democracy, mainly to Western Europe."

Sausage Migrants

"Sausage migrants are those people who have money," Nikita explained, employing a Russian metaphor for emigrants seeking economic prosperity dating back to the scarcity of sausage and other meat products during Soviet food shortages. "After the war, their life became inconvenient for them; that is, Netflix was canceled, they could not watch movies or access WhatsApp and Instagram. Stores like Zara, IKEA were closed, so they decided to move to other countries if they could·afford it. But even the sausage migrants – purposeless, self-indulgent, materialist, YOLO ['You only live once'] – they still understand what's going on."

He looked down at his left forearm, which was covered in a spiderweb tattoo.

"Every Russian has a choice: to be silent and do nothing to resist, or to leave," Nikita continued. "In the case of Ukraine, it was not possible to be silent. For the middle class, there was always an implicit deal with Putin. As long as people have peace and a comfortable, stable life, they are not so afraid of what is happening abroad and they would stay quiet. But when the sanctions began and the Internet began to be blocked, that deal was broken and it meant the emigration of the middle class."

Like other multinational firms that employed Russians, Nikita's company was concerned they would be subject to sanctions and actively facilitated their employees' departures. When the war started, they allocated a one-month advance payment to employees who wished to leave. Nikita didn't hesitate.

"I've never been an activist," he said. "I tried to sign a few petitions against war or corruption, but I always stayed inside the boundaries of Russian law. I did not support [the late opposition politician and anti-corruption activist, Alexei] Navalny. I wasn't really politically active until the 24th of February. For me, the start of the war crossed a red line. And even though it will eventually end, the regime will not change. And there's no chance of a revolution … unless Putin leaves power."

The sausage migrants may not be ideologically driven, but they are often liberal and cosmopolitan. Many are software programmers or have other jobs in the information technology industry. With the·outbreak of war, they were able to work remotely, typically for overseas companies that paid in foreign currency. Others opened new business entities in Serbia.

Just over a month after Russia invaded Ukraine, 323 companies with Russian founders were registered in Serbia – 25 percent of all active Russian-founded legal entities in Serbia on record. In March 2022, an average of nine companies were founded per day.[36]

According to Serbian law, Russians are able to enter and remain in the country for thirty days before needing to briefly leave the country to restart the clock. Russians who are ineligible for a visa or residency but wish to remain in Serbia take a monthly daytrip to Bosnia for a "cup of coffee," and drive back across the border. Some Russians are known to have lived this way for decades.

Evacuees

Still, a large number of Russians in Serbia were indeed ideologically driven and destined for liberal democratic states in Western Europe. Many expressed a sense of isolation and sudden danger before they fled their homeland.

"The IT workers are people with an open worldview, they don't want to support the war with their taxes; they are mindful, self-aware. We, who arrived recently, are evacuees," said Masha, a forty-one-year-old tourism agent from Moscow who had lost her job with the onset of the pandemic in 2020. "*Evakuashka*. It is a person who was forced to flee the country, urgently evacuated to wherever he could."

Initially, Masha had doubts about leaving Russia right away. She hesitated to leave her furniture, appliances, and other material belongings behind. However, most of her friends decided to leave Russia after the first day of the war. Those who stayed in Russia were not financially stable enough to depart and neither was she really.

"It's a matter of values," she said, draping her saffron scarf over her shoulder. "[They're] more important than your salary. I don't want to associate myself with Russia because of the war. I can give up my passport. Besides, the value-driven people are leaving, and the revolution has departed ... The more people leave, the less chance there is for change."

Inna was no more prepared.

The thirty-six-year-old St. Petersburg-based fitness trainer was visiting an old friend in Belgrade when war broke out in Ukraine and she never returned. Dressed in an olive sports bra and a shiny, black puffer coat with her brown hair pulled back, Inna had just left the gym. Before becoming a trainer, she had worked for an organization that educated and prepared election observers in Russia.

"My duties included short-term observation of the elections during the voting – making sure voting is fair – and there I saw how the whole system works," she said. "One day, when we were counting the votes and the results of the elections for the State Duma [the lower house of the Federal Assembly of Russia], the woman who was responsible for counting the votes of the opposition simply took a whole box of voting cards and ran out, so that we could not determine how many votes there were. I was so surprised by what people were willing to do for money.

And she was a primary school teacher. If she does such things, then what will she teach our children?"

Inna wants to move to Western Europe, but is struggling to gain entry. When we spoke, she had already written letters to the embassies of twenty-six European Union countries. Few close friends remained in St. Petersburg, she said, and only one of them supported her when Inna decided to stay in Serbia. Her parents stopped all communication with her, even on her birthday a few weeks before.

"There is nothing left for me there," she said.

Ana and Grigor felt equally despairing. But mostly, they were just scared for their lives.

Struggling artists from St. Petersburg, Grigor was earning 450 euros per month as a book illustrator in Belgrade, while Ana worked as a minimum-wage cleaner. On March 2, 2022, their families chipped in to pay for their tickets from Moscow to Belgrade, where they were living with friends. Grigor's mother was born in Odessa, but he and Ana were both staunch supporters of Ukraine and ultimately wanted to move there once the war concluded.

Ana, thirty-six, was in a canary-yellow trench coat and round glasses with thick lenses. Grigor, twenty-three, wore a maroon jacket with a Ukrainian flag pinned to his left sleeve and a "Free Russia" flag pinned to his right. The latter was a Russian Federation flag drained of its "blood"-red pigment, leaving a light-blue stripe between two white stripes.

As a youth, Grigor had been very affected by the 2015 assassination of Boris Nemtsov – a Russian physicist, opposition politician, and former deputy prime minister – and later by the poisoning of Alexei Navalny.

"There were black days for me," he said. "The weight of the situation crushed me. And it drove me to politics."

As a teenager, he protested Russia's 2014 annexation of Crimea and Navalny's 2021 arrest, always with a Ukrainian flag on his sleeve. But the January 2022 protests against the buildup of Russian troops on Ukrainian borders before the war commenced, he said, "gave you the feeling of doing something very dangerous."

"There was the smell of something very rotten in the air," he elaborated. "Provocateurs placed in the crowd, radicals, freaks who came to destroy it. There seemed to be a small army of undercover police, entering the grounds. You got the sense that they wanted to eat you. When we ran from the chaos, it felt like we were being chased by a pack of mad dogs. I have no money, but I try to do whatever I can."

Shuffling cigarettes around in the ashtray, Grigor said, "I'm resentful of Russia's creative class because they are complicit with the regime."

To the extent that other observers have suspected something like a Democratic Drain phenomenon taking place in world affairs, they have focused on the exceptional circumstances of events like those of 1989 and 2020 in Hong Kong and 2022 in Russia. But if Democratic Drain were limited to such extraordinary occasions, it would be a localized trend, specific to crises. To the contrary, I have argued that, while Democratic Drain may intensify at these turning points in political development, it is more commonly characterized by the steady depletion of democratic human capital – and so it must be driven by something far more mundane.

The findings from Chapter 2 show how those inclined to leave for economic or family reasons will bring disproportionately liberal democratic proclivities with them. Now in this chapter, I show that those who depart voluntarily for political reasons do not need a once-in-a-generation crisis to mobilize them. Something far more routine has much the same effect: national elections.

OUTVOTED

Mass emigration from Russia is not new, even after the end of the Cold War. In the first 19 years of Vladimir Putin's rule, 1.6 to 2 million people left the country, though the rate had been declining since 1999. However, when Putin returned to the Russian presidency in an election marked by fraud and protests in 2012, departures spiked again – suggesting the effect of disappointing national election results on citizens' decision-making.

And indeed, emigration has long been understood as a response to unwanted political change in a variety of contexts, beginning with Albert O. Hirschman's 1970 model of "voice," "loyalty," and "exit." When people who do not wish to, or cannot, voice their political opinion, Hirschman expected many to leave a polity entirely – what has been called "voting with one's feet" – as a rational response to political conditions.[37]

But people who study world politics have focused principally on the departure of elite dissidents following elections. Political opponents have prominently emigrated from such regimes in places such as Algeria, Chile, Egypt, Nicaragua, Nigeria, South Africa, and Uganda, among others.[38] Those leaving Cuba and Nicaragua in the wake of the ascent of left-wing regimes in both nations were noticeably richer and more educated than previous emigrants from those countries.[39] Similarly, many private-sector elites emigrated in the wake of President Alberto Fujimori's victory in

Peru and the victory of President Evo Morales in Bolivia.[40] Emigration is a commonly understood reaction to elections, but only among those who have personally lost power – people closely affiliated with a losing party or a group that stands to be disfavored or oppressed by the new regime.

As an extension of my findings from Chapter 2 about the liberal democratic proclivities of prospective migrants, I explore the possibility that – even if they are not directly impacted by the politics of an elected party or candidate – average people may similarly wish to emigrate when authoritarians gain power and threaten to roll back precious rights and freedoms, deepen corruption, or undercut institutional integrity. I expect that these sociotropic conditions would be specific to weaker democratic states teetering on the edges of authoritarianism when authoritarian-leaning candidates are elected. This is a possibility that has not been examined across countries before.

Elections as Triggers

To test this possibility, I return to the Gallup World Poll leveraged in Chapter 2 to better understand the demographic and ideological attributes of the world's prospective migrants (see Figure 3.1). From this earlier analysis, we already know that people with negative views about the democratic quality of their respective countries' public institutions are more likely to report their interest in emigrating – part of the phenomenon

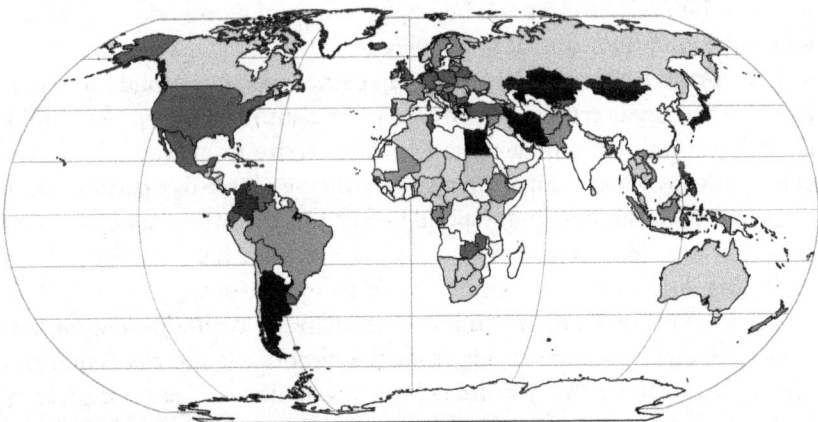

FIGURE 3.1 Countries included in the elections analysis.
Note: Countries in white are not included in the analysis. Countries in shades of gray are included in the analysis. Darker shades indicate a greater number of elections included for a particular country. For example, six elections are included in the analysis for Argentina, while only one for Peru.

I call Democratic Drain. But does interest in emigrating spike after an election in which authoritarian-leaning candidates gain power?[41]

In their pursuit of samples that comprise thousands of people nationally, Gallup's extended periods of data collection often immediately precede, immediately follow, or are actually intersected by national elections. This provides an opportunity to examine people's responses just before, just after, and both before and after election results are released. Because survey administrators collect respondents' data in a random sequence – respondents contacted before the election are not observably distinct from those contacted afterward – any differences in their preferences and views can be attributed to the effect of the election results.

Focusing on respondents interviewed within the last 81 days before and within the first 81 days after national elections,[42] it is possible to study these dynamics around 234 elections across 125 countries between 2004 and 2022 – a total sample of 225,442 respondents during a period during which the world witnessed significant democratic backsliding in many regions. (See Appendix C for a list of countries and election years.)

To determine which elections produced democratic backsliding, I distinguish between "deconsolidating" and "consolidating" elections.[43] Using the three most meticulous evaluations of democratic institutions available worldwide – V-Dem Polyarchy, V-Dem Liberal Democracy, and Polity[44] – I define a deconsolidating election as one where the country's annual score drops in the year following the election compared to the year before the election. Inversely, a consolidating election is one where the country's annual score increases.[45]

In Figure 3.2, the results from the three measures of consolidation present a common pattern. In countries that are consolidating (in light gray), the proportion of respondents indicating a desire to migrate to another country drops when comparing results from the ninety-day period before the election to the ninety-day period after. On the other hand, in countries that are deconsolidating (in dark gray), the share of respondents indicating a desire to migrate to another country grows.

These results hold even if the data is analyzed with different parameters – at different time bands from the election, if the case countries are limited to those that feature neither strong democracies nor severely authoritarian regimes, if the sample is limited to survey periods intersected by an election, and if we focus only on people who not only intend to emigrate but who have explicitly made plans. Interestingly, while women are marginally more likely to be dissatisfied by government institutions, consistent with findings from Chapter 2, they are marginally less

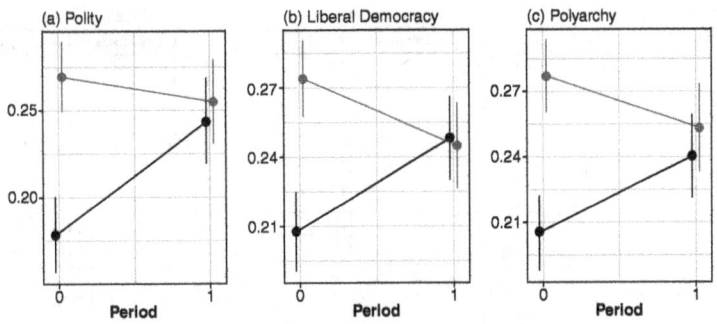

FIGURE 3.2 Migration intention and democratic consolidation and deconsolidation.
Note: Panels (a), (b), and (c) show predicted values before and after the election for consolidation countries (light gray) and deconsolidating countries (dark gray).

likely to wish to emigrate. (For the results of alternative analyses, please see Appendix C.)

Put plainly, improving democratic conditions are correlated with less interest in emigrating, while weakening democratic conditions are correlated with more interest.[46] The prospect of democratic decline motivates large numbers of average people to emigrate in a way not demonstrated before.

Voter Mobilization

To truly constitute the Democratic Drain phenomenon observed in Chapter 2, however, election results promising a democratic decline would specifically spur *people who hold democratic values*. The effect would be more pronounced among respondents who express concern about the status of liberal democratic institutions.

To test this hypothesis, I estimate a model similar to the one using the Gallup World Poll data earlier in this chapter, but interacting my concern with the period immediately before and after elections, my previous measures of democratic consolidation, and also individual-level views about democratic quality.

As I explain in Chapter 2, the Gallup World Poll asks respondents about their migration plans and also the quality of public institutions in their countries, a proxy for liberal democratic values. Specifically, the poll asks whether people have confidence in the honesty of elections and in the national government, whether people believe there is corruption within the government, and whether people believe that individuals and members of the media possess the freedom to express their views and

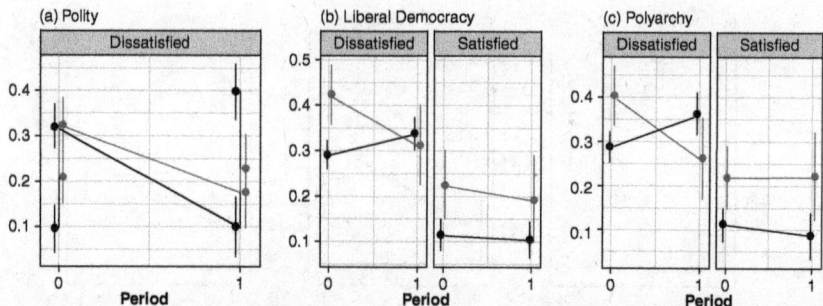

FIGURE 3.3 Democratic consolidation and individual views on democratic institutions.

report news accurately – five indicators that I aggregate into a single, scaled measure of liberal democratic values.

As Figure 3.3 shows, among respondents with the most negative views about the quality of their country's democratic institutions, a consolidating election triggers a reduction in the desire to migrate, whereas a deconsolidating election triggers an increase. Meanwhile, among respondents with the most positive views about the quality of their country's democratic institutions, neither consolidating nor deconsolidating elections have an influence on their desire to migrate. This is true across three different approaches to measuring democratic deconsolidation, panels (a), (b), and (c).

The left and right plots in each panel of Figure 3.3 also reflect the findings from Chapter 2. Among respondents with the most negative views about democracy in their country, the desire to migrate is higher – both before *and* after the election – than for respondents who have a positive view about the quality of the democracy in their country.

VOTING OUT

Taken together, these results reveal the mechanics of the Democratic Drain phenomenon. Democratic values are not only associated with people's desire to emigrate. The prospect of democratic decline spurs people with liberal democratic proclivities to leave their countries of origin and – according to my findings from Chapter 2 – to migrate to places with stronger democratic institutions. Migrants are indeed democracy's carriers, but they are also democracy agitators and democracy seekers.

To the extent prospective migrants' plans to exit are realized, this has massive consequences. Examining protest data in authoritarian regimes, researchers have found that, when economic opportunity exists abroad and people are free to emigrate, countries with higher levels of emigration experience fewer political protests thereafter.[47] And much like Hong Kong – whose citizens were thought to be far less connected to their country of origin – emigration likely spiked in the countries I studied in the period after the election of authoritarian-leaning public officials.

Alas, it is very challenging to connect people's expressed desire to migrate with real-world demographic trends. This is because global bilateral flow data – which accounts for country-to-country movement each year – is not available outside the world's high-income nations, most of which are already consolidated democracies. Future work would do well to connect elections that swing power to more authoritarian parties with emigration trends thereafter. For now, as the next chapter shows, the best chance to witness the demographic manifestations of Democratic Drain is to see whether there is a sliding scale of liberal democratic values descending from destination states to migrants' countries of origin.

4

The Sliding Scale

Szabadság Tér – Liberty Square – sits at the center of Budapest's centermost neighborhood. It was once the site of an old prison where Prime Minister Lajos Batthyány was executed following the Hungarian Revolution in 1849. But today it is a leafy sculpture garden surrounded by stately ministerial and diplomatic buildings, all adjacent to Hungary's striking, neo-Gothic parliament (Figure 4.1), which was completed a few years after the jail was razed in 1897.

The square's monuments are a reflection of twentieth-century Hungary's countervailing political forces. A larger-than-life statue of US President Ronald Reagan stands at the rounded north end of the park (Figure 4.2), directly opposing a memorial devoted to the Red Army he opposed. Three decades after the conclusion of the Cold War, the Soviet memorial is the last of its kind in Budapest. At the southern extreme, there is a statue of Hungary's polarizing, right-wing interwar leader Miklós Horthy, hailed as a hero by some and decried as a fascist by others. But most controversially, the Hungarian government established a 2014 memorial to "Victims of the German Occupation" that critics have argued whitewashes Hungary's complicit deportation of its Jewish citizens to Nazi death camps during the Second World War. Since its erection, protesters established an ever-changing "countermonument," the Living Memorial – an assembly of artifacts, photos, and flowers that has become Hungary's most prominent site of civic protest (Figure 4.3).

FIGURE 4.1 Parliament, Budapest, Hungary.

The entire scene is a dignified assortment fittingly in the foreground of Europe's most polarizing government – overseen by Prime Minister Viktor Orbán, himself a paradoxical figure.

One of the founding members of the Fidesz political party – originally an acronym for "Alliance of Young Democrats" – Orbán was a fierce young advocate for free elections and the withdrawal of Soviet troops in the late 1980s. He was the beneficiary of a scholarship to study political science at Pembroke College, Oxford, from Hungarian billionaire George Soros' democracy-promoting philanthropy. In January 1990, Orbán left Oxford to run for a seat in Hungary's first post-communist parliament.

But over the next two decades, Orbán evolved from a center-right liberal into the global face of far-right nationalism – an iconic model for illiberal, populist politicians across Europe.[1] A pariah in pro-democracy circles, Orbán has undermined the independence of Hungary's news media and judiciary, inserted party loyalists to direct the country's universities and cultural institutions, and redrawn electoral districts to disenfranchise his opposition. He has tenuously maintained Hungary's membership in the European Union (EU) and reaped the benefits of its subsidies and market access, all while denouncing Brussels and its

FIGURE 4.2 Szabadság Tér, Budapest, Hungary.

cosmopolitan liberalism. He and Fidesz won three consecutive national elections in 2010, 2014, and 2018, and surmounted a historic, unified opposition in April 2022 to win another four-year term and a parliamentary supermajority – a backbreaking defeat for Hungary's liberals and progressives that, as Chapter 3 anticipates, likely generated outflows of demigrants.

FIGURE 4.3 The Living Memorial, Budapest, Hungary.

To demonstrate the extent of this Democratic Drain, I have primarily focused until now on numerical evidence that shows that the depletion of democratic political capital is not merely an exceptional occurrence or something specific to certain regions or circumstances, but actually a global phenomenon. Like many global phenomena, Democratic Drain is the accumulation of millions of microeconomic, household-level decisions.

In this chapter, I engage with these decisionmakers – in Hungary but also Serbia during the same time period.[2] Their stories are matters of family, romance, and dreams, but also principles, values, and integrity; and often violations, disappointment, and trauma. These illustrations ground a global trend in the everyday considerations of average people.

I then leverage a unique study of European public opinion to reveal the way that Eastern Europeans who move West under the EU's free mobility rules hold more liberal democratic proclivities than those in their countries of origin who wish to migrate, and how those prospective migrants hold more liberal democratic proclivities than their countrymen who don't wish to move at all – a "sliding scale" of liberal democratic views among people with the same origins.

THE JEWISH QUARTER

A short walk to the east from Liberty Square, Budapest's Jewish Quarter is a holding pen for Hungary's eager aspirants (Figures 4.4, 4.5, 4.6, and 4.7). It is a hip, central neighborhood that was once the flourishing hub of Hungarian Jewish life from the late eighteenth century until the Second World War and Holocaust. After German and Hungarian Nazis turned the area into a ghetto – and killed, starved, or displaced hundreds of thousands of Hungarian Jews – the quarter declined during the communist era. But since the end of the Cold War, it has experienced a revival. Retail shops, ruin bars, and stylish restaurants have moved into the hollowed spaces near the Dohány Street Synagogue – Europe's largest – and converted the quarter into a convivial district that attracts fashionable locals and tourists in equal measure. The designer stores and trendy dining, framed by rustic exteriors blackened with time and tattooed with bright graffiti, symbolize Budapest's grit and creative energy. The contrast is catnip for Hungary's bright young things.

FIGURE 4.4 Deák Ferenc Tér, Budapest, Hungary.

FIGURE 4.5 Jewish Quarter, Budapest, Hungary.

On a late Monday afternoon – one week after Orbán and Fidesz were reelected in April 2022 – bars were already filling up with a mix of twenty- and thirty-somethings, seemingly all of whom were on their way out of Hungary or just returning from time abroad.

Rita

I met Rita outside Fekete Kutya, The Black Dog pub on Dob Street, three blocks north of the synagogue. Swimming in an oversized lavender hoody and black puffer vest, she was joining a friend for a casual beer. Rita was training to be a psychotherapist, but she was the one who was feeling disturbed that day.

"The election was a very big slap in the face for us, for our community, friends and family; the bubble that we live in just burst," she said, rubbing her forehead and lifting her sunglasses up to hold back her ample brown hair.

"Fidesz was not even the biggest tragedy," she said, referring to Mi Hazánk, the "Our Homeland" Party, an extreme far-right party that won

FIGURE 4.6 Erzsébet Tér, Budapest, Hungary.

seven parliamentary seats and nearly a million votes in 2022. "We weren't expecting that they would get into the Parliament, let alone with this many seats. Mi Hazánk is a way of thinking; it means that people who voted for them support their ideas. I don't want to be dramatic but there is a reason why people call them 'Nazis.' It's because they have the same ideology."

FIGURE 4.7 Astoria Metro Station, Budapest, Hungary.

Rita said that she planned to leave Hungary and was open to different destinations. She had spent a year in Spain a few years ago and would consider returning, or moving to an English-speaking country.

"Before the elections, everybody said to me, 'I understand that you want to leave but please don't,' and, 'Just try to change things for the better here.' But now, everybody is on the same page; they're leaving. Now everybody understands that there is no hope left."

She took a sip of her beer. "It doesn't matter what you do. If you go to protest, to strike, things won't change."

Exasperated, she peered down the colonnade.

Gergő and Dávid

A few seats away, Gergő was no more hopeful. A thirty-three-year-old product designer from Kecskemét – a small city fifty miles southeast of Budapest – he and his fiancée had hinged their plans to move to Berlin on the outcome of the election. They were willing to stay in Hungary, so long as Fidesz did not win a parliamentary supermajority, the two thirds of the chamber required to pass changes to the national constitution.

"I have a flat here and I still pay the mortgage on it, so I was just trying to be calm and realistic, and think it through if we really want to leave," he said.

"After the elections I was like, 'Okay, now it's over.' You know, I have feelings for my country. I love it. I want the best for the Hungarian people and for the country too. I pay my taxes here. I work here. And I volunteer here. So I really want to make it better. But on the other hand, I am thinking forward to my future children. Do I want to raise my children here? Would it be good for them here?"

Gergő wore a black jacket and a turquoise cycling cap with the brim flipped up to reveal his fleshy, unshaven face. Gergő had the friendly, open demeanor of someone earnest who felt somehow violated.

"One of the biggest problems is that the people, the nation, they think what Orbán thinks," he continued. "But to be honest, I am the angriest at the opposition. There is no real alternative from Fidesz ... There is no debate between the two sides in Hungary. Fidesz has shut down the debates.

"Another big problem is that Fidesz polarizes society. Words like 'liberal' have become a swear word and the ideas that I agree with have become dirty. Classic values like dignity, conversation. Fidesz doesn't believe in these values but they talk just in keywords and stop critical thinking. All the important institutions are in Fidesz's hands – all media, and all the universities."

He paused to greet his colleague, Dávid, who had just arrived.

Dávid was also a graphic designer, from Kaposvár – a town 100 miles southwest toward the Croatian border. Tall, slender, with deep-set eyes and a receding hairline, he had just left work and overheard the end of our conversation.

He didn't blame Gergő for departing to Berlin, but he didn't think the most recent Fidesz victory was any more reason to emigrate than the party's earlier triumphs. For Dávid, Hungary was not a country that wanted liberal democracy. In fact, he doesn't think Hungarians want democracy at all.

"Hungary has never been a free country," he said as a point of fact. "If you look at Hungarian history, we never had democracy. We have had a democratic system only for the last 30 years. And so we never knew how to act in a democratic system. We have never been introduced to how to think as citizens; we were always told what to think. Even in the last 30 years, in the beginning, they tried to introduce this way of thinking – critically, and as citizens. But then the government stopped trying. Politicians always wanted to decide for us.

"The campaign of Fidesz said that we are going forward, but actually we are going backward." He looked briefly at Gergő. "Or at least we are staying where we always have been, at a stage where there is no freedom."

Marci

One block away, I met Marci, a twenty-four-year-old commercial media professional, at Dobrumba – a mod, vegan-friendly Levantine restaurant (Figure 4.8). She had just spent several years in Germany and Poland and was prepared to leave again.

Even if the opposition coalition had defeated Fidesz, she planned to move to London the following year. It was a decision she had made years ago, but she wanted to first finish her finance degree in Budapest.

"It wasn't even this election," she said. "I was already thinking about leaving four years ago after the previous election. And I decided to move because, okay, the political climate is one factor, but there are professional reasons too. I work in the media and you know there are more opportunities in my field abroad. I want to work in directing and the business side of the media, and this doesn't exist in Hungary. I think if the press would be freer in the country, there would be more opportunity."

She particularly admired RTL, a privately owned Hungarian television channel with a younger, urban audience. RTL has been one of a few television networks to be openly critical of Viktor Orbán and the Fidesz government since they rose to power in 2010. As a result, it has been the target of frequent scrutiny by Fidesz-controlled media regulators and a proposed 2014 policy that would have taxed up to 50 percent of

FIGURE 4.8 Dobrumba, Jewish Quarter, Budapest, Hungary.

commercial television networks' advertising revenue. Fidesz ultimately backed down from the tax proposal under pressure from EU, German and Luxembourgian officials, and after RTL threated to file a lawsuit with the International Court of Justice. In order to protect the station's independence from the Orbán government, RTL moved the licenses of its Hungarian stations to Luxembourg.

"After the [2022] elections, all of my friends reacted as if the end of the world had come," she continued. "But I think actually everything will stay the same. If the opposition had won, there might be some hope. But with these results, everything will stay the way it is as the country slowly radicalizes. They do it really professionally, Fidesz. It's not like things change from Day 1 to Day 2."

She slid her fork under the leaves of her Fattoush salad.

"I think it's problematic what happens on the policy level. Fidesz advocates for nationalism and anti-EU ideas in their institutions and at every level of Hungary … Hungary has turned into a place where people think in a nationalist, anti-Western way. I've come to the point where I can't identify with the society around me, and that is one of the biggest reasons for leaving. I don't feel home in this society anymore."

For many people like Marci in Hungary's cultural spaces, the profes-sional has become inescapably political. Accordingly, they see emigration as a path to fulfill their values *and* their career goals.

Kata

Kata, even more directly, has experienced the politicization of profes-sional spaces (Figure 4.9).

She came to the Jewish Quarter that evening in a sheer mauve top lay-ered over a silky bubblegum blouse, both pressed under an ivory corset. Fair and slender, she wore iridescent teal eyeshadow, red lipstick, and small pearls affixed to the top of her cheeks like lustrous freckles. With her marmalade hair in a styled bob, Kata stood out from her concrete surroundings.

Her appearance was as thoughtful and outspoken as her views. A feminist activist, lately she had been far more agitated by the Fidesz government's series of legislation targeting gay, lesbian, bisexual, and transgender people. In 2020, the parliament prohibited same-sex cou-ples from adopting children and prohibited gender changes in citizens'

FIGURE 4.9 Kata.

personal documents. Then in 2021, public officials outlawed communicating with people under eighteen years old anything that the government considers to be promoting homosexuality or gender fluidity. The law also banned companies from running advertisements that expressed solidarity with gay people and restricted television shows and films from featuring gay characters or even a rainbow flag.

The series of laws, which followed similar prohibitions in Poland and Russia, were immediately condemned by global civil society groups but also a coalition of EU peer governments, which decried Hungary's overt discrimination against gay, lesbian, bisexual, and transgender people and its failure to protect citizens' freedom of speech and expression.

A twenty-year-old photography student who grew up attending a private, alternative high school for the arts, Kata had worked in the fashion industry since she was sixteen. She had made numerous friends who were affected by the new policies and by the casual, homophobic rhetoric it licensed inside Hungarian families and workplaces. Kata came to realize that the laws did not just constrain the freedom and rights of gay people, but also their allies.

A few months before, she applied to Budapest's Moholy-Nagy University of Art and Design, which asked photography degree candidates to prepare a portfolio that responded to the prompt, "*Egy régi történet margójára,*" or "To the margins of an old tale." Channeling her frustrations with the homophobic legislation, she shot a series of photos of her "feminine" boyfriend to reflect on the alienation of average Hungarians from the traditional values the government sought to impose.

"I don't want to be labeled," she said. "I can be attracted to anyone who I like."

However, in the final-round interview, she faced a panel of evaluators who told her that the subject matter was "overplayed." She recounted, "They asked me how it is okay to fight for LGBTQ rights while nationalists cannot say their opinions?"

Initially, earnestly, she tried to view the feedback as thought-provoking and felt compelled to answer it sincerely as a generative exercise. "But then they started to say more homophobic and sexist things," she said. "After I talked about how important feminism is for me, they answered that they believe that today men are more oppressed than women."

Kata's evaluators were connected to Hungary's Nemzeti Együttműködés Rendszere, Orbán's "System of National Cooperation" – the catchphrase for Fidesz reforms since its second election in 2010. Presented by Fidesz as a social contract between citizens to implement a new approach to governance, the system has steadily shifted control of higher education, but also institutions related to culture, health care, agriculture, and memory politics, to private foundations managed by leaders appointed by the Fidesz party to long, and in some cases unlimited, terms. Doing so has tightened the party's control over everything from curricular matters at universities to the management of government-owned mansions, resorts, ports, parks, theatres, clinics, and public–private enterprises. It also ensures that the party's loyalists continue to control these government-funded institutions independently of who wins future elections – a tactic previously employed in the late 1980s by the technocratic elite of Hungary's last communist government to salvage their influence.[3] Similar supervisory authorities oversee Hungary's Media Council, Energy Authority, and its regulator of tobacco and gambling.

Kata ended up enrolling at the University of Fine Arts, but she plans to depart for the Netherlands as soon as she completes her degree.

"It's just so fucking bad that I will have to leave," she said bitterly. "I now have a lot of [professional] connections. So I have my career here. But most importantly, my friends, and my family. Also, I love Budapest. I love the city and the people. So why should I leave if I have a career here? But I won't have a reason to stay. I cannot imagine living in Hungary."

She straightened her posture and reflected for a moment.

"The elections shocked me," she admitted. "I didn't think it was going to be this bad, that the whole map will be orange [for Fidesz]. After the elections, all my friends said that they want to leave too. If my friends leave, and the people I love, then my career here is replaceable."

"Before the elections, I thought it was super selfish to leave the country because, if we leave, then who will stay? But now, I think it might be selfish, but my personal well-being is more important for me than Hungary."

Áron

Áron has made the same calculation. In fact, he made plans to leave Hungary the day after the 2022 election.

"After the elections I only focused on myself," he said. "I think it is quite a normal psychological reaction that after a shock you focus on yourself. I was like: it's totally fine that I quit my job. You know I have everything here at the moment. I have a flat, I have a job, I got a cat a year ago. But I decided that it doesn't matter, I can rent out my flat, I can give my cat to one of my friends to take care of him. It would hurt, but I could do that in order to live my life freely. Because I think that it is more important that I could live freely."

Áron is a twenty-four-year-old psychologist and social worker who had devoted the entirety of his young career to supporting disenfranchised Roma minorities in Hungary (Figure 4.10). After volunteering at his organization for four years as a teenager, he has worked for them since 2018. Slim and handsome, he wore his chocolate-brown hair in a ponytail, which emphasized the square jawline framing his friendly smile.

"To my story, I think it is important that I'm gay," he said frankly. "I have an amazing situation in Hungary, and I always envisioned living in Budapest for the rest of my life. I love the city, I have the people who I love here — my friends, my family. And I have this really strong mission in my head; I want to do what I do now. There is so much injustice in Hungary, in schools and other areas of life, for Roma. So I have been really planning to stay in Hungary.

FIGURE 4.10 Áron.

"Last year I made a 25-year plan for my future," he confessed some-what sheepishly. "Because I studied psychology, I planned to do a PhD here and then develop a method to project children's socioeconomic [potential]. But on the other hand, I have another plan that, when I will be 30 – which is not so far from now – I might want to start a family. And for that I want to live in a place where I have the freedom to have a family. I am not certain but I know that I want to have that option for myself. And at the moment, it seems like Fidesz will stay in power for a long time and even Mi Hazánk is getting stronger. So I could not have a family here, and I'm struggling with this decision. Because I need to choose. I need to choose between my profession, my career – into which I already put years of effort – and my private life."

Áron had searched for job opportunities in Berlin and Madrid, his preferred destinations, and he joined a Facebook group for Hungarian psychologists abroad to solicit professional advice.

"I think Spain is economically kind of on the same level, so I won't be 'the poor Hungarian' there. But at the same time, Spain is emotionally totally the opposite of Hungary; it is more warm, more welcoming."

But it's not Spain's warmth that is drawing him there. And it's not encounters with homophobia in Hungary. The issue is with the govern-ment and its policies.

"I can live my life in this leftist, liberal Budapest bubble, so I don't really meet with homophobic people. My family is quite okay with the situation too. It is only an issue sometimes in the Roma settlement where I work, but most people there don't know that I'm gay and the ones who do have known me for quite a long time, so they don't really care anymore.

"People start to feel that they are the minority in Hungarian society and therefore they don't feel that good here anymore.... It makes me really angry and sad at the same time, that I have to choose between my personal livelihood and seeing my niece growing up."

He smiled politely, pinching the sides of his mouth. The emotion swelled.

"I think people want to leave," he said, pensively. "I talked to my cousin, a friend of mine, and also a lesbian colleague about it. We were always talking about leaving Hungary, when the government made its stupid laws, but it was always just a conversation. And to be honest, I'm not sure everybody will leave; most people will stay. ...But I think in the following years the social movement will become weaker, there will be fewer people here who want some change; and the people who voted for Fidesz will — as we say in Hungarian — eat the meal they cooked."

My interviews in Budapest's Jewish Quarter reveal the vacillating nature of migration decisions, particularly when they are voluntary choices. For successful Hungarian professionals, they must consider the investments they have made in their country of origin – their network of friends, their jobs, their family, their property, their pets – in the context of Hungary's inevitable democratic deconsolidation. While some feel personally implicated by the loss of rights, freedom, and contestation, others are more indirectly affected. Either way, their evaluation of their future in Hungary is weighed against their uncertain prospects abroad. Remarkably, many demigrants are willing to tolerate substantial uncertainty. This may mean restarting their careers and their social lives, becoming the outsider in a new place. But much as economic or family migrants may sacrifice some degree of political power, demigrants demonstrate that they are prepared to sacrifice the unity of their families and the stability of their professional life in order to live in a liberal democracy where they enjoy certain freedoms.

STARI GRAD

Stari Grad – Belgrade's old city – is perched on the Šumadija ridge in the shadow of the city's ancient Kalemegdan Fortress. With Roman origins in the third century BC and rebuilt over time by the Romans, Byzantines, Huns, Austrians, and Ottomans, the citadel overlooks the confluence of the Sava River into the Danube, 200 miles downstream from Budapest (Figures 4.11 and 4.12).

The heart of Belgrade, Stari Grad is today the site of the city's most important landmarks and the seat of Serbian government. Its residents are the liberal descendants of Serbia's old intelligentsia and urban professional *arrivistes*. But since President Aleksandar Vučić's reelection in 2022, the neighborhood has been flooded with protestors commuting from across the region to condemn him and the ruling Serbian Progressive Party (Srpska Napredna Stranka, SNS).

Opposition groups and international watchdog groups have long accused Vučić and his government of corruption, ties with organized crime, violence against political opponents, and the curtailment of media freedoms – allegations he has vociferously denied as Serbia vies for EU membership.

But the discontent intensified in March 2023, when a senior SNS official removed special prosecutors one day after they brought charges against six people accused of embezzling $7.5 million at a state-owned utility company. The action came shortly after the Serbian government

FIGURE 4.11 Knez Mihailova Street, Stari Grad, Belgrade, Serbia.

had passed constitutional amendments that depoliticized the appoint-
ment of investigators and judges. It electrified SNS's opponents and the
city center swelled with demonstrators.

A few weeks later, after two young men went on separate killing
rampages that left eighteen Serbians dead over a two-day period in
May, protestors returned to Belgrade's center weekly to accuse the

FIGURE 4.12 Kafana SFRJ, Stari Grad, Belgrade, Serbia.

government of permitting a culture of violence in its circles and on the media outlets they control. After a month of demonstrations demanding the resignation of Vučić and his ministers, on May 26, 2023, the SNS bussed in tens of thousands of people from across the Balkans to rally in a show of support for the government. But the following day, Vučić stepped down as leader of the SNS and appointed his defense minister – and family attorney – as his successor. The president accused his opponents of exploiting the tragic shootings for political ends, calling them "vultures" and "hyenas."

Vučić, nevertheless, remained the head of the state, and the protests persisted. Week after week, demonstrators – many subsequently donning images of vultures and hyenas – filled the streets of Stari Grad, processing from the central government building to the President's Office and on to Serbia's National Assembly. After the marches continued into the fall, Vučić dissolved parliament and called an early election, hoping to cement his authority with an outright legislative majority.

Though the election presented an opportunity for opposition leaders to chip away at SNS power, in interviews conducted in Stari Grad, many Belgraders were deeply disillusioned. Vučić was first elected president in

2017, and after five years of accusations of corruption, intimidation, and rights violations, he was reelected in a landslide in 2022 with the support of his national media machine and the largest party membership in Europe. People were planning their departures.

Aleksandar

After the 2017 election, Aleksandar was a sixteen-year-old estranged from his parents in a residential neighborhood of Belgrade, and seeking a sense of purpose (Figure 4.13). His neighbor asked if he might like to volunteer as an SNS activist. Seeking greater community engagement, Aleksandar eagerly agreed and worked in a local marketing and community outreach capacity.

"I wanted to see it from the inside," he said. "And unfortunately, I did. I saw how the fraud works, the pressure they put on people. Everything the opposition talks [about], which sound like crazy accusations. But the truth is much worse."

Clean-shaven and bespectacled, Aleksandar casually tied his bleached blonde hair into a bun and rolled up the sleeves of his dark teal Henley shirt.

FIGURE 4.13 Aleksandar.

"The fraud is mainly from the bribes," he said plainly. "Fraud is not new to Serbia; [it has been occurring] ever since the 1990s. We're accustomed to fraud and we are starting to think that this is normal; we were born into this. People see bribes as a normal thing. My parents once asked me, 'How do you expect me to vote for opposition if they don't give me anything?!' And then there are Bulgarian trains."

A method of vote-buying that originated in Bulgaria but since became prevalent throughout the Balkans, "Bulgarian trains" are a way for corrupt party activists to cast pre-filled ballots. Outside of polling stations, activists distribute pre-filled ballots to voters who are willing to sell their own. These voters then cast pre-filled ballots and exchange their empty ballots for payment by the handlers, who pre-fill them for the next voter.

"Not many people are checking the regularity of elections," Aleksandar said. "It's possible to vote multiple times, as the UV [invisible ink to mark voters] is often not sprayed. We have many witnesses. When I was working with SNS, I saw where the voting boxes were put. After the elections, they were stored in the common room of the building, but it was actually an incognito SNS headquarters, where they would take the results, calculate them, and then compare to what results should be in other Belgrade municipalities [before reporting them]. The opposition cannot fill all polling positions, so SNS inserts their people and registers them as monitors from the opposition."

He took a sip of a frothy cappuccino.

"Close to my building, there is a Romani camp," he continued. "The Roma are a target for election fraud because they are easy to buy. The [living] conditions are terrible and the SNS bribes them with a false idea of security. They threaten them by saying that the turnout has to be high in their community; otherwise, they threaten to kick them out of the welfare system."

Before Vučić and the SNS's rise to power, Serbia's previous government removed a large Roma settlement under Belgrade's Gazela Bridge with the support of the city's then-mayor, Dragan Đilas. With Đilas now leading the country's principal opposition party, Roma communities expect little improvement were the SNS to lose power. Still, Aleksandar said he was stunned by Romas' debilitation and the SNS's audacity.

"It shook me how you can talk to a poor person and threaten to take away their bare necessities," he said. "And it also shook me how little [the Roma] wanted to improve. I don't understand how they can survive that humiliation. But then, I realized that it's not only Romani people; it's everyone living on the margins."

He summed up his time with SNS in one word: "Trauma."

Today, Aleksandar is finishing a university degree in anthropology. After volunteering for opposition groups, he has spent the last two years working as a journalist.

"It's a way to use my voice to reach out to people and educate people," he said. "But this year I realized that it doesn't matter how big of a fraud Serbia's elections are; these people really do support this government. You cannot steal that many votes. Vučić was just very strong in the presidential elections. People actually look up to him. So at this point, I am not afraid of political corruption or of the government; I'm more afraid of the voters. These elections are the reason I definitely want to move. I want to finish University first, and then [move] westward."

Staša

Staša is a twenty-six-year-old communications professional working at an anti-poverty nonprofit in Belgrade (Figure 4.14). Slender with straight, walnut-colored hair, she wore a cream-colored shirt under a matching jacket. A frequent protestor for many years, Staša even met her

FIGURE 4.14 Staša.

boyfriend – a Serbian British dual national who works for a civil rights organization – during a demonstration.

"I felt like something was going to change after years of protesting, but in the last year and a half, it all came down," she said. "Hope has evaporated. [There is] no hope of change in the elections. We cannot even grasp how many [ways] they rig the elections, and how our votes don't count. What I want does not matter in this country; it's as if I am not a citizen. We have no meritocracy; there are incompetent people in power because they are in with the [SNS] party.

"So I changed from wanting to stay for the first time in my life to a perception of things never changing and becoming worse in terms of censorship, the media, et cetera," Staša said.

She and her boyfriend are now making plans to move to London, where his employer is based anyway.

"I didn't have hope for the recent elections. I was supporting one movement and I was living in a bubble, so I thought that it was bigger. But when results became available, the reality hit. What was I thinking? I'm not apolitical, but this moves me further towards that side – that I cannot make a change, so it makes me think more about London."

She peered out a window toward the Terazije Fountain.

"My mother says that I can always come back and contribute here later."

Slavica

Slavica actually did come back. A single graphic designer, she spent two years in Singapore and another six in Italy, before returning to Belgrade in 2010 to help care for her sick mother. Now fifty-four, she is readying to move abroad again.

Slavica initially moved abroad as a disenchanted democrat. She was a member of Serbia's Democratic Party, which was in power between 2000 and 2012, but has since fractured into a weak opposition group. She looked up to Zoran Đinđić, the former Belgrade mayor and reform-minded Serbian prime minister (2001–2003), who sought to mitigate the power of organized crime and increase accountability before he was assassinated on March 12, 2003 as part of a conspiracy between Serbian mafia bosses and former officials from Yugoslavia's secret police.

"After he was killed, so was the hope for change in the world," Slavica said, shaking her head. She left for Singapore shortly thereafter.

"I cannot live in this mess; the political situation is not suitable for me," she said of the current circumstances in Serbia. "It's been 30 years in the streets, of protesting, of hope. But just like 15 years ago, nothing is changing; life and time are standing still. The hope that at least some part will change or get fixed is what kept me going. But I realized that it will stay like this for the next 10 years, and there is no progress in that for me."

She untied the bright red, floral scarf around her neck, laying the folded corners against the front of her black, wool coat.

"There [used to be] hope of seeing light at the end of the tunnel. But now, after the [2022] elections, I do not see it anymore.

"I don't want my employment to be conditioned on joining the party. My last job was for only a couple of months in a private company, and they had no complaints with regard to my output, but they criticized me for not being a member of SNS and support in the opposition.

"Eighty percent of my generation already left during the 1990s and never came back. Now, after numerous years, [those who stayed in the 1990s] are looking to move abroad. In the past six months, I haven't heard of a person who doesn't want to leave – educated people, who want to leave normally, with dignity.

"I was a monitor at the most recent elections," Slavica added. She observed the Pinosava precinct in Belgrade's suburbs. "In the morning, when I arrived [at the polling station], I saw four big and strong guys, hooligans, who were in charge of establishing order in that polling station. Later I saw people without hope, bribed, poor, old people and their grandchildren extorted [to vote for Vučić for a job] or for societal status. In that polling station, people en masse voted for Vučić. I cannot understand what kind of urge one would have to be pushed deeper into the grave. They were driven by cars, organized transport; it wasn't voluntary."

Slavica said that she would be in Croatia or Slovenia within five months.

Jovana

Jovana does not want to leave Belgrade. But, she says, the circumstances provide little reason to stay.

Twiggy and pretty, she is a thirty-seven-year-old psychologist with a British husband and a two-year-old son (Figure 4.15). She says she is part of Serbia's "lost generation," who experienced war, sanctions, and poverty during their most formative years. The daughter of a Serbian father and Slovenian-Croat mother – a "Yugoslav family," she said – she was

FIGURE 4.15 Jovana.

deeply opposed to the Milosevic regime in the 1990s, was equally against the rise of the SNS twenty years later, and now affiliates with a Belgrade-centered opposition party.

"In general, there is no hope – but our hopes rise two weeks before every election," she said. "Ultimately, Serbian democracy is just democracy on paper. I was a monitor at the most recent elections, and the rigging happens outside of polling station. They're ticking boxes for the European Union, but they're not changing anything really. I don't have a relationship [with] the state. I don't owe anything to the state. If the government was working for the people, I would have a different attitude, but I've never lived in a state like that.

"Having a child changed my perspective," she added. "Previously, I didn't think about ecology or air pollution. But once you have a child, you start thinking about where you want them to grow up."

Yearningly, she looked toward the street. The descending afternoon sun cast orange light and longer shadows on the pavement, where pedestrians busily passed each other, smoking cigarettes and checking their phones. She pulled a black cardigan closer over her sage-colored blouse.

"I like life here," she said, nodding. "I just hate politics."

Jovana acknowledged that she and her husband could return to Britain anytime. They could also join her sister in Germany, she said. They just didn't think they would be as financially comfortable. The couple recently purchased a flat in central Belgrade, but they were also thinking ahead about their son's educational prospects.

"Some of my activist friends have indeed been migrating," she said. "They are all liberals, but they did not leave for political reasons.

"If you leave, you admit that you wasted your time here fighting. [...] Our movement will be weakened if I move, so this further keeps me here. I feel a little bit of responsibility for that, but on the other hand, [that] does not supersede giving my child a future."

My conversations in Belgrade reveal the many ways that the corruption and illiberalism of Vučić's SNS touched average people and activists alike. My interviewees lacked the professional credentials of those I interviewed in Budapest. On the one hand, they would lose less economic status were they to depart. But on the other hand, their economic future in countries like Croatia, Germany, Italy, and the United Kingdom was far less secure. Their stories show that the decision to emigrate is grave for demigrants of all classes and that a number had already once left their homeland for other countries, only to return and find a worse political landscape. With Vučić's reelection, they were prepared to leave again.

THE SLIDING SCALE

For Hungarians like Rita, Gergő, Dávid, Marci, Kata, and Áron and Serbians like Aleksandar, Staša, Slavica, and Jovana, their aspirations to depart are not exceptional. Hungary and Serbia – but also neighboring countries like Bulgaria and Poland – are depopulating.

According to a 2019 United Nations report, of all the countries worldwide whose populations are projected to decrease between now and 2050, fifteen Eastern European countries are in the top twenty.[4] Indeed, many otherwise nativist Eastern European citizens are more concerned about emigration trends than immigration trends.[5]

East–West European mobility has been understood as an economic phenomenon, motivated by Eastern Europeans' desire to access higher wages, greater social mobility, and better living standards in the West. I have already shown that this understanding veils the fact that ostensibly economic migrants hold disproportionately more liberal, democratic values than the countrymen they leave behind, but also the political motivations of many emigrants – especially after the election of authoritarian-leaning parties and candidates.[6]

Still, because I cannot identify those who actually move before they do so and follow the trajectory of their journeys – let alone their values and impact – I can only present evidence of Democratic Drain's fundamental mechanics. It is difficult to observe Democratic Drain "in action" over time.

This is a common challenge for observers of slow-moving and uncertain phenomena. As an analogy, consider astronomers who wish to observe the life cycle of stars. Stars' formulation over millions of years has been believed to begin in nebulae, climax in a supernova, and often end in a black hole. Without time to record this glacial process or notice when great changes will take place, scientists have collected data about the status of elementary materials from snapshots of celestial bodies at different stages in the process and pieced it together to suggest a long-term trajectory. In this book, I am identifying a phenomenon of human behavior, but I can use the same logic to link simultaneous snapshots from different places.

The politics of contemporary Europe present such an opportunity.

After being ruled by a mix of liberal parties in the wake of communism's collapse in 1991, many of Europe's primary migrant-sending states elected a wave of illiberal, populist leaders after 2010. Their victories have been part of a greater trend across Europe, where voters have redistributed electoral power to a greater share of far-right and far-left fringe parties than the continent has seen in its democratic history. In May 2019, this trend crested in European elections when far-right, nationalist parties increased their share of European Parliament seats from 20 percent to about 25 percent. And it has continued to grow since then.

Eastern Europe has been illiberalism's anchor. Since 2010, fringe party leaders from the left and right have been elected prime ministers in Hungary (Viktor Orbán), Greece (Alexis Tsipras), Poland (Mateusz Morawiecki, Beata Szydło, Jarosław Kaczyński), and Slovakia (Robert Fico, Peter Pelligrini), and have entered prominently into coalition governments in Austria, Italy, Latvia, and Lithuania. Far-right parties now control more than a tenth of the national legislature in Eastern European countries including Bulgaria, the Czech Republic, Estonia, Hungary, Latvia, Poland, Romania, Slovakia, and Slovenia.[7] Together, these countries have sent millions of immigrants to Western Europe since the end of the Cold War.

If Democratic Drain might help explain these developments – limited to snapshots of the different population subgroups at a single moment in time – we would expect to observe a "sliding scale" of democratic values from West to East, in which:

SNAPSHOT 3: Eastern Europeans who choose to stay longer durations in Western European countries hold stronger liberal democratic values than those who recently arrived from the same set of countries.

SNAPSHOT 2: Eastern Europeans who actually move West under the EU's free mobility rules hold more liberal democratic proclivities than those in their countries of origin who wish to migrate but have not departed.

SNAPSHOT 1: Prospective migrants in Eastern Europe hold more liberal democratic proclivities than their countrymen who do not wish to move.

SNAPSHOT 0: Eastern European citizens who do not want to emigrate hold relatively illiberal and undemocratic values.

Illiberalism in Context

As in Chapter 2, I consult my 2020 survey of nationally representative adult samples in nineteen European countries including Austria, Bulgaria, the Czech Republic, Denmark, Estonia, France, Germany, Hungary, Italy, Latvia, Lithuania, the Netherlands, Poland, Romania, Slovakia, Slovenia, Spain, Sweden, and the United Kingdom.[8] Again, to discern the extent to which respondents hold liberal democratic values, I solicit respondents' approval or disapproval of a variety of state actions that violate minority rights, suspend voting rights, break secular norms, infringe upon freedom of speech, and threaten judicial independence. Responses are then scaled into a measure of illiberalism (0 to 1, where 1 is more illiberal) that approximates the one I use in my research on destination preferences in among prospective migrants in the Middle East and North Africa in Chapter 2.[9] I also measure vote shares and party favorability ratings (on a 0 to 10 scale) for all major parties across the full sample from the nineteen countries.[10]

When I compare the liberal democratic values of prospective migrants from Eastern European countries (Snapshot 1) to those of their countrymen who do not plan to emigrate (Snapshot 0), the results demonstrate that prospective immigrants from Eastern Europe (0.41) are incrementally but statistically significantly more liberal than their countrymen (0.44). While the difference is not large, the massive scale of East–West migration greatly amplifies its effect. This reflects the same differences I observe in Middle Eastern and North African countries and reinforces my expectation that, over time, migration is depleting Eastern European countries of their more liberal elements.

When I compare the liberal democratic values of Eastern European immigrants in Western European countries (Snapshot 2) to prospective Eastern European migrants who have yet to depart (Snapshot 1), I find that the prospective migrants (0.41) are more illiberal than those who emigrated from 2015 onward (0.39). Because of the relatively smaller number of foreign-born people in my Western European samples, the difference is not statistically significant.

Looking at Eastern Europeans who have resided in Western Europe for longer than ten years (Snapshot 3) compared to more recent arrivals (Snapshot 2), I find that those with shorter durations of stay (0.39) are more illiberal than those with longer durations of stay (0.38). Due to smaller samples of Eastern European migrants, this marginal difference is not statistically significant either, but taken together, the bottom four points plotted in Figure 4.16 visualize the sliding scale.

Remarkably, Eastern European emigrants – who initially arrive with limited exposure to liberal democratic norms or governance – report views that are nearly as liberal as the average Western European (0.36). Tellingly, if I examine native-born Western European far-right

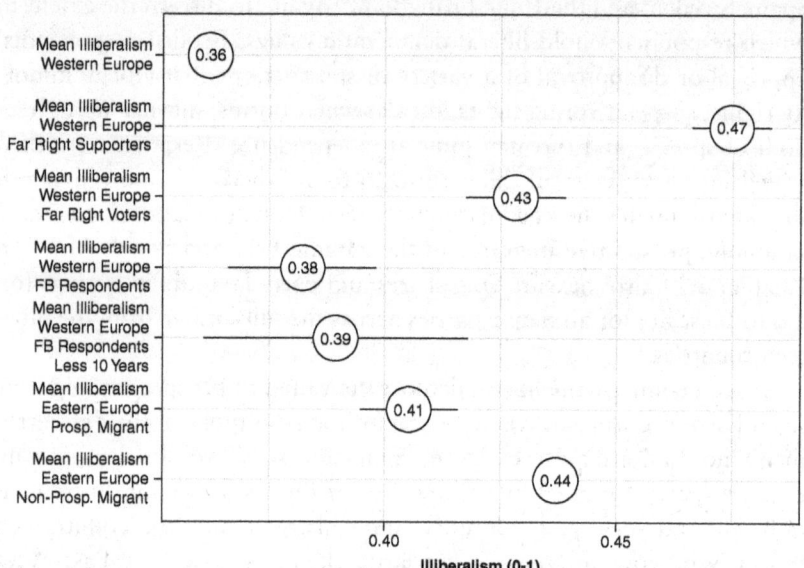

FIGURE 4.16 Mean levels of illiberalism across foreign-born and far-right groups.

supporters, they are actually more illiberal than Eastern European immigrants and prospective migrants. Westerners who vote for far-right parties report an average illiberalism score (0.43) that is higher than the Eastern European average. So are the illiberalism scores for those who favor far-right parties (0.47) – a remarkable disparity from the regional average that surpasses the average of Eastern Europeans who have no intention of emigrating.

The novel illiberalism scale I introduce in this book is a consequential factor in understanding the rise of the authoritarian far-right in Europe, just as it was in my analysis of results from the Middle East and North Africa. But as I emphasize in my discussion in Chapter 2, this is a "hard" test of true principles that may underestimate the extent of liberal democratic values among respondents. The abstract and absolute nature of the questions might incline respondents to be more cautious with their choices in countries without a tradition of liberal democracy in the first place, which is almost as true for Eastern Europe as it was for the Middle Eastern cases. For this reason, again, the results should be interpreted as

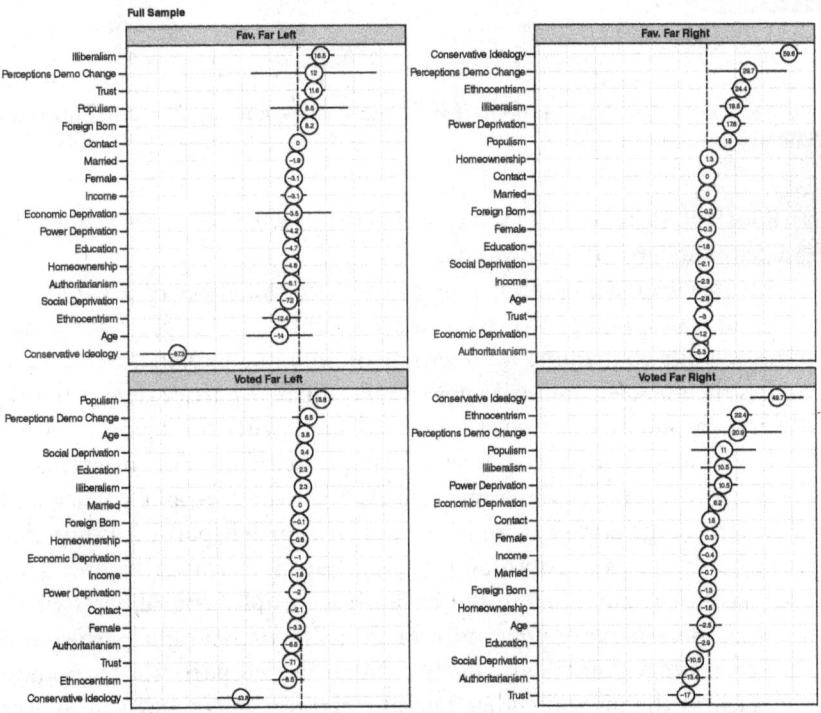

FIGURE 4.17 Predicted support for fringe parties across nineteen countries.

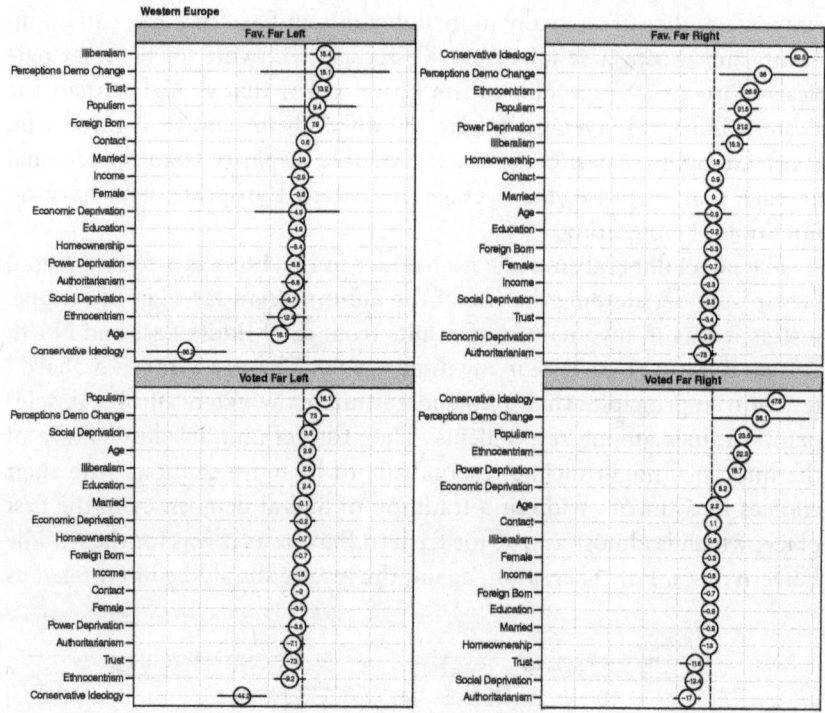

FIGURE 4.18 Predicted support for fringe parties among Western European countries.

a "floor" of liberal democratic values in the selected countries and render greater confidence in their validity.

Advanced modeling allows us to estimate the effect of a variety of different attitudinal perspectives on the likelihood of support for fringe parties, while controlling for a variety of potential explanatory factors. Across the nineteen countries with a mix of fringe parties (Figure 4.17), illiberalism emerges as positively correlated with the favorability of *both* far-right *and* far-left parties. People with illiberal orientations are 19.5 percentage points more likely to favor far-right parties and 16.5 percentage points more likely to favor far-left parties. While this trend holds across Western and Eastern European states (Figures 4.18 and 4.19), it is amplified in the East where people with illiberal views are 32.9 percentage points more likely to favor far-right parties and 22.1 percentage points more likely to favor far-left parties. This finding underscores the pivotal choice liberal emigrants make when they elect to depart. Liberal, democratic parties in Eastern Europe, if they are to ever win office, rely on their support.

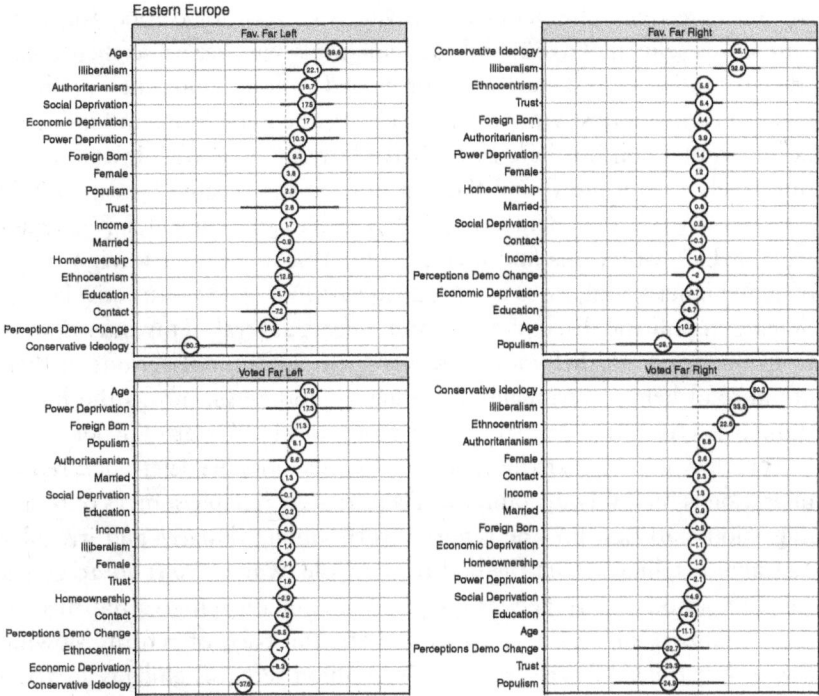

FIGURE 4.19 Predicted support for fringe parties among Eastern European countries.

A SELF-SUSTAINING CYCLE?

Taken together, these results display the sliding scale of liberal democratic values descending from Western Europe to the East. Though smaller samples of Eastern Europeans in Western Europe leave some uncertainty, the snapshots corroborate the implications of Democratic Drain. And the stories of young liberals from Hungary and Serbia in the aftermath of their respective April 2022 elections exhibit the logic of prospective demigrants before they depart their countries of origin.

Interestingly, these results also suggest that Democratic Drain may be a self-sustaining cycle because the initial election of far-right authoritarianleaning parties and candidates may not only push out future generations of people with liberal democratic values; it may deter those abroad – who appear to grow more liberal with prolonged durations of stay – from returning to their countries of origin. Researchers find that the departure of many emigrants from European countries is correlated to frustrations and grievances that drive far-right populist support in the regions they leave behind – reinforcing this broader effect.[11]

This deterrence eliminates a well-validated tool for democratization. Numerous scholars have found that emigrants who return to their countries of origin instill democratic norms and values among their country-men. Returnees boost voter turnout, electoral competition, and influence nonmigrants' political behavior, particularly in areas with lower education levels.[12] In Central and Eastern Europe specifically, returnees hold more positive views of democracy as a system of government, have greater trust in EU institutions and increased interest in EU and foreign news, display higher voting rates in European elections, and more actively participate in political discussions.[13] And indeed, several of my interviewees from Budapest and Belgrade who had spent substantial periods of their life abroad held governments in Hungary and Serbia up to the higher standards typically expected from democracies in Western Europe.

Whether or not it's attributable to migrants' possible deterrence, return migration is relatively uncommon. There are few reliable sources of return migration statistics, but the rate of return among refugees and irregular migrants is telling. From the end of the Cold War in 1991 to 2022 – a 31-year period – only between 28 and 30 million refugees returned to their countries of origin worldwide, with the pace of returns slowing down over time.[14] There are over 117 million refugees globally in 2024 alone.[15] In the EU, over 300,000 foreign nationals are ordered to leave the EU each year because they have entered Europe irregularly or are staying irregularly. However, only around 21 percent of them return to their home country or to the country from which they travelled to the EU.[16]

In the decades since the end of the Cold War, however, many prominent destination countries like Canada, Australia, Japan, Singapore, and countries in the Arabian Gulf region have shifted to migration policies that emphasize temporary labor admissions, raising the likelihood that migrants will return to their countries of origin. But even in this new landscape for global mobility, scholars estimate that around 25 percent of international migrants return to their country of origin.[17] Return migrants tend to be concentrated in Africa and Latin America,[18] though some migrants move to a third country.[19] Most sources confirm that the majority of migrants stay abroad.

With return undesired by many migrants, unwelcomed by their governments, and generally unlikely, the only way demigrants might continue to push for democratic reforms in their countries of origin is through diasporic politics. In Chapter 5, I explore the potential for expatriates' power to offset Democratic Drain's steady depletion of democratic political capital. I also discover its limits.

5

Democratic Gain

In March 2017, an edgy tension beset the streets of central Istanbul. After President Recep Tayyip Erdogan curbed a number of fundamental rights and freedoms in response to an alleged coup attempt the year before, he became the target of a wave of anti-government protests in Taksim Square and Gezi Park.

Steps from the police-filled plazas, several unmarked salons were reserved for two days of closed-door meetings in the basement of the Point Hotel (Figure 5.1).

Attendees spoke only Arabic in the meetings and avoided the five-star property's street-level lobby, preferring to exit via a side door when they needed to smoke. Almost exclusively men, they dressed in blazers but went tieless, and frequently stepped into the empty, carpeted corridor to accept phone calls in a variety of other languages. One spoke in French. One in German. Another in Italian. Many in English, some with British accents and others American.

Inside the meeting rooms, the most prominent members of the Syrian diaspora coordinated a democratic government-in-waiting. They represented multiple parties affiliated with the National Coalition for Syrian Revolution and Opposition Forces, also known as the Syrian National Coalition or "Etilaf" – an assembly of opposition groups in the Syrian Civil War that was founded in Doha, Qatar, in November 2012. Etilaf assembled the Syrian Interim Government, an alternative government that controlled some areas of Syria and claimed to be the sole legitimate representative of Syria.

FIGURE 5.1 Bosphorus Strait, Istanbul, Turkey.

The al-Assad family had been untouchably in power since 1971, when General Hafez al-Assad transformed the Syrian republic into a dynastic dictatorship, empowered by a cult of personality. When Bashar al-Assad succeeded his father in 2000, he leveraged the loyalty of Syria's Alawite clans and the *mukhabarat* secret police to secure his control over Syrian society. In the face of discontent within a year of taking power, Bashar al-Assad squelched the so-called Damascus Spring of cultural and political activism against the regime – which accentuated a four-decade period of violent humanitarian violations that produced hundreds of thousands of refugees even before the Syrian Civil War began.

Many of the expatriates in Istanbul had left Syria in the years since the outbreak of the civil war that followed uprisings across the Middle East and North Africa in March 2011. After protests broke out in Dara'a and Damascus, demonstrators tested the state's tolerance of dissent amidst simultaneous rebellions in Tunisia, Egypt, Libya, and Bahrain. The al-Assad regime was initially able to retain control with a violent crack-down but, by 2012, army defections and militarized bombardments severely escalated the conflict.

At that point, thousands of professionals and dissidents fled for second homes in London, New York, Paris, Rome, Vienna, and Washington, where some held citizenship or residential visas. Others joined family abroad. They were among nearly 7 million seeking refuge in other countries and another 6 million internally displaced. Ultimately, 13.5 million Syrians would find themselves in humanitarian need and 500,00 were dead – from an estimated pre-war population of 22 million.[1]

Some delegates at the meeting had been abroad for decades. They had attended overseas universities or joined family members in North America or Europe and become physicians, lawyers, engineers, and entrepreneurs, but maintained ties with friends and relatives in the Levante. These long-time expatriates and their recently departed colleagues represented dozens of population sects and parties as diverse as those inside Syria, but they all sought to liberate their homeland from the clutches of totalitarian tyranny and ultimately install a new democracy.

During the Istanbul sessions, they held internal elections and strategized about how they may support their brethren in territories controlled by the Free Syrian Army, strengthen their militias' resistance against attacks by Syrian President Bashar al-Assad's forces, and facilitate more support from their North American and European allies.

So far, I have shown the way that the departure of such educated professionals with democratic values can deplete their country of origin of political demand for liberty, individual rights, and the institutions that protect them. In the Istanbul secret meetings, these Syrians were testing the possibility that they might leverage their freedom and resources abroad to advocate for liberal democracy back home – a sort of democratic "gain" that could counter the adverse effects of Democratic Drain on their home country's politics.

New forms of digital communication have rendered democratic political activists abroad enormous capacity to connect with the people and movements they left behind. However, there are limits to their power, as politics remain stubbornly subject to local relationships, provincial subjectivities, and government suppression. And just as activism has become transnational, so has the reach of this suppression. It has become clear that there are constraints on diaspora influence,[2] contingent on the extent to which they are able to maintain connectivity and legitimacy in the eyes of the people they support.

In this chapter, I explore the extent to which Syrian leaders were successful in order to better understand the prospects and limitations of a coordinated democratic "gain" counter-phenomenon. In particular, I ask under what conditions do external opposition leaders communicate and establish legitimacy with homeland dissidents? A valid response requires an understanding of both the way the diaspora engages in transnational activism and the way that average people in the country of origin perceive and interact with members of the diaspora.

Most examinations of diaspora politics observe only one angle at a time – those at home or those abroad – or look at the effects of diaspora activism in hindsight after pivotal political events, rather than concurrently with them. Focusing on Syria in 2017, six years into a merciless civil war, I leverage a rare, large-scale survey of people residing in opposition-held territory and contemporaneous interviews with members of the exiled opposition leadership to undertake an analysis of public attitudes and over 1,000 respondents' social networks.

LONG-DISTANCE NATIONALISTS

With the growing reach and sophistication of the internet, scholars have documented transnational activism and the dynamics of political advocacy from abroad.[3] Researchers have noted the impact that diasporas have held on elections, wars, and other political disputes in countries of origin as diverse as Sri Lanka, Nagorno-Karabakh, Mexico, and states in the Balkans.[4] Particularly for diasporas from authoritarian states, it is thought that migration renders new opportunities for political activism as "long-distance nationalists" against previously untouchable regimes.[5]

The Istanbul gathering of Syrian exiles was an attempt to organize diasporic activism at an extraordinarily high level, bankrolled by Western and Arab governments invested in toppling the al-Assad regime. Most activism, however, is the isolated effort of individuals on tight budgets during their limited free time – an Iranian dissident producing a podcast from a bedroom studio in West Los Angeles, a Turkish party activist registering voters at mosques around Berlin's Kreuzberg neighborhood, a Bangladeshi elder organizing a hometown association meeting in East London. What democratic "gain" can this bring?

Agents of Democratic Diffusion

On one hand, overseas activists have been shown to act as "agents of democratic diffusion who help strengthen democracy in their countries of origin."[6] They direct attention to the victims and perpetrators of human rights abuses.[7] They also contribute to peace processes,[8] democratization,[9] international development,[10] post-conflict reconstruction,[11] and transnational social movements.[12] Party officials have been observed to share vote-winning strategies they saw abroad along with rhetoric that encourages greater participation.[13] With access to a greater variety of less biased sources of information, exposure to democratic norms, and technological savvy to communicate their ideas, diasporas and emigrants are thought to endow their homelands with values associated with liberalism and transparency.[14]

But the practical impact of these activities is very much in question.

In Mexico, high-migration towns are far less inclined to participate in politics and more likely to view politics as ineffective in serving their needs; the higher a municipality's migration rate, the lower its turnout was in federal elections.[15] And democracy in Mexico remains a work in progress. During an era in which many highly skilled Indians have been recruited to Western democracies, the ruling Bharatiya Janata Party has simultaneously sought to engage their diaspora and turned increasingly nationalist and authoritarian. In the Dominican Republic, emigrants' political participation has been described as reinforcing the "government of politicians" rather than instilling strong and genuine democracy.[16] In a study of Lebanese political parties' outreach to the diaspora in Australia, researchers found that the campaigns were not interested in adopting emigrants' ideas for democratic reform; they just wanted votes.[17] Candidates and parties actively ignored diasporic voices they deemed to threaten their preexisting agendas.

Even if many emigrants hold more liberal democratic values than their countrymen, these studies suggest that the net effect of their political activism from abroad is questionable at best.

"Transnational Repression"

Transnational political activity is one thing. Transnational political power is quite another. Given the amount of consultation, deliberation, and resources required to build and establish successful democracies, examples of democratization enacted from abroad are rare. Diaspora politics are constrained by conditions in both migrants' destination country and their countries of origin.

In countries of destination, diaspora power is subject to whether emigrants choose to settle in free, stable countries that offer the resources and platforms for activism.[18] Even inside conducive destination states, competition among subgroups of a national diaspora for financial support can generate divisions.[19] And when support comes from the destination government, this association can undermine organizations' legitimacy in the homeland.[20] But even with stable, apolitical support in conducive destination societies, diaspora mobilization can be undercut by homeland institutions that weaken or frustrate immigrants' enthusiasm.[21] Diaspora power relies on regular, high-frequency contact to overcome doubt and inspire nonmigrants to stay informed.[22]

In countries of origin, authoritarian regimes often seek to exploit these weaknesses and repress diaspora activism in a variety of ways. Protest abroad has long been viewed as traitorous by homeland regimes that do not tolerate dissent at home,[23] and a number of governments have taken action to suppress it. According to the Notre Dame sociologist Dana Moss, "transnational repression" has three components: (1) spreading fear, mistrust, and division between conationals; (2) significantly constraining individuals' abilities to speak openly about the home country politics; and (3) limiting anti-regime mobilization to "fringe" exile groups.[24]

Between 2019 and 2024, the US Justice Department has charged dozens of suspects with acts of transnational repression.[25] In one 2022 case, a Chinese intelligence operative enlisted a private investigator to hunt for any mistresses or tax problems that could upend a New York congressional campaign led by a former student leader of the historic Tiananmen Square protests.[26] In a 2023 case, after an Iranian journalist and activist criticized Iran's human rights abuses, Tehran hired an Eastern European organized crime gang to scout her Brooklyn home and plot her murder.[27] In a shocking example of how even ostensible democracies might also engage in such actions, in 2023, the Canadian government accused its Indian counterparts of murdering a Canadian citizen who was a prominent Sikh nationalist. A year later, American authorities in New York filed charges against an Indian government employee they say was involved in a failed plot to kill another separatist leader who is an American citizen.[28]

Beyond such targeted assassinations, techniques have involved threats of retribution,[29] surveillance,[30] exile,[31] the withdrawal of scholarships, and the punishment of relatives as proxies.[32] Such overt actions are designed to intimidate.[33] Many such governments and other actors have turned digital spaces into new areas of surveillance, intimidation, and counter-mobilization.[34] Some governments create and employ "troll" networks – organized efforts to use fake and real social media accounts to promote regime-backed agendas and threaten dissidents.[35]

According to a large 2024 report by Human Rights Watch entitled "We Will Find You," its authors report over 100 cases of transnational repression, more than three-quarters of which occurred in the past 15 years, committed by dozens of governments.[36] They have reportedly targeted human rights defenders, journalists, civil society activists, and political opponents, among others, deemed to be a security threat. Many of these targets are asylum seekers or recognized refugees in their place of settlement.

According to the report, methods of transnational repression include killings, targeting of relatives, abuse of consular services, online harassment or surveillance, and unlawful removals like expulsions, extraditions, deportations, abductions, and enforced disappearances. Some governments also misuse the International Criminal Police Organization (Interpol) to target critics abroad. These tactics often facilitate further human rights violations, such as torture and ill-treatment.

Financial Remittances

Recent research also shows that, even if emigrants' political remittances can defy transnational repression to inspire demand for greater liberty, democracy, and transparency, their financial remittances can indirectly drive support for authoritarian incumbents. The logic is that the more than $800 billion in remittances sent by emigrants worldwide reduce deprivation among home country citizens and make them more likely to support whatever regime is presently in power. Inversely, when people experience a drop in remittances, they become less satisfied about their household economic situation and attribute responsibility to the incumbent at home.[37]

Researchers acknowledge that remittances can reduce families' dependence on patronage and state-provided public goods and thus reduces recipients' government dependency and undermines authoritarian patronage systems.[38] However, if remittances are used to provide what are otherwise public goods or reduce pressures for redistribution, they can simulate the effect of state-delivered public goods. Like welfare, remittances are often countercyclical – they increase during economic recessions and after natural disasters – but because they don't come from state coffers, they can help governments avoid financial crises and sudden currency devaluations.[39]

As a result, remittance recipients exhibit greater support for incumbents relative to nonrecipients.[40] In more autocratic countries, unearned foreign income received reduces the likelihood of government turnover, regime collapse, and outbreaks of major political discontent.[41] The potential fungibility of patronage and remittances allows actors, in particular the government, to engage in certain behavior that would not be possible in the absence of these funds.[42] And together, these forces act as a further counterweight to any power that pro-democratic activism may hold.

After Eritrea gained independence from Ethiopia in 1991, the new Eritrean government actually imposed a "diaspora tax" on its expats worldwide. At the time, most Eritreans abroad accepted the new levy as an opportunity to contribute to the rebuilding of a country devastated by thirty years of conflict and to help the veterans of the liberation wars.[43] The widespread understanding was that the tax was a temporary measure to be lifted once the new parliament became fully functional and the economy stabilized. But as the Eritrean parliament has not convened since 1997, the tax stayed in place and is one of the main sources of revenue for the repressive regime of President Isaias Afwerki.

The diaspora tax continues to be collected by Eritrean consular offices around the world because they demand proof of tax payment to provide even the most basic consular services. Diplomatic officials refuse to issue ID cards or any other legal documents until the tax is paid. Citizens who do not pay cannot sell their properties in Eritrea or go home to visit their relatives. People who have never paid the tax can also face demands for massive back payments whenever they need any services from the Eritrean government.[44]

Warring Factions

If authoritarian states' diasporas can avert the unintended effects of their financial remittances to remit their political ideas, their influence has not been especially democratic. Frequently, migrants support one warring faction over another in their countries of origin. Indeed, where diasporas have measurably influenced homelands in the past, they have been more successful in support of paramilitary and illiberal groups, not democratization.

For example, the Tamil Tigers of Sri Lanka and the Kosovar Liberation Army – both of which benefited from substantial foreign donations and support in the 1990s and 2000s – were engaged in bloody battles of ethnic conflict. In the historic 2011–2012 Egyptian election, researchers found that people with family members who emigrated to the Arabian Gulf region voted heavily for Islamist and Muslim Brotherhood-affiliated parties, which hold weak democratic values.[45] The Armenian and Jewish diasporas in the United States are well organized and well resourced but many of their members have recently backed illiberal governments in Armenia and Israel, respectively.[46] The Filipino diaspora was once a critical source of resistance against the dictatorship of Ferdinand Marcos between 1972 and 1986. But today large parts of the diaspora support right-wing, authoritarian-leaning leaders like Presidents Rodrigo Duterte and Bongbong Marcos.[47]

Many researchers suggest that diasporas fleeing wars often maintain and inflame the conflicts from abroad.[48] The escalation of violence may intensify transnational connections and contestation.[49] As a result, scholars of civil wars and ethnic conflict have begun to examine the transnational dimensions of these clashes.[50] In these contexts, secessionist movements are prone to reach out to the diaspora for money, support, and connections.[51] Immigrants and exiles have become "conflict entrepreneurs,"[52] take up arms,[53] and pursue contentious political causes.[54] Ethnic conflict may even radicalize members of the diaspora previously characterized by inclusive pluralism and accommodations of difference.[55]

Such examples demonstrate how concepts of "gain" presume a country of origin that is in fact receptive to the ideas and capital that expatriates seek to remit and emigrants whose democratic values extend to their preferences in less democratic spaces. Authoritarian states are typically not interested in the transfer of democratic perspectives from their diasporas.[56] And often, emigrants find their destination countries' governments to be inaccessible to their lobbying.[57] Meanwhile, illiberal and authoritarian factions are happy to receive material and tactical support, so long as their agendas are not questioned or undermined.

There are notable exceptions where democrats return to office in their homelands, but they are not examples of people who advocated for liberal reforms from abroad. Ayad Allawi was the prime minister of postwar Iraq but was effectively installed by the United States' occupying forces. Mohammed Nur returned to Somalia from London to be the mayor of Mogadishu, but he was appointed by local, unelected officials. A stronger example comes from the exiled members of Tunisia's Islamist Ennahda Party, who returned to stand for election after 2011. However, the party's leadership had previously advocated for an Islamic state and justified political violence.

Taken as a whole, this body of research implies that diaspora activism is significantly subject to external actors' capacity to communicate with and retain a sense of legitimacy among people in the country of origin. Indeed, diaspora power derives from their duality – their capacity to exist "outside the state but inside the people"[58] as "transnational brokers" connecting otherwise disconnected citizens.[59] However, we know far less about the dynamics and contingencies of these connections, particularly in the context of war and suppression when remittances will not hold a counteractive effect. Understanding this requires a concurrent view of both the diaspora and people in the country of origin. Alas, due to limits on access and the difficulties of studying dispersed diasporas and people in conflict zones, few studies can offer such a bifocal lens, like the perspective offered by the attendee of the Istanbul meetings.

SYRIA VIA ISTANBUL

In the midst of a civil war fought by multiple factions on the ground and by multiple proxies abroad, the covert meetings of Syrian democratic opposition leaders in Istanbul encapsulated a striking case of the challenges and conditionality of diaspora power.

On the one hand, the mobilization of the Syrian diaspora opposition had been undermined by interventions directed by the al-Assad regime for decades. There have been numerous reports of relatives in Syria being harmed after expatriates spoke out against the regime,[60] and other reports of threats and intimidation.[61] The Syrian government and its affiliates have also reportedly installed malware on thousands of dissidents' digital devices that enables the regime to track their location, read their data, and access their cameras and microphones.[62] Under such long-term transnational repression designed to engender mistrust between conationals, Syrian politics has been subject to a disposition of silence.[63] Indeed, Etilaf – the party that gathered in Istanbul – did not form until the civil war.

On the other hand, the Syrian diaspora has been strengthened by four structural factors that had emerged by the time of this study. First, whatever weaknesses existed in the diaspora before the Syrian Civil War erupted, the Syrian opposition had six years to build a governing and communications infrastructure with supporters of the movement – which had accumulated the financial backing of Arab Gulf monarchies and Western democratic powers eager to see al-Assad fall. Diaspora activists had already contributed to efforts to advance accountability, truth, and victim recognition.[64] They met regularly with diplomatic officials and in global summits that attempted either to unify the opposition or negotiate a resolution to the conflict.

Second, despite regime attempts at surveillance and intimidation, Syrian dissidents abroad benefited greatly from the accessibility of the internet, which made information easily transmittable across enemy lines to people on the ground. Many Syrians publicly criticized and protested their government using digital media.[65]

Third, the deterrent power of regime threats against them and their families dissipated with the intensification of conflict. Syrians came out against the regime once regime violence affected their families or forced their families to flee; once the scope and brutality of regime violence transformed their objects of obligation beyond family members; or once they perceived the al-Assad regime's increased use of collective and arbitrary violence to mean that there were no additional risks of public opposition.[66]

And fourth, because of the contrast between the totalitarian oppression at the hands of the al-Assad regime and the relative liberty of Syrian expatriates abroad, the ability of the diaspora to demonstrate the discrepancy in rights and freedom between those living inside and outside the regime was exceptional. Anyone abroad – anywhere, in almost every possible circumstance – could passively transmit the virtues of more liberal environments and what is possible elsewhere. And even before the 2011 rebellion, the Syrian diaspora was very large.

Under these circumstances, Syria would appear to be fertile ground for an influential diaspora. Governments in exile have functioned and held legitimacy before, including in eras with far weaker communication technologies at their disposal.[67] Many such governments were established in London during the Second World War. More recently, the diverse leaders of the Iraqi National Congress played a critical role from the Persian Gulf War in 1991 until after the 2003 US invasion of Iraq, despite skepticism about its credibility related to its ties to the US Central Intelligence Agency (CIA). Earlier research on post-communist countries finds that defeating authoritarian leaders requires not only a united opposition but also the involvement of external actors, such as foreign governments and international civil society groups, which can provide resources and legitimacy.[68]

With such resources in-hand, one might expect Syrian dissidents in opposition-held territories to be both informed about their leadership abroad by 2016, but also sympathetic about these leaders' displacement. Indeed, by that point, half of the country's citizens were internally displaced or abroad and advocacy from within Syria was almost impossible. Therefore, it is reasonable to estimate that any limitations to external opposition leaders' communication and legitimacy with homeland dissidents in Syria are likely to be present in other authoritarian states or warzones.

If democratic "gain" were in fact taking place through the relations of Syrians at home and activists abroad, we would be able to observe the diffusion of democratic values. This diffusion might be ultimately visible in the expressed values of people who remained in Syria's opposition-held territories by 2017. But as a precursor, and at a minimum, it is reasonable to expect an awareness of the activities of Syrian democratic leaders abroad. Are these leaders well known among their constituents? Are their social networks connected? Do they have credibility? And what challenges do diaspora leaders perceive in their efforts to connect with citizens under siege?

From December 2016 to October 2017, I examined the attitudes and social networks of 1,000 Syrians living in 10 regions outside the control of al-Assad's forces. Partnering with a Syrian polling firm, I undertook a rare, large-scale survey of 983 people in Syrian territory, which included a small subgroup of Syrians residing across the border in the Turkish municipality of Gaziantep.[69] (Please see Appendix D, available online, for a detailed description of sampling methods and Appendix E, available online, for disaggregated results across the survey's indicators.) This polling was complemented by twenty-four further interviews with elite members of the international opposition, many of whom gathered in Istanbul. (Please see Appendix D, available online, for further detail about this qualitative research.) Together, this research offers a unique look inside Syria during the civil war and an analysis of social networks within and beyond Syrian borders.

INSIDE FREE SYRIA

A central component of the Democratic Drain phenomenon is that people who emigrate tend to hold more liberal, democratic values relative to the countrymen they leave behind. While I have already shown how this depletes the home country of popular demand for more liberal, democratic leaders and government policy, it also implies weaker receptivity at home to liberal, democratic appeals from members of the diaspora. Syria is no different.

Consistent with levels reported in Chapter 2 from my research in other Arab countries such as Jordan, Lebanon, Libya, Palestine, and Tunisia, overall support for liberal democratic values is low among the Syrians sampled. Across the Syrian sample, there is weak support for freedom of speech (9 percent of those sampled) and more moderate support for checks on executive power (35 percent) and a separation of church and state (29 percent). Where respondents exhibited more liberal democratic values, a fraction asserted these values "strongly," whereas substantial shares of the sample "strongly" *opposed* checks on executive power, secular separation, and freedom of speech.

Responses varied rather widely by region, but displaced Syrians in Gaziantep reported the highest mean levels of liberal democratic attitudes in the sample, A majority of Gaziantep respondents supported checks on executive power (56 percent) and a secular separation (66 percent). It is unclear whether this support is because Gaziantep respondents felt freer to express democratic values or because of their exposure to Turkey's relatively more democratic institutions. But based on more recent research, it is likely because Syrians who fled to Turkey and other more Western states already possessed stronger liberal democratic proclivities before their departure.[70] Naturally, this also conforms to the sliding scale I observed among Eastern European emigrants and prospective migrants in Chapter 4.

Certainly, these results reveal the challenge for members of the pro-democracy diaspora who wish to instill more liberal values and mobilize resistance back home. The starting point is very low. However, this approximates the state of liberal, democratic values in other regional countries that are the targets of their respective overseas activists. If the appetite for democracy were high, many of these countries would have robust social movements already organizing for new institutions and not require "democratic gain" from abroad.

Ideal Leaders

Despite their unity in resistance to the al-Assad regime, the pro-democracy opposition movement in the territory controlled by the Free Syrian Army was fragmented due to ethnic and sectarian differences, regional dispersion, and a war with multiple enemies on multiple fronts. For this reason, it was unclear what rank-and-file members of the Syrian opposition value in the profile of their leaders.

While such intelligence would help opposition leaders determine how to best reach and mobilize their supporters, direct questioning about these values is unhelpful because these perceptions of "legitimacy" are never determined in isolation; rather, leadership profiles feature multiple attributes that combine to create the people they embody.

To ascertain individuals' latent perceptions of legitimacy, I employed a conjoint experiment. The conjoint experiment presents respondents with the profiles of two hypothetical leaders of the pro-democracy opposition movement. These profiles randomly vary background characteristics, including whether the leader was:

- previously a part of the al-Assad regime;
- was an early revolutionary; and
- is currently outside of Syria.

Respondents were then asked which of the two candidates for public office they prefer. This design permits an estimate of which attributes are most influential on respondent choice or decision-making, without directly querying respondents about a specific attribute.

The results suggest that respondents were 17 percent more likely to identify a leader as "legitimate" when they were located inside Syria. Potential leaders were penalized for joining the revolution late (-19 percent) and for previously being part of the Assad regime (-19 percent).

Given that the probabilities are additive, one implication of these findings is that a former member of the Assad regime located within Syria would have roughly equal legitimacy to a leader located outside of Syria who has never been associated with Assad. In other words, living outside the warzone is as incriminatory as a previous affiliation with the enemy itself. It is a mark of illegitimacy.

Some demographics were more sensitive to foreign residency than others. Respondents from Ar-Rastan – a region near the North Lebanese border where protests, army defections, and a battle took place early in the civil war – were 30.7 percent less likely to identify with a leader who lived outside Syria, an effect larger than those observed in all other regions. This constituency was also 33.7 percent less likely to identify with leaders who were previously associated with the al-Assad regime. Compared to the remainder of the sample, Syrians polled in Gaziantep found greater legitimacy in leaders who had fled like them.

Foreign residency hurt leaders' legitimacy more in the eyes of Syrian people with university educations (a 22.4 percent penalty) and those who had never been displaced (a 19.5 percent penalty). Respondents who had never been displaced were also far harder on leaders who were previously affiliated with the Assad regime than respondents who were displaced. The results do not suggest significantly more or less sensitivity to leaders' foreign residency among any other demographic. It is a broad trend and, for would-be leaders in the diaspora who envisioned themselves bringing democracy back to Syria on a shining white horse, a latent but damning bias against expatriates.

But why such bias? Some resentment, surely. Perhaps even a sense of betrayal. But possibly also because those who remained in Syria felt so disconnected from those who had departed.

NETWORKS UNDER SIEGE

Social network analyses ask survey respondents to list the people they speak to on a regular basis – frequently or not. To account for people's sensitivity about identifying others during wartime, I did not ask for the names of these contacts, but I did ask for their general location, the level of closeness, and the nature of their relationship.

The results suggest that Syrian information networks tend to be comprised of localized networks of friends, neighbors, and family members, who are highly trusted even if not personally close to each other. The majority of contacts resided in the same town or governorate – a highly closed network consistent with those that social network experts tend to observe in very closed groups such as resistance or terrorist organizations. These networks often prove difficult to penetrate – even by a supportive, pro-democracy diaspora. (Please see Appendix F, available online, for detailed and disaggregated results from the social network analysis.)

Name Recognition

Only 19 percent of respondents could name a single leader of the opposition movement without prompting by survey enumerators. Even when the most prominent members of the Syrian opposition movement were named by survey enumerators, the majority did not recognize them. Those who were able to name a leader were more likely to rely on communications media, via internet news websites, television, or social media like Facebook, WhatsApp, or Twitter. However, the use of these social media is contingent on the availability and strength of erratic mobile internet reception – which only reinforces a propensity to "hunker down" in a society under siege.

Awareness of opposition leadership was low everywhere. It peaked in Ar-Rastan (40 percent) and Jarjnaz (39 percent), but was lowest in Kafr Nabudah (4 percent) – a city in the northwest part of the Hama governorate that was held by rebels until a 2019 counteroffensive by the Syrian Army with Russian support. Across demographic subgroups, there was greater awareness among men (23 percent), people with higher educations, people between forty and forty-nine years of age (28 percent), and people who had never been displaced (21 percent).

Even after being prompted, respondents still exhibited low awareness of opposition leaders. The leaders with the greatest name recognition were Muaz Al Khateeb (36 percent), a former Damascus imam and former president of the Syrian National Coalition (or Etilaf); Riad Hijab (36 percent), the former Syrian prime minister and highest-ranking defector from the Syrian government; Burhan Ghalioun (18 percent), a French-Syrian sociologist and first chairman of the opposition's Syrian National Coalition; George Sabra (17 percent), a longtime dissident and former president of the Syrian National Coalition; and Bassam Jaara

(15 percent), a London-based journalist and spokesperson for the Syrian National Coalition.

There was 0 percent name recognition of Abdulelah Fahed and 2 percent recognition of Anas Al-Abda, respectively the Secretary-General and president of Etilaf, the pro-democracy group that met in Istanbul, at the time I conducted my fieldwork.

Mass Communication

My social network analysis examined the breadth and insularity of respondents' social networks, but also the extent to which they were connected to sources of information. Across the sample, the most commonly used sources of information were television (53 percent), Facebook (51 percent), WhatsApp (49 percent), and internet news (34 percent).

Men were significantly more likely to gather information from all sources of information than women, although both watched television news at similar levels. Similarly, respondents with post-secondary educations and people under forty years of age were also significantly more likely to gather information from all sources of information. Television is particularly common among those without a vocational or university degree, people over forty, and people who had never been displaced by the conflict.

Respondents who could identify pro-democracy opposition leaders and those who were optimistic about the opposition movement's fight with the al-Assad regime were more likely to consume all types of informational media across the board. The only exception was that people who thought an al-Assad regime victory was "very likely" were more likely to get information from internet news sources. Among all the media forms, the use of Facebook was most associated with increased confidence in the pro-democracy resistance movement and awareness of its leaders.

Reliable Sources

Beyond forms of mass communication, I was especially interested in the extent to which people relied on direct, interpersonal communication for trusted information. I asked respondents to report the approximate number of people they have "directly spoken to (in-person, by phone, or by internet) to receive trustworthy information or news about the situation in Syria" over the two months prior to the survey.

Looking across demographic subgroups, more casual informants were reported by men, the highly educated, the younger, and the more religious. Those with more casual informants were also more likely to name resistance leaders and be more confident in the opposition movement's likelihood of victory.

The survey asked for detailed information on four casual informants from whom respondents most regularly receive trustworthy information on the situation in Syria. While the average number of casual informants reported was greater than four across all regions polled, the average number of specific contacts listed was 2.02. This may reflect either an exaggeration of the number of individuals that respondents speak to regularly, uncertainty about the identity of the contact, or discomfort with revealing information about these contacts.

Among those informants listed, trustworthy connections were likely to be with friends (37 percent) and family members (35 percent). Contacts were unlikely to be formed at mosques (1 percent) or with public officials (1 percent). Neighbors (13 percent) and colleagues from work (11 percent) constituted a minor share of informants. Overall, 93 percent of the entire sample reported speaking to their principal informants at least once a week.

Respondents' reported networks of informants were founded on trust more than on a personal sense of closeness. About 73 percent of the listed informants were thought to be trustworthy and 95 percent were thought to be worthy of at least moderate trust; but a mere 57 percent of the informants were personally close to those surveyed.

To determine the density of these networks, I also asked about the relationship between respondents' informants when more than one was specified. The scale ranged from contacts "who know each other" to those who reported "a very close relationship." Relative to network density outside of Syria, the scores were consistent with very cohesive groups with their backs against the wall.

The high-density insularity of social networks is reinforced by their local nature. A large number of informants were based in the same location as the respondent. The share of these neighboring informants comprised around 70 and 80 percent of all informants in many internal provinces. This would be high in almost any context, but it also contrasts with the networks of Syrians in Gaziantep, where only 11 percent of respondents' informants were in the same location. Very few respondents cited informants from outside of Syria, and even fewer from outside the Middle East region. Respondents in Douma and

Mzeireb – located in close proximity to Damascus – were particularly isolated from the information network spanning other opposition locations.

Respondents who were more confident in an opposition movement victory and those who were familiar with its leaders were 13 percent more likely to have informants outside of their local region and 9 percent more likely to have informants outside of Syria. Looking at demographic subgroups, the profile of people who tended to have more interregional and international informants were men, fifty years old and over, with higher educational attainment, and displaced. The magnitude of these trends was greater when examining the share of international informants. Across the sample, informants outside of Syria were almost exclusively friends and family members. These international informants were characterized by higher levels of trust but, again, not necessarily greater closeness.

In sum, my sample of Syrians in opposition-held regions maintained hyperlocal networks of high frequency contact and high trust. In other contexts, this might represent a highly cohesive society. However, these data suggest that – under siege – Syrians were "hunkering down" and connected to only the most highly trusted sources of information. Compounded by reduced internet access, this makes their communities harder to reach, if not downright impenetrable.

ELITE CIRCLES

Combined with interviews of Syrian diaspora leaders, these data about Syrians' public attitudes and network dynamics permit a better understanding of the challenges they face. (See Appendix D, available online, for a discussion of my methodological approach.) For their part, the Syrian diaspora elites reported a relatively diffuse social network among themselves and an observable sense of disconnection from Syrians on the ground. In total, the 24 respondents I interviewed reported relationships among 161 people. The network density – the interconnectedness among the 161 people – was low.

Informational exchange across political organizations was rare. People are more likely to maintain relationships with others inside the same political party or subgrouping. Several individuals emerge as key figures who engage with more elite informants than others. But among them, only Nasr al-Hariri – a member of Syria's parliament who resigned in protest in 2011 and eventually served as president of the Syrian National Coalition – was known at all by survey respondents in Syria (about 8 percent of survey respondents). None of the others held much public salience outside elite circles, which corroborates my findings about the atomization of Syrian citizens from the leaders of the pro-democratic opposition movements.

I also conducted a different analysis that evaluates the degree of status or "prestige" inside the network – how many times individuals are nominated by others. From this angle, a different individual emerges as a critical node in the opposition social network: Hadi Al Bahra, who was the president of the National Coalition for Syrian Revolutionary and Opposition Forces between 2014 and 2015. In 2017, at the time of my interviews, he was referenced as a highly trusted informant and confidante by multiple members, particularly those who reported wide networks of their own. However, Mr. Al Bahra – who would be reelected president of the opposition again in 2023 – was effectively unknown by the large-scale sample inside Syria (and ostensibly uninvolved in the military effort that ultimately felled al-Assad in 2024).

Freedom without Legitimacy

In the interviews with opposition elites in the diaspora, there was enormous frustration with a pervasive sense of disconnection from Syrian citizens on the ground in rebel territory. Respondents, who were granted anonymity to protect them from retribution by the al-Assad regime, underscored a number of reasons for this, but all related to flawed systems of governance that rendered the exiled opposition little credibility and the isolating social effects of a treacherous warzone.

Local councils in Syria were a critical liaison for the opposition elites. These municipal-level organizations provide information, distribute resources, and acted as lieutenants on the ground. It is for this reason, one leader said, that the councils had been the target of regime and Islamic State attacks.

"I used to work closely with the local councils and so I have a huge network with them," he said. "We help them to further their work with the humanitarian agencies and international NGOs [nongovernmental organizations]. That was until 2014, when Der Ezzour came under Islamic State occupation. We then had to stop all the work in Islamic State-controlled areas due to international policies. Humanitarian aid was stopped. The international view was that assistance in those territories would also support Islamic State. There was also a fear that aid workers would eventually be accused of assisting terrorists. So 138 local councils stopped working there.

"Elsewhere," he continued, "the regime targeted the local councils and bombarded them so that they would not be able to provide services. [Assad] felt less threatened by the [army] than by the local councils and the services they provide because they were the alternative to the Assad government. They provided education, health, electricity, and water."

Another opposition leader lamented that, even in the regions with functional local councils, the opposition was challenged by its reporting structure. The gap was often filled by foreign governments and international civil society groups, which undermined the legitimacy of the opposition movement.

"The greatest challenge we have is the absence of a proper structure and hierarchy of reporting," he said. "There are people in crisis right now [and] when the Coalition hears the demands of these people, it doesn't have the appropriate tools to support them. And without those tools, you can't support those people and it makes us lose credibility in front of them. Then if a [transnational] civil society organization comes to their aid, they cut contact with us.

"[If] your needs are being provided by foreign governments, [people in Syria] stop listening to political bodies like us," he added. "If we had a supportive, functioning hierarchy and support was delivered through its channels, we would provide good governance and earn more legitimacy. Our voice is lost when that support comes from others."

Insiders on the Outside

This disconnection has been exacerbated by the realities of communicating in a warzone. Elites were unanimously reluctant to discuss, let alone reveal, their sources of information. These contacts operate in the shadows of encrypted telecommunications, in constant fear for their lives. And while this protects these precious sources, it also inhibits any sense of a coherent, collective movement.

One respondent said, "I stopped communicating with [my connections in Syria], because contact with the opposition is sufficient to have them executed. I started to get my information from public resources. And because I'm not very much of an extrovert, my connections were limited to the [party] and diplomats. The nature of my position gives me access to sensitive information, and so I stay away from being overly social to avoid embarrassing situations. This includes not being active on social media."

Another opposition leader said, "Even to members of Etilaf, I give them headlines, but not details. This is a life and death battle on the ground."

This secrecy made coordination difficult between people on the inside and people on the outside. On the one hand, most respondents felt that they were far more able to mobilize and advocate for their countrymen when they were based inside Syria. On the other hand, most recognized that such advocacy was perilous or simply impossible given current conditions inside the country.

"On the outside, you have the freedom to move and meet people, to hold conferences," one leader said. "That would be impossible inside Syria. Inside, they have a lot of energy but don't have the freedom to organize or meet. Our success is related to the agreement between those inside and outside to create harmony in our work."

Still, even were there to be greater cohesion among the elites and stronger connections with Syrians on the ground, the interview data reveal exiled elites who possess more liberal democratic norms than those expressed by survey respondents. I asked both samples the same questions about liberal democratic values related to checks on power, a separation of church and state, and freedom of speech. The sample of elites was categorically more supportive of such norms than the people they represent.

Transition Costs

In many cases, political leaders abroad are also taxed by the cost of adjusting to their destination societies. Emigrating and resettling is hard enough.

One source, once a leading Syrian human rights activist, said, "In the beginning of my time in the United States, I was working on my activism and maintaining my connections. After that, I started selling coffee in the streets."

He began to weep.

"I thank God for what I have."

Also based in the United States, a former Syrian opposition party leader thought back to the days before the Syrian Civil War. "I remember 12

Syrian asylum seekers who came to the US in 2008. Only two of them have stayed active and at the lowest level. Others have language difficulties, financial difficulties, or lack the academic credentials to contribute here [in the United States]. They came here with the hope of a better life, but [miss] the dynamics of society and the way of life in Syria – where you can always stay with your family and not pay the rent or utilities.

"There are dozens of cases like this ... There is a culture of shame and it is difficult to [rebound] from this to resume their activism ... The attrition rate is higher than 90%. Less than 10% are able to maintain their activism. Many you don't hear from after one year."

Other activists cited the temptation to leave homeland politics behind and the unfamiliar pressure to focus on asylum applications and other legal documentation. Nearly all subjects – independent of their location and the duration of their time abroad – expressed some degree of estrangement from their country of origin and its people. And this is precisely what autocrats hope for when they expel or pressure their opponents to emigrate.

There are a number of prominent examples in which autocrats would have been better positioned had they expelled their political competition, rather than imprisoned them. Aung San Suu Kyi attracted a great deal of attention despite her house arrest for much of twenty years after being elected the presumed prime minister of Myanmar in 1990.

Imprisoned for twenty-seven years, Nelson Mandela became the subject of an international campaign for his release but also for the anti-apartheid movement until his election in 1994.

Soviet nuclear physicist and human rights activist Andrei Sakharov was subject to a six-year internal exile in January 1980, during which his hunger strikes garnered worldwide attention and sympathy. This set an example for Vladimir Putin's more recent antagonist, Alexei Navalny – the opposition politician and anti-corruption activist who was repeatedly jailed and poisoned by the Russian government, until his alleged murder at Putin's order in February 2024.

In the 1980s, the imprisonment and torture of Ennahda's leader, Rachid al-Ghannouchi, inflamed his Tunisian supporters before his exile in 1992. Ghannouchi's infamy receded during his time in Europe, before his opportunistic return in 2011.

And as with Ghannouchi, many governments slander democratic leaders as "treasonous" both before and after they leave their countries of origin. This tarnishes leaders' reputations and disables their influence and mobilization efforts. According to data collected in interviews, this appears to be a widespread means that autocratic governments employ to discredit voices from abroad. Respondents report false accusations of being a "double agent" and being "tarnished" by a "yellow press," an extension of a longer trend of "fifth column" accusations in authoritarian states.[71]

The former Syrian party leader who is now based in the United States told me, "After being away for so many years, it's not easy to return and say, 'Hey, I'm back! Let's do something together.' You look like an opportunist. And I don't blame them for thinking that. Arabs tend to believe that a rise to power is synonymous with a rise to wealth. All of our rulers are wealthy. ... It's difficult to persuade that a campaign is about power for good and not personal enrichment."

In these ways, emigrants' engagement in pro-democracy movements is hindered by personal obstacles, but also by various forms of resistance to their ongoing advocacy.

FAMILY TIES

Despite the power and resources of its diaspora, the case of Syria – and indeed various others – throws cold water on the idea of "democratic gain." A reasonable counterargument, however, might say that – despite all the advantages associated with the Syrian opposition's international support – a warzone is a challenging place to transmit liberal democratic values. And while the evidence suggests that Syrians were no more able to transmit these values during peacetime before 2011, it is worth exploring the possibility that democratic gain takes place more subtly in the casual conversations of intimate family members and friends who maintain their relationships across borders.

Very few studies address this possibility. On the one hand, leveraging surveys across six Latin American countries, Norte Dame political scientist Abby Córdova and Vanderbilt political scientist Jonathan Hiskey found that individuals who have strong cross-border ties that connect them with relatives living in the United States are more likely to participate in local politics, sympathize with a political party, and persuade others to vote for a party.[72] In a separate study of Mexico, however, sociologists at the University of California, Los Angeles (UCLA) find that such effects are conditional on migratory patterns and the extent to which emigrants contribute to the provision of public goods.[73]

On the other hand, Harvard economist Alberto Alesina and UCLA economist Paola Giuliano have found an inverse relationship between

strong family ties and political participation. The more individuals rely on
the family as a provider of services, insurance, and transfer of resources,
the lower their civic engagement and political participation.[74] In short,
strong family ties appear to be a substitute for generalized trust, rather
than a complement to it.[75] Still, they also found that cultural preferences
diffuse through diasporic relations.

While Alesina and Giuliano focus on preferences about economic
redistribution, the implication is that emigrants communicate and
influence values and attitudes back home without necessarily being political advocates.[76] Do people who have friends or family members living abroad hold different values from their countrymen without such
relationships?

To address this question, I return to my study of public attitudes across
ten countries in Eastern Europe – many of which have experienced democratic backsliding in peacetime, but have large, more democratically
inclined diasporas in Western Europe, as shown in Chapter 4.

And indeed, the results show an interesting difference between people
with and without such diaspora connections. In Eastern European
countries, people who have friends or family living abroad are 9.1
percent more likely to consider emigrating than those without such
ties.[77] This may be because prospective migrants feel more confident
that there will be support available to them upon arrival or because
the stories and observations that emigrants share inspire countrymen
to emigrate too.

However, this does not mean that emigrants similarly transmit their
political values, too. People with friends or family members abroad score
1 percentage point lower on the authoritarian personality scale and
1.5 percentage points higher on the scale of liberal democratic values
than people without friends or family living abroad.[78] If emigrants are
attempting to reorient the authoritarian values of their countrymen who
plan to stay back home, the effect has been minimal.

A ONE-WAY PHENOMENON

In sum, this chapter shows that diaspora activists possess the freedom,
resources, and organizational platforms to affect social, political, and
economic life in their countries of origin in many ways. But according to
a number of different studies, grave challenges inhibit the transmission
of democratic values.

Despite a civil war that freed diaspora leaders to more stridently criticize the Syrian regime with the political and financial backing of Western democracies and numerous Arab monarchies, their political movements were barely known inside Syria. Despite their presence on websites, messaging apps, and social media, the pro-democratic opposition's leaders were nearly anonymous to their countrymen. Worse, the conjoint analysis shows that leaders in the diaspora were viewed as less legitimate; their emigration was as damning to their favorability as a previous affiliation with the al-Assad regime would have been. The diaspora leadership struggled for years after my research, and when the al-Assad regime finally collapsed on December 8, 2024, it fell at the hands of Syrian militants associated with the Islamic State and Al Qaeda extremist groups.

Syrian leaders acknowledged their sense of disconnection and attributed it to the challenges of being outside the theater. For people inside Syria, there were severe safety risks associated with communicating with opposition officials amidst state surveillance. Other leaders believed foreign governments did not share credit for the infrastructure investments, military support, and humanitarian aid the diaspora galvanized. Still others struggled to attract their countrymen's attention, even when the distinction between the free and authoritarian worlds could not be clearer. But for so many, the life of an immigrant abroad posed so many challenges that distracted them from their activism or undercut the extent to which they could advocate to and for the cause of bringing democracy to Syria. Earlier research has also emphasized the challenges of such external interventions in regions where people hold weak democratic values in the first place.

The best chance for "democratic gain" may emerge from the passive diffusion of democratic norms and values in the social remittances from friends and family – not activists – in democratic destination states to loved ones back home.[79] When these intimate transnational relationships are sustained, scholars have found that gender norms, education trends, labor activism, and even fertility rates change among people in the country of origin relative to their countrymen.[80] Higher regional emigration rates positively correlate with improved institutional quality and citizens' demand for accountability, particularly in countries that send migrants to democratic, high-income destinations.[81]

A variety of country-specific studies reinforce this conclusion. In the Balkans, researchers found that people with friends or family abroad are less likely to bribe local public officials and more likely to see bribe taking by public officials as unacceptable.[82] In the Dominican Republic, receivers of remittances see emigrants as catalysts of positive change because the emigrants witnessed fairer, more organized, and equitable political systems that they then communicated to those back home.[83] In India, elite migrants are credited with creating space for new political elites from historically disadvantaged groups.[84] Mexicans with friends or relatives abroad have expressed greater dissatisfaction with the country's democracy than those who do not know anyone living outside the country.[85] The same study found that Mexicans with diasporic ties are also more likely to participate in a civic organization and organized protests. In Moldova, transnational democratic diffusion has been credited with diminishing support for the Communist Party, contributing to its fall in 2009–2010 and Moldova's eventual alignment with pro-democracy and pro-European policies.[86]

My analysis of the European data presented in Chapter 4 corroborates this earlier research elsewhere, offering a flicker of promise in the power of personal relationships. Eastern Europeans who do not wish to emigrate, but have a close friend or family member abroad, hold slightly more democratic values than their countrymen without overseas ties. Therefore, while formal political advocacy from abroad is subject to severe limitations, "democratic gain" may be limited to interpersonal calls and messages between the people they trust most under conditions that permit the free flow of information. These findings add to an extensive amount of scholarship that both recognizes the potential power of diasporas but also questions their effect on democratic political development.

The evidence suggests that Democratic Drain is principally a one-way phenomenon with weak countervailing trends that might otherwise offset it.

6

A Human Base

Majid worked as a public advocate and attorney in Syria for twenty years. He inherited the Damascene law practice his father had run for over sixty years – its two offices and a library of half a million books. He had long leveraged the firm's success to pursue his passion for human rights. Trained by some of Syria's top lawyers, Majid defended asylum seekers, political prisoners, and people on death row over the decades, often working closely with European embassies.

By 2009, this work was enough for the Syrian government to imprison Majid, too. Authorities pressured the Syrian Bar Association to disbar him and then convicted him on charges of "weakening the sentiment" and "morale" of the nation in a sham trial. After being detained for two years in 2011, he was released under a special amnesty just before the Syrian Revolution began. Once he was reissued a passport, the Spanish Ambassador to Syria inserted a Schengen visa good for two years. At the time, there was already a sense that everything was about to change and the visa offered an escape route. Rebel insurgents had just attacked the highway to the Damascus airport and various government offices.

Very shortly afterward, Majid was mentioned in a series of US diplomatic cables publicly posted by WikiLeaks – the nonprofit media company praised and condemned for its release of state secrets and classified documents in the name of justice.

"I told my colleagues that I needed to run to the pharmacy," Majid recalled. "I booked a ticket to Cairo and left two hours later in the clothes I was wearing. The people in my office, I left them. I didn't have time to close the door or turn off the lights.

"When I was in Cairo, I found out that the Syrian government was in discussions with the Egyptian military council to extradite me. So I left for Paris within 24 hours using my Schengen visa."

Majid and I met at Marseilles, a French brasserie on Ninth Avenue in New York City's Hell's Kitchen neighborhood, a few blocks from the headquarters of Majid's American peers – partners from white-shoe law firms like Cravath Swaine & Moore or Skadden Arps. Majid now shuttled people like them around Manhattan in his limousine. The soft-spoken lawyer-turned-chauffeur was clearly traumatized.

Despite the Assad regime's brutal repression, Majid had always sustained faith that many Syrians continued to privately yearn for democracy. Over the years, he canvassed to recruit support for liberal reforms or accommodations and recalled the sacrifices people were willing to make in the name of freedom.

"One day, [when I was being pursued by the police], a boy took me by the hand and led me into his house, where his mother hid me in an internal room. The forces cut off the fingers of her older son outside, but the family never revealed that I was hiding inside."

He looked away, poignantly recalling the family's heroism.

"For years, there was no opposition," he said. "There were just individual people. But the political conditions made organizing them impossible – parties, projects, programs, charities, the whole infrastructure of politics. When [exiles] established the opposition abroad, it was not a natural development; it was *in vitro*."

He paused to reflect.

"There are moments in history, just moments, that politics should not waste," he said. "But if you're not prepared for that moment, it will not happen. This is not magic. Democracies are not pulled out of a hat.

"Democracy requires two things: It needs a base. And it needs tools. It's not just an idea. We need a human base.

"By 2011, very few democrats were left. Our problem is that our moment came too late."

Dissidents without Demigrants

The disintegration of the so-called Arab Spring in 2011 diminished hopes for democratization in many countries all over the Middle East and North Africa. Today, the region is characterized by conflict and instability in collapsed autocracies like Libya, Syria, and Yemen, collapses that have produced new autocracies in Egypt and Tunisia and teetering autocracies seeking to avoid or suppress the unrest as in Bahrain, Jordan, and Morocco – but little democracy. Even Israel, a democracy in the troubled region, has been tested by the authoritarian tendencies of Binyamin Netanyahu, whose government has sought to weaken the judiciary and violated human rights.

This book introduces the possibility that one reason would-be democratizers have struggled to consolidate support behind liberal political development during the so-called Arab Winter is that these societies lack sufficient numbers of liberal democrats.

As democratically inclined people leave their authoritarian countries of origin, pro-democratic pressure on the regime wanes. When industrialized democracies lure highly skilled migrants and refugees from authoritarian states with the promise of social mobility and freedom, these emigrants bring the seeds of economic growth – but also democratic reform – with them. And so those who might otherwise support and even advocate for democratization in Cairo, Damascus, and Tunis leave for London, Washington, and Paris.

Indeed, as Middle East politics scholar Samer Shehata mused about post-revolutionary Egypt, its politics became dominated by democrats who are not liberals (Islamists standing for election) and liberals who are not democrats (authoritarian secularists).[1]

Democratic Drain is an incremental mass phenomenon that may not be detected until its effects are plain to see, much like climate change or a decline in fertility rates. Like these other global meta-trends, to evaluate and understand Democratic Drain, it must be measured in a standardized way as universally as possible. This was the goal of the preceding chapters, which present evidence that the relatively liberal, democratic proclivities of emigrants and prospective emigrants is depleting their countries of origin worldwide of precious political capital that might otherwise be the foundation for more democratic institutions, transparency, individual rights, and freedom.

However, there are people who do not need to see this evidence to be persuaded about the existence of Democratic Drain – dissidents, the leaders of democratic movements themselves. People like Majid.

For most of this book, I have focused on "demigrants," democratically inclined emigrants, and I have primarily employed large-scale statistical methods to understand the dynamics and mechanics of this mass phenomenon. While some leave their countries of origin in response to illiberal or undemocratic political developments, others depart in response to a career opportunity or a chance to reunite with family members abroad – unlike Majid, all voluntarily.

But it is also critical to consider the plight of dissidents because, if they depart, they too become part of the Democratic Drain phenomenon, an elite component of an otherwise massive sorting effect. After all, dissidents lead the institutional reform efforts that rely on the mobilization of citizens with democratic proclivities. From their perch, they offer a unique perspective about the challenges of democratization in more authoritarian settings because they have devoted their lives to the cause. In this chapter, I conduct in-depth, interview-based research – much as I did with the Syrian exiles leading pro-democracy efforts from abroad – to observe Democratic Drain from the perspective of the people who have devoted their lives to mobilizing people with democratic values to make freedom and rights-based claims of the state.

In interviews with twenty-four activists from across the Middle East,[2] I solicit these leaders' postmortems about their struggles to bring institutional change to their countries of origin four or five years after the 2011 Arab uprisings.[3] In almost every interview, discussions about the political turned very personal. As authoritarian governments sought to discomfort or remove these democratic actors from their countries' political spaces, their countries' stories of Democratic Drain became their own personal stories. Crucially, the leaders describe the ways millions of demigrants have left over the years. Through their reflections, we can see the extent to which their political movements rely on rank-and-file supporters. It's a matter of human resources.

HUMAN RESOURCES

In interviews, activists spoke at length about how the ranks of liberal democrats in their countries of origin had been severely depleted, particularly how few people were even prepared for their outreach because of both the departure of democratically inclined emigrants and state suppression of democratic ideologies.

Abdullah originally fled Libya in 1976, but devoted his career thereafter to training and mobilizing democratic movement leaders across the Middle East and North Africa. With the collapse of the Ghaddafi regime in 2011, he returned to Benghazi to focus his energy on his own countrymen again.

When I arrived, I felt like there was a yearning for something like democracy but with zero education. Democracy needs more than yearning. Democracy is not just elections. The candidates were mostly remnants of the old regime. There was no underground group of democrats. They could not survive in the country.

They were forced into exile, imprisoned or killed. The education system did not produce [democrats] and people were not exposed to free media. It was a controlled society.

Still, when I was inside, I was more effective. Meeting and training the people, I could touch base with women, children, nurses, teachers. Whenever I finished a workshop, even with the hardcore Islamists, they would tell me that they'd love to help more.

But ultimately, democracy did not take root because we had no roots. Democracy is a culture that you have to develop in society. That's why I've tried to do workshops about citizenship – knowing your rights and doing your duties. The 42 years of indoctrination created a culture of individualism in the worst sense. We got rid of one Gadhafi and he left 6 million more.

Faisal, a Syrian human rights activist, had similarly participated in trainings and democratic mobilization before.

The US State Department has spent billions on sending the International Republican Institute, the National Democratic Institute, Freedom House to the Middle East, trying to educate the public about respect, coexistence, accepting electoral defeat. And some Arabs accepted that this is the best way to move forward to build better nations. We need to reach them. But most of the people we convince then leave the country, because they know they will not realize that promise in the conditions of their native countries. Democratization starts with taking away deprivation, then education, and then asking people what they want. Those that we trained to believe in democracy looked around and couldn't find other people to join them.

Others witnessed the steady loss of democratically inclined people over the years in their respective political spaces. Much as Chapter 3 reveals, political milestones like elections – but also their dismissal amid broader instability or regime change – often triggered departures.

Maher, an Egyptian human rights activist, said:

Previously there were three groups in Egypt – the military regime, Islamists and democrats. Now there are no democrats. This took place earlier in Egyptian history [gradually] until 2003, when Egypt started taking baby steps toward reform and opening as a response to the war in Iraq. During that period, more people were joining the democratic movement than leaving the country – until [Sisi's coup in] 2013. That's when there was another [mass] departure, when every major reform was cancelled, and the regime became more repressive than any time in the last century.

Zaki, an activist and researcher in Yemen, said:

Since 1962, there are no statistics about which democrats have left Yemen, of course. But the elites have left. There is a strong correlation between democracy [preferences] and education [attainment]. They tend to be more urban, living in cities. Much of the country's people are illiterate, and they just listen to the radio or watch television. They do not know what a constitution is. Many [democrats] returned with hope, but they despaired and left for good. We are like many people around the world who left for the United States and Britain. This impacted democracy, because the only people who remained were against democracy.

Malika, a Tunisian activist, believed that the world held false hope for Tunisia after its 2014 elections yielded a democratic parliament for the first time in its history. Six years before President Kais Saied suspended parliament, deposed the prime minister, and consolidated power on July 25, 2021, Malika warned me that Tunisian democracy was more the product of a temporary political détente than a reflection of true political will:

The initial revolution did not request democracy. They requested food, jobs. When you throw out the police state, the most common choice was democracy because none of the pre-existing opposition groups were very strong and the military was an independent unit. [The political party] Ennadha will talk about the sacrifices they made [for democracy], but the truth is they had no choice. They were not strong enough to control the country by themselves. Nobody was.

The primary advocates for democracy were not previously democrats. Democracy served their interests. They claim that they believe in democracy, but they were as radical as anyone else and they had an agenda to advance. The only truly democratic party was Ennadha, which held elections inside the party, consulted widely, and have been consistent in their position. I was speaking to one of their leaders over breakfast the other day and when I told him that even Ennadha doesn't want power right now because they don't want to be blamed for the country's early struggles, he smiled and said, "No comment."

I don't follow any one party. I have friends in all of them, but stay independent because I listen to their perspectives and think, "Oh my God, none of you are democratic."

There was no movement for democracy before or during the revolution. You can see it in the election results. We are 12 million people, 8 million eligible voters, 5 million registered, and only 3 million who actually voted. What does that tell you about the democrats in Tunisia? Americans say that this is similar to their turnout. But Tunisia is a new democracy. People should be excited about democracy! But they didn't vote. How beautiful is that story?

Egypt, Libya, Syria, Tunisia, and Yemen are disparate countries, each with their own histories of institutional development, colonialism, and conflict. They have unique political cultures informed by ethnoreligious differences, regional dynamics, and colonial affinities. But these civic leaders describe a similar feeling of leading a charge, only to peer behind them to discover fewer and fewer people following them. It's not merely disinterest they describe; democracy also relies on civic skills and values that are not necessarily learned in long-authoritarian spaces.

DRIVERS OF EMIGRATION

For reform-minded leaders, pro-democratic citizens were the critical constituencies they sought – as Majid said, "a human base" that could scale their activism into a movement, a revolution, a government. And because many of these leaders had already emigrated once themselves, they were acutely sensitive to and familiar with the calculations behind the departure of so many would-be supporters from their countries of origin over the years. From their perspective, what are the mechanics behind the emigration of democratically inclined citizens?

People's Preference for Political Rights

So many observers of migration assume that prospective migrants' choices are consumed by economic calculations. But Chapter 2 clearly shows the way political considerations also shape migrant behavior and decision-making. However, my interview subjects, without any prompting, were already acutely aware that prospective migrants actively seek political freedoms as they weigh other attributes in destination states.

Emran, a democracy advocate from Egypt explains, "Mainly the Islamists and [Islamist] youths are in Turkey or Qatar … Others who had better opportunities went to Europe or the United States for work or education. More democrats are going to the United States and Europe. The reason is the mindsets. The position that Turkey and Qatar have taken is considered against [the regime of] Sisi. The question is where would you feel safe as a member of the opposition?"

Mariam, a leader in Yemen's democracy movement, says, "The 300,000 to 400,000 people who have migrated [from Yemen] to Saudi Arabia are those who are willing to accept their policies on human rights, immigration, women, and education. We would rather stay in Yemen than go there."

Faisal, a former Syrian party leader, says, "The Syrians I meet who recently left have accepted American conceptions of democracy, but believed it is impossible to live that concept unless they move to Germany, France or the United States."

But prospective migrants are also seen to be receptive to liberalizing policies enacted by the government. Unlike Egypt, Syria, and Yemen, Morocco has been characterized by general stability since King Mohammed VI loosened his grip over public affairs after the Arab Spring.

According to Mounir, a liberal activist there, this has also softened people's appetite for a renewed democratic movement.

"Many activists from the parties have left," he says. "During the Arab Spring movement, all political parties prohibited their activists from participating in the demonstrations. That leaves a problem. Political parties like USFP [Socialist Union of Populist Forces] and PJD [Justice and Development Party] who should be and are considered to be acting for democracy refused to participate in an effort toward a transition to democracy. Meanwhile, the people demonstrating were independent Islamist or Liberal activists who refused their party recommendations – a minority. The leaders of the democracy were too close to the regime."

Western Immigration Policies

Western democracies' immigration policies increasingly aim to recruit skilled labor migrants from the developing world.[4] Since around 2005, European states have modified admissions standards to make entry and settlement more difficult, if not impossible, for low-skilled migrants from outside the European Union (EU). Concurrently, settler states like Canada and Australia have pursued points-test policies which evaluate migrants on a range of criteria and favor applicants who possess technical skills, higher education credentials, and language fluencies. This narrows the economic and, potentially, the political profile of those who leave authoritarian regimes.

Amal, a nongovernmental organization (NGO) activist from Yemen, says, "Right now, most of my friends who were part of the pro-democracy revolution in 2011 want to leave Yemen. They feel very hopeless, that things are changing for the worst, and that there is little to do. So they are looking for education and jobs abroad. They are generally very highly educated, speak English, have traveled before to attend conferences and workshops. They have a network of colleagues abroad, and many have worked for international NGOs. People like that. So those who have the opportunity to leave, do."

Aliyah, a former democracy activist from Egypt, says, "A lot of people left Egypt because, if you have a business or have the opportunity to get US or Canadian citizenship, you go. They just became more focused on their business and making it work. They are still activists but not as visibly. A lot of them left to pursue other things and their own futures. They didn't necessarily give up on Egypt, but it's like a time-out. They're focusing on their businesses, their families and immediate needs."

She continued. "If you have that chance, another nationality, why not? And often times, this is what gets them in trouble with a government who accuses them of people a double agent. And it's easy, there's a mood of doubt. People will find a way to hold your personal life against you. And then you're tarnished. The yellow press is very irresponsible, and you don't have the tools or energy to really respond. If you've been away for so long, you have to reintegrate yourself into the realities. And that's a real disadvantage. You have to rebuild your networks. Either you know someone or start from scratch. Otherwise, you are completely out of the game."

Expulsion or Forced Emigration

Many would-be democratizers – highly educated or not – are pushed out of their authoritarian homelands. Authoritarian regimes are bolstered when dissidents emigrate and, in some cases, actively facilitate or force their emigration.[5] Even under the Sisi regime, Egypt continued to announce restrictions on NGOs that require increasing government control and restrictions on foreign funding.[6]

Many respondents from Egypt described informal notifications about their imminent arrests. Syrian respondents recalled national police stationed in front of their homes. Others depicted outright expulsions, assassination attempts, and threats against family members.

Malika, a liberal activist from Tunisia, says, "Historically, Tunisian democrats were abroad in France, the United States and England. They were refugees from the regime, especially the ones in Europe. These people were the educated. They were professionals. Each had a different story, aside from being educated and a likely affiliation with [the Ennahda Party]. Most of these people stayed in the US or Europe after the revolution. They had lives abroad, families, and they just didn't think that they could make a difference back in Tunisia."

Amir, a former Egyptian party leader, says, "The majority of the democratic leaders in Egypt, the most important ones, are either in prison or in voluntary exile. They are in Lebanon or Turkey or America. We have 50 young people in prison from our [movement] … There has been [a lot of] immigration of our liberal people outside of Egypt. It started 60 years ago. After the 1952 revolution, many left. They go out to escape prison and arrest … [If they were to have returned before the Arab Spring], it would have been very important. It would have been beneficial. They would have helped us reform."

Amir departed Cairo a few weeks after Sisi gained power in a July 3, 2013 coup. "There were threats of arrest when I left, and media campaigns against me. I was imprisoned five times for a total of five and a half years. We were exposed we were exposed to big pressure [by the regime]. They destroyed our headquarters. They shut down our party newspaper and organized big media campaigns against us. They slandered us, they accused us of being agents of America or being with the [Muslim] brotherhood.

"The current is still there, the liberal current," he says. "But it is weak."

Supranational Organizations

Ironically, the supranational organizations that train local democratic activists may actually disrupt their momentum by extracting activists from their context. Organizations like the National Endowment for Democracy, Amnesty International, and the United States Agency for International Development (USAID) pluck high-potential democracy advocates from their national contexts with the best of intentions. After selected fellows and trainees become acculturated to Western, liberal environments, a substantial number of leaders pursue broader advocacy directions in those environments that distract their attention from their original struggles. Their homelands will never know what their impact might have been.

Others may return to their countries of origin, equipped with new vernaculars, demands, and ideas that fail to resonate with other citizens. A further consequence is that activists' contact with other émigrés abroad may build a network that facilitates their own future emigration. Recent research has emphasized the role played by such social ties in labor migrant decision-making.[7]

In interviews, the temptation to stay abroad was strong.

Ahmed, a once-influential Egyptian journalist, says, "The American Embassy in Egypt nominated me to take up a 3-week scholarship about journalism in three US states. So I thought why not stay and learn a new situation, learn English? I'm not trying to escape but I want a new experience. But if I return, I think I will be perceived as a risk by security and intelligence people. Also, I'm worried that if I return, I will not be able to re-enter the United States."

Maher, the Egyptian human rights activist, says that he was given a five-year tourist visa from the American government without solicitation.

"When I applied for a visa to the United States two years ago, I was planning to stay for only two weeks for a tour organized by [the Project on Middle East Democracy]. I was meeting several activists and members of Congress. I assume they either didn't want me to ask again, or they were giving me a back-up plan."

Mariam initially left Yemen on a Fulbright scholarship. She says, "Now I don't want to go back. There is no room for people like me [in Yemen]. People throw rocks at people like me. I moved for my career, but also for my safety. To get my job now in Yemen, I would have to yell, fight and commit myself to the Muslim Brotherhood."

Across interviews, people with democratic proclivities are subject to a variety of circumstances that facilitate or motivate their emigration. Expulsion and exile act as Democratic Drain "push" factors. Freedoms, rights, and supportive constituencies abroad act as Democratic Drain "pull" factors. Admissions standards imposed by Western democratic governments deliberately drive Brain Drain and inadvertently drive Democratic Drain.

Emran, the Egyptian democracy advocate, described nearly the entire range:

These are really trying times.

One group of people flees indications of their pending arrest or imprisonment. Knocks on the door, phone calls, a warrant, their friends go to prison.

Another group of people feels completely frustrated that their revolution was stolen in December 2011. It's a new round of military rule. It's over.

A third group of people leaves due to intimidation or fear.

A fourth feels there is no professional opportunity left. The economy is providing no jobs or anything else. This is part of the Brain Drain. It happened in 1967. The best elements leave, the people of the middle and professional class.

A fifth is people who over the years were used to some kind of political activities that are no longer available. Preparing for revolution or party belonging. I have known so many people who were not under pressure who still left. And they didn't have to.

There is this feeling of deep guilt, because of the feeling that those who stay are better. But then I realize that I would be put in jail, and I would not survive. But who is left? Who will reignite? Who will lead the second wave?

DANCING ON THE HEADS OF SNAKES

These currents can be understood discreetly in the almost scientific way Emran classifies them. But in the personal stories that other activists tell, we can see how the different push and pull factors often converge. Their narratives reveal how different people responded to this confluence of outward pressure in different ways – often jumping between emigrating and adapting, adapting and emigrating.

Ibrahim, an Egyptian youth activist who I interviewed in Washington DC, said:

I don't consider myself an exile. I'm not seeking asylum. But I don't think it's suitable to be back in Egypt soon. Until it's safe, my new plan is to pursue a PhD and finish my graduate studies. I don't think I'll be back after this fellowship.

Many democrats have activism that is separate from their daily job. So among liberals, democrats, and leftists, it is a very individualist path and not all of us are keen to leave because people have businesses at home and some try to survive against the regime.

Egypt doesn't have a history of activists abroad, like Tunisia or Syria. But even that work only reaches a few million people, not the population. It's never as effective as being inside. But I cannot believe in a shadow government from abroad or a national coalition. All of these things are useless.

Many people are trying to leave. And almost anyone can go to a place like the Emirates. But they won't let you in if you have liked a Facebook post that criticizes the regime, so many democrats choose to be silent in exchange for jobs with good salaries. One of the biggest minorities in Qatar are Egyptians, and they have a full variety of views – silent Democrats alongside Muslim Brothers and regime supporters.

Ibrahim's experience reveals how the boundaries of democracy and authoritarianism abroad define his ability to advocate for reform in his country of origin. For Middle Eastern activists at least, emigration to one of the rich Gulf monarchies can constrain any possibility of diaspora activism and democratic gain – particularly if the cause is affiliated with the Muslim Brotherhood.

Hakim, a journalist and researcher, had just returned to his native Yemen from a fellowship in Washington, DC. His time in the United States produced some letdown when he arrived in Sana'a.

"We need more work from people interested in democracy. Many of the international organizations already left or keep limited resources here. Most of the international NGOs are suspended because of the Houthis' breakthrough and to a limited extent, Al Qaeda's activities. About 20% of the leaders left the country. And many of those remaining stopped their work because they think it is a hopeless case. The Yemeni Spring had the chance to develop new leaders, but recent developments will lead people to lose their interest. The people abroad stay abroad for two reasons. They have a career opportunity, or they apply for asylum."

"What made you return?" I asked.

"It's my country," he said pointedly. "And my chance here is better here than elsewhere. I found that the year I spent outside provided me with good knowledge and a good life for my children, but I was also expecting that Yemen would have improved during my period away. I was approached to work on Arabic-language television based in the United States, and I had a chance to be a reporter for that station. I was also advised to apply for other fellowships, and my wife had some opportunities as well."

"If you did not see the opportunities in Yemen at the conclusion of your fellowship, would you have still returned to Yemen?" I asked.

"No, I would have stayed in the United States."

"What if the situation gets worse?" I pressed.

"This is what separates me from other activists," he said. "I maintain those connections."

Ibrahim and Hakim both reiterate the irony that one of the Syrian expatriates lamented in Chapter 5 – that on the outside, activists have the freedom to network and advocate, but lack the legitimacy and immediacy they need; and on the inside, they have all the legitimacy and immediacy, with none of the freedom to organize. This fundamental tradeoff informs the emigration decisions of all dissidents.

In the case of Sabina, a Yemeni feminist from a wealthy family in Sana'a, she cycled between casual humanitarianism and formal activism for years, while the option of moving abroad lingered in the background. Her story is compelling:

My first milestone was in high school. At 15, I had President [Ali Abdullah] Saleh's granddaughter as a classmate. And I remember being in a history class with her, when the teacher praised a state figure. I intervened and told her that they were not good people – that they steal people's money and kill them. [Saleh's daughter] cried, and the next morning, her brother came to school with soldiers and demanded that I apologize.

At the university, we had a deep struggle with the military, who occupied the campus. Police came to search students, and they harassed me. Another classmate was beaten and locked in a wire cabinet because his brother was a journalist who protested Saleh's rule. I participated in a series of protests against the military occupation of the university.

When I decided to do my graduation project, we conducted research on women in the central prison in Sana'a, sentenced for so-called moral crimes. This is when my identity as a feminist began to form. It was a completely different world. I was 21 and I witnessed two executions, and ten cases of public lashing. I used to go to the Mufti to ask questions about what I found.

To earn money, I taught English during my time in university, where I met many activists. I participated in women-led protests against the wars that took place between 2006 and 2009. Many men were scared to protest back then, because of [aggressive] security services. The year after I graduated, the uprising started. The first protest that called for the overthrow of Saleh came the day after Ben Ali fled Tunisia.

I was in the Square every day until September 2011, when the armed conflict started. The first few months were this romantic dream, but it became increasingly dangerous as the days went on. I planned a silent march, I worked secretly with the Red Cross to provide medicine and food. I learned how to give first aid. Eventually I realized that I was not protesting for the same causes as the men. I wanted to topple the regime too, but I also protested to gain acceptance from these men. At the time, permission was needed for me to go to the protest.

At the time when imprisonment and torture was on the rise, people took opportunities to leave and claim asylum. During the 1968 Civil War, many Southerners left. Then in the 1980s, when many of the Communists and Leftists from the North. In 1994, there was another wave of Southerners who wanted to secede. And then again, during the six wars of Saleh. And then in 2011, I began seeing people I know leave.

Many sons and daughters of Liberal leaders claimed to be in danger and used the crisis to enroll in education programs abroad, and never came back. But those famous civil society figures are not the leaders. The maximum that they can do is post their status on Facebook. Those whose lives are really in danger have stayed. The hard core have stayed, but this might change soon. This is the worst time to seek democracy ever.

Saleh once said that ruling Yemen is like "dancing on the heads of snakes." It's difficult to make claims against the military. There is no bureaucracy, no state. It's a racist, theocratic, armed militia. Saleh was a dictator who oversaw a corrupt system, but there is no system now – and so there is real danger. Many liberals may now leave to claim asylum or to take advantage of professional opportunities abroad.

It is a time when you feel like everything is moving backward. Maybe it's an illusion, but I feel like my work can take us somewhere. As long as I can go to my office in the morning and open up my studio, I'll be okay. Once that is taken away from me, then I may need to leave too.

Much like other activists in authoritarian contexts, Sabina came to realize she couldn't dance alone. To extend the metaphor further, there were simply fewer snakes from which to skip. As authoritarian forces consolidated power in Yemen and elsewhere, the space for democratic activism attenuated. Advocates were either with the regime or a threat to its endurance.

As an extreme, Sabina's concerns about Yemen's shrinking democratic spaces will resonate with activists in countries subject to democratic backsliding, where democratically elected governments are stifling opponents by prosecuting independent media organizations, demanding loyalty from civil servants, altering the composition of judiciaries, and making constitutional reforms that gerrymander electoral districts or remove institutional checks to their power. As journalists, jurists, and bureaucrats depart, the infrastructure of democracy weakens. And when the plumbers, professors, and professionals follow, person by person, its popular support disappears, too.

POSTMORTEM

The persistence of authoritarian regimes in Egypt, Libya, Morocco, Syria, Tunisia, and Yemen is far more complicated than the departure of democratically inclined citizens can singularly explain. Analysts of the Middle East and North Africa must weigh the power and actions of entrenched dynasties, the thirst for oil and natural resource wealth, Islam and Islamism, greater geopolitics, and a lack of broad-based economic development.[8] By drawing attention to Democratic Drain, I do not suggest that observers' attention to these structural factors is unfounded. Rather, this book shows that the persistence of authoritarianism and democratic backsliding – through structural change or otherwise – is enabled by the sorting effects of human mobility and demographic change.

Even if the world continues to debate the reasons why democracy takes root in some societies and not others, even if the world debates the true impact of liberal-minded people's departure from more authoritarian spaces, the evidence that Democratic Drain is taking place is quite clear and phenomenal in scale.

In multimethod research across as many as 149 countries, I find that prospective migrants hold less authoritarian and more democratic political values than their countrymen, such that if they depart, the society they leave behind will not only become older, less educated, and more insular, but also less democratic and more authoritarian in its orientation. While the differences between these "demigrants" and their countrymen are not always great, the effect is exponentially amplified when over 9 million people per year move to a country that is substantially more democratic than their country of origin.

I find that demigrants' initial destination preferences draw them to democracies that reflect the political and civic values they hold, even if this means sacrificing their material well-being to some extent. Even if these preferences are sometimes overridden by the draw of family members and work opportunities in less democratic spaces, this suggests that emigrants are not merely inclined to leave their countries of origin; they deliberately self-sort according to their political values.

I find that people's interest in emigrating spikes in the immediate aftermath of elections, particularly those which have the effect of weakening democratic institutions in the years thereafter. This effect is concentrated among people who hold democratic values and expectations of institutional integrity. Those who question the honesty of the election, suspect corruption among public officials, or feel that freedom of speech is constrained are significantly more likely to say they would like to leave.

Despite this evidence, some may doubt that the difference in political values between prospective migrants and those who wish to remain in their country of origin is significant enough to truly undercut democratic political development. They may also point to uncertainty about whether people who wish to emigrate – even those who claim to have made plans – actually *will* emigrate. And ultimately, a challenge faced by all scholars of human mobility is that it is nearly impossible to study people's behavior and attitudes for long periods of time, particularly when they are on the move. However, my analysis of public opinion data across Europe's intracontinental migration corridor suggests that Eastern Europeans who do move West under the EU's free mobility rules hold more liberal democratic proclivities than those in their countries of origin who merely wish to migrate – implying the actual mobility of people across borders to create a sliding scale of liberal democratic views among people with the same origins.

Others may doubt that democratically inclined citizens hold more power to influence politics in authoritarian home countries than they would if they enjoyed full freedom to advocate from abroad. However, the evidence I gather suggests that the impact of diaspora activism is largely weak and, when it is stronger, not necessarily liberal or democratic. Even in the midst of an active revolution, where diaspora leaders have geopolitical backing and great platforms for influence, I find remarkably low domestic receptivity to their advocacy. Interviews with diaspora leaders themselves reveal the challenges of sustaining cross-border political relationships and sustaining their livelihood as exiles and refugees.

Here in Chapter 6, I corroborate this research with interviews of democratic organizers and leaders who witnessed the collapse of the 2011 Arab Spring's democratic movements in the years that followed. After capturing the world's attention by taking down entrenched dictators, they lamented the way their street protests ultimately produced new authoritarian regimes because, among a variety of factors, they simply lacked the critical mass of liberals and democrats to form a popular base. It is impossible to know what would have transpired if the Middle East and North Africa's authoritarian aspirants had to account for an organized, liberal, democratic movement with identifiable leaders.

In my interviews with them, activists place the behavior and migratory choices of individual actors at the center of democratic political development. Indeed, without a sufficient corps of people with democratic values, democratic political development moves to the periphery.

THE NEXT WAVE

Where might we expect Democratic Drain to take hold next?

Democracy does not always decline dramatically. It can be a subtle process in which rights and freedoms are steadily chipped away, in which independent institutions are incrementally weakened or corrupted, in which electoral rules marginally but meaningfully limit the ability of opposition parties and activists to compete. After all, much of the authoritarian world remains, to some extent, competitive.[9] And so, like countries such as Hungary, Serbia, and Egypt, there are even less conspicuous examples of backsliding in places like Georgia, Myanmar, and Nigeria.[10]

Far more conspicuously, the democratic world has been stunned by recent political developments in Israel, Turkey, and the United States, each of which may trigger substantial Democratic Drain in the near future, if not already.

Israel

In early 2023, Israel's Justice Minister Yariv Levin and Prime Minister Benjamin Netanyahu's coalition introduced reforms that limited the Supreme Court's power to exercise judicial review, granted the government greater control over judicial appointments, and abolished the "reasonableness" doctrine, which previously allowed the Supreme Court to check executive actions. Hundreds of thousands of Israelis filled the streets during several months of protests. Despite the widespread opposition, the Knesset proceeded with the reforms, leading to a significant decline in public trust in political institutions and international condemnation.[11] The traumatic onset of the Gaza War on October 7, 2023 only deepened Israel's democratic decline. Netanyahu was accused of war crimes associated with the deaths of Gazan civilians and of pressuring the head of Israel's internal security service, Shin Bet, to prioritize personal loyalty over constitutional and legal standards. Netanyahu also suppressed media freedom when the Israeli government permanently shut down Al Jazeera's operations in the country in May 2024, citing national security concerns.

While limited evidence is currently available because of the recency and speed of political developments, Israeli emigration reportedly spiked by 25 percent after the judicial reforms.[12] In a March 2023 survey of nearly 2,000 Israeli academics, 73 percent reported that they were likely to leave Israel within the next year, with 76 percent attributing their potential departure to political circumstances.[13] Such an immense exodus of academics has not yet taken place, but there has reportedly been a significant evacuation of other high-skilled Israelis since – particularly medical personnel and professionals from Israel's potent technology and startup industry. About 8,300 high-tech employees, 2.1 percent of the sector's workforce, left the country in the 9 months after the Gaza War began.[14] These workers tend to be more secular, educated, and liberal in their political orientations. Meanwhile, those who remain are disproportionately ultra-Orthodox citizens, who tend to support Netanyahu and far-right parties. This only compounds the brain drain of earlier years, but also the sorting effects associated with different fertility rates between Israel's more secular, liberal population and its more authoritarian-leaning Orthodox population.

Turkey

In March 2025, Turkish President Recep Tayyip Erdoğan's government arrested the mayor of Istanbul – and future opposition leader – Ekrem İmamoğlu on dubious corruption charges, sparking worldwide protests. This terminated his ongoing mayorship and prompted Istanbul University to invalidate his diplomas, effectively disqualifying İmamoğlu from running for president in 2028. The arrest was consistent with Erdoğan's increasingly authoritarian tactics since a failed coup attempt in July 2016. During a two-year "state of emergency," his government dismissed or detained over 100,000 public officials including judges, military personnel, academics, and civil servants for their alleged links to the Gülen movement, which the government accused of orchestrating the coup. Numerous media outlets were shut down, many journalists were arrested, thousands of academics were dismissed, and many judges and prosecutors were removed from their posts – leading to a significant decline in press freedom and a less independent judiciary.

Even before İmamoğlu's arrest, previous developments inspired an exodus of highly skilled professionals and educated youths motivated by economic opportunity abroad and democratic decline at home. In one survey, 95 percent of Turkish university students expressed an interest in studying abroad,[15] and 75 percent of those abroad said they do not plan to return to Turkey, citing the absence of free speech and job prospects.[16] In a 2022 survey of Turkish young adults, 77 percent of respondents said they do not trust politicians, 70 percent preferred to live elsewhere, and 60 percent did not see a future for themselves in Turkey.[17] In a 2021 workshop run by the opposition Republican People's Party, emigrants said they were not only motivated to depart by economic factors, but also the extent of corruption in Turkey and the lack of freedom of speech, rule of law, and an independent meritocracy.[18] With the emigration and democratic decline of the previous decade, the 2023 Turkish elections were still competitive despite evidence of electoral manipulation and the 2022 arrest of Mayor İmamoğlu, then for insulting public officials.[19] Should a new wave of emigration take place – and Turkey's economy has not been strong – it is unclear that future elections will remain competitive. İmamoğlu's 2025 disqualification dashed any hope of liberal democratic reforms in the near future and, by the time such hope returns, millions of democrats may have already left.

United States

Finally, in the United States, Donald Trump began his second term in the White House with a dizzying series of actions that weakened or violated the US government's system of checks and balances and consolidated presidential power. In his first 100 days between January and April 2025, Trump signed 139 executive orders – many of which were subject to immediate legal challenges or struck down – surpassing the number of these once-extraordinary mandates by any modern president in such a short period. Most notably, the actions closed offices and agencies created by congressional appropriations, dismissed inspectors general, politicized a variety of historically nonpartisan offices and institutions, and defunded a variety of government-backed institutions independent enough to resist or criticize White House orders. Trump has also made extortionary threats to compel law firms, media publications, universities, and technology companies he deems adversarial to bend to his will. His administration opened investigations into political rivals and the Democratic Party's fundraising apparatus, and ignored judicial orders to return wrongfully deported immigrants and US citizens.

It remains too early to determine whether the millions of Americans directly affected or concerned by these actions will depart the United States or stay to commit themselves to resisting Trump's government at home. While the United States has long boasted the world's most robust economic conditions – which might normally mitigate the number of people seeking to depart – Trump's actions against private companies, independent regulatory agencies, and his trade war combine to destabilize markets and threaten future growth. Given the strained state of US civil society and the tight margins of recent US elections, the emigration of liberals and democratic activists could have an outsize effect on American politics.

IMPLICATIONS

The policy implications of Democratic Drain are complicated.

This book has focused principally on the effect of emigration on political development in countries of origin, but extensive evidence suggests that immigrants' *arrival* is fueling the rise of authoritarian-leaning populists in destination states, too. In other words, the arrival of – even relatively liberal and democratic – foreigners is not offsetting the nativism and nationalism their presence triggers. The post-2010 transatlantic wave of populism is comprised of disparate parties and candidates, but its *sine qua non* is a strong aversion to immigrants and a nostalgic desire to return to a previous era before their arrival.[20]

It is thus possible that human mobility – in so many ways an expression of human freedom and spur of human development – simultaneously contributes to the suppression of freedom and development in both sending and, because of democracy's majoritarian dynamics, receiving states too. This paradoxical possibility pressurizes the need to persuade voters in destination countries to accept newcomers and recognize the way they contribute to the achievement of national interests.[21]

But, in a more novel way, the Democratic Drain phenomenon places two of democracy's most important national interests in ostensible conflict with one another: its interest in seeding and reinforcing liberal institutions abroad and its interest in strengthening the national population and economy at home.[22]

Immigration is ultimately an engine of economic growth and, in the face of severe population aging across the world's wealthy democracies, a demographic salve. Immigrants bring their ingenuity, entrepreneurial spirit, and mobile human capital to countries with a voracious appetite for innovation and labor. Educated immigrants – such as those who are most likely to hold liberal and democratic values – are typically net contributors to national welfare states and job creators, and are characterized by great intergenerational social mobility. Lower skilled immigrants have higher fertility rates and fill significant labor shortages in critical industries like construction, agriculture, health care, food production, and food services.

As critical as these individuals may be to the democratic political development of their home countries, denying them entry to wealthy democracies on this basis would – for even those governments most concerned with spreading democracy and freedom worldwide – prioritize a foreign policy prospect over domestic interests in population stability and economic growth. As problematic as brain drain is for low-income countries, democratic governments are no more inclined to deny entry to highly skilled professionals seeking a visa.

Doing so would also ignore the agency of emigrants who themselves are navigating the conflict between their own concern for the political development of their homeland with their household's prosperity, security, and freedom. In doing what's best for themselves and their families, they face a collective action problem similar to the one faced by policymakers in the world's wealthy democracies.

Rather than a problem to be solved, Democratic Drain should be interpreted as a negative externality of a global boon. Setting aside nativist backlash in countries of arrival, the emerging challenge is to identify policies that might mitigate its enablement of authoritarian politics in countries of origin. (As people from rural regions flood metropolitan areas worldwide and alter local political culture and partisan distributions, the same logic might be applied to domestic political dynamics as well.[23])

Unlike brain drain, which offers the silver lining of "brain gain" – where emigrants inspire and often invest in the economic development of their countries of origin – emigrants struggle to inspire or transplant democracy from abroad. Authoritarian governments welcome the diaspora's financial remittances far more than they welcome their advocacy, particularly when expats' political views contradict those of the regime. And indeed, whereas skilled emigrants are often incentivized to return to their homelands to open businesses, transfer technology, and set up satellites of their overseas operations, dissidents usually cannot return to advocate. Demigrants and dissidents alike will be less inclined to return and forfeit the freedom, rights, and institutional accountability they likely sought in the first place. And as the world sorts into more and less authoritarian regions, the prospects for return dim.

My analysis of European data offers a flicker of promise in the power of personal relationships. Eastern Europeans who do not wish to emigrate, but have a close friend or family member abroad, hold slightly more democratic values than their countrymen without overseas ties. This introduces the possibility that pro-democratic advocacy might be better delivered in interpersonal calls and messages between the people we trust most than formal political advocacy from the outside. Alongside contributions of resources to parties and organizations in countries of origin, this may be a private way for activists to sustain the cause of liberal democracy. Still, the difference in values between Eastern Europeans with and without relatives abroad was slim and governments will struggle to find policy levers that facilitate the maintenance of these personal relationships any more than the global telecommunications industry already has.

This turns the policy focus to foreign governments' work with dissidents, not demigrants.

Democratic governments seeking to counter the depletion of people with democratic values from authoritarian-leaning spaces have been tempted to invest in the advocacy of diaspora activists, to strengthen them beyond the resources they can generate from their own ranks. But my research shows how even well-funded, government-backed overseas activists struggle to reach people in their countries of origin, sustain their credibility, and build institutions from the outside. Many are even attacked or intimidated by their home country's security and intelligence services. Every dissident I interviewed was convinced that their work must ultimately be pursued "on the ground" – precisely where such a "human base" is steadily disintegrating.

Currently, a number of democratic governments invite activists to democracy training, education, and leadership programs that they organize in their respective countries. The conclusions of this book suggest that they would do better by investing resources in programs that can be executed on the ground inside the "partly free" societies they wish to influence. They should also select candidates who demonstrate a clear commitment to remain in their country of origin in the future. They should then return prospective leaders to their work with a mentorship agreement in place.

This model was once pursued to a limited extent by USAID, which relied on "Foreign Service Nationals" – foreign citizens employed by the American government – to pursue agendas related to the promotion of democratic governance and human rights in their countries of origin. In the same spirit, the US Fulbright program requires scholars to return to their country of origin at the conclusion of their fellowship for a period of time before they are permitted to migrate to the United States. Similarly, governments can financially incentivize civil society organizations that receive their financial support to stay in countries of origin when they might be tempted to relocate.

But perhaps the greater issue is precisely this insistence on dividing the pursuit of global democracy into the atomized projects of specific nations, when the consolidated human base of democratic activists and resources across countries would outnumber any one country's authoritarians.

Anne Applebaum, the journalist and scholar of democracy and autocracy, has recognized this and proposed what she calls "Democrats United." Applebaum notes that while pro-democracy movements around the world act independently, autocratic leaders in countries such as Russia, China, and Iran tacitly and explicitly coordinate because of a clear understanding of their common interests.[24] "Democrats United" is the counterbalance: an international coalition of pro-democracy activists, including the diasporas of autocratic countries, to coordinate efforts on anti-corruption, anti-disinformation, and other common challenges that affect democratic advocates everywhere.[25] This might also include media strategies that seek to reach and connect the citizens of countries subject to democratic backsliding with radio, television, and social media content.

Any such effort would do well to focus on the liminal states at the edge of democracy and its deconsolidation and states where democratization is within reach but tenuous or fragile. Much of Eastern Europe, yes, and other young democracies like Bolivia, Guatemala, Kenya, Peru, and Tunisia. But also critical regional powers like Brazil, India, Indonesia, South Africa, and Turkey, which are in need of reinforcement. The evidence I gather in this book suggests that, since the 2011 uprisings in the greater Middle East, states like Egypt and Yemen are no longer so liminal.

And this is the broader context of Democratic Drain – that human mobility ultimately constitutes a sorting effect. Migration concentrates the world's most intrepid, highly skilled, entrepreneurial people in the top economies. And it concentrates people with liberal democratic values in the world's most stable liberal democracies.

Rich countries get richer. Democratic countries get more democrats.

Appendix A

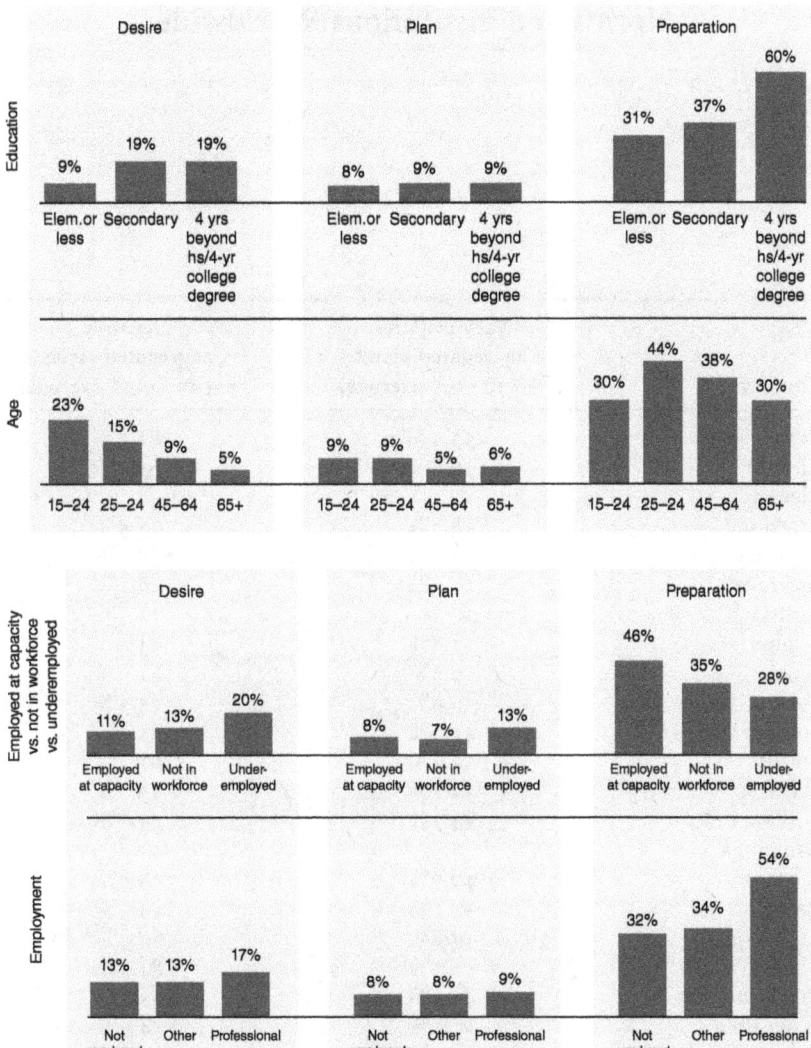

FIGURE A.1 Desired, planned, and prepared emigration worldwide by education, age, and employment status, 2011 (Gallup, Inc. 2011).

Appendix B: Aggregated and Disaggregated Views of Democratic Norms and Institutions Worldwide

Country	Very negative aggregated views (−1 to −0.5 average)	Negative aggregated views (−1 to −0.01 average)
Afghanistan	53.5%	82.2%
Albania	36%	63.5%
Algeria		
Argentina	28.8%	77.5%
Armenia	27%	55.3%
Australia	11.7%	48.1%
Austria	7.7%	23.1%
Belgium	12.8%	53%
Benin	19.3%	44.7%
Bolivia	36.8%	74.3%
Bosnia Herzegovina	43.2%	85.1%
Brazil	19.2%	61.3%
Bulgaria	53.1%	85.7%
Burkina Faso	24.7%	55.6%
Cambodia		
Cameroon	40.9%	68.8%
Canada	21.6%	44.3%
Chile	39.8%	80.3%
Colombia	52.2%	84.5%
Congo Brazzaville	40.7%	63%
Costa Rica	17.6%	54.9%
Croatia	40.2%	73.8%
Cyprus	30.7%	67.2%
Czech Republic	22%	62.9%
Denmark	10.5%	47.4%
Dominican Republic	15.5%	51.1%

(*continued*)

Country	Very negative aggregated views (−1 to −0.5 average)	Negative aggregated views (−1 to −0.01 average)
Ecuador	28.9%	60.6%
Egypt	15.8%	49.6%
El Salvador	19.4%	43.1%
Estonia	17.5%	42.9%
Finland	3.1%	20%
France	13.6%	37.9%
Gabon	57%	80.3%
Georgia	41.8%	72.8%
Germany	8.7%	26.1%
Ghana	18.9%	48.9%
Greece	27.8%	64.7%
Guinea		
Honduras	43.3%	83.3%
Hong Kong	81.7%	88.8%
Hungary	64%	85.3%
Iceland	10.4%	29.9%
India	11.8%	34.6%
Indonesia	27.3%	51.5%
Iran		
Iraq	41.2%	79.5%
Ireland	5.6%	16.2%
Israel	14.1%	42.9%
Italy	19.5%	50.3%
Ivory Coast	29.2%	57%
Jamaica	20.9%	63.4%
Japan	32.3%	65.9%
Jordan	23.3%	45.8%
Kazakhstan	40%	70.8%
Kenya	28.3%	61.4%
Kosovo	11.8%	39%
Kyrgyzstan	25.8%	61.5%
Laos		
Latvia	30.6%	57.9%
Lebanon	41.1%	87.5%
Lithuania	37.1%	63.3%
Malawi	21.9%	62.1%
Malaysia	33.3%	59.7%
Mali	21.6%	53.4%
Malta	19.5%	45.1%
Mauritius	44.8%	69.4%
Mexico	32.6%	65%

(*continued*)

(continued)

Country	Very negative aggregated views (−1 to −0.5 average)	Negative aggregated views (−1 to −0.01 average)
Moldova	35.4%	60.5%
Mongolia	38.4%	88.4%
Morocco		
Mozambique	23%	47.4%
Myanmar	41.1%	84.2%
Namibia	15.8%	52.9%
Nepal	12.9%	37.9%
Netherlands	18%	45.1%
New Zealand	7.8%	23.4%
Nicaragua	43%	61.7%
Nigeria	49.5%	87.8%
North Macedonia	38%	75.1%
Norway	4.6%	16%
Pakistan		
Panama	33.7%	74.3%
Paraguay	22.4%	76.9%
Peru	29%	75.5%
Philippines	29.6%	63.4%
Poland	49.7%	78.1%
Portugal	10.9%	37.7%
Romania	21.9%	72.8%
Russia	74.8%	90%
Saudi Arabia		
Senegal	21.4%	54.5%
Serbia	47.6%	69.7%
Sierra Leone	12.9%	26.8%
Singapore	12.1%	22.8%
Slovakia	21.3%	55.7%
Slovenia	20.3%	66%
South Africa	25.4%	55.4%
South Korea	26.3%	58.6%
Spain	12.9%	49.1%
Sri Lanka	26.8%	63.6%
Sweden	8.6%	28.4%
Switzerland	0%	8.8%
Taiwan	32%	64.7%
Tajikistan		
Tanzania	12.5%	29.8%
Thailand	69.3%	91%
Togo	36.9%	62.7%
Tunisia	21.8%	67.3%

(continued)

Country	Very negative aggregated views (−1 to −0.5 average)	Negative aggregated views (−1 to −0.01 average)
Turkey	72%	86.8%
Uganda	36%	61.8%
Ukraine	51.6%	75.7%
United Arab Emirates		
United Kingdom	3.6%	23%
United States	11%	53.4%
Uruguay	18.1%	49.5%
Uzbekistan		
Venezuela	81.8%	92.8%
Vietnam		
Zambia	8.6%	24.6%
Zimbabwe	34.6%	56.3%

Country	Low confidence in elections	Low confidence in government	Corruption	No free speech	No free media
Afghanistan	86.3%	74.7%	98.2%		67.8%
Albania	72.6%	59%	93.4%		50.6%
Algeria					55.8%
Argentina	77.2%	86.1%	92.9%	83.8%	37.3%
Armenia	57.7%	76.7%	83.3%		28%
Australia	41.6%	72.7%	63.6%		26%
Austria	26%	43.7%	71.2%		18.3%
Belgium	50.8%	78.9%	77.8%		20.2%
Benin	56.1%	31.4%	69.4%		48.4%
Bolivia	77.8%	79.3%	88.2%	91.4%	45%
Bosnia Herzegovina	84.4%	86.1%	95.2%		52.2%
Brazil	62.4%	77.3%	79.9%	87.6%	36.5%
Bulgaria	86.5%	85.8%	95.3%		64.8%
Burkina Faso	62%	52.9%	80.1%		40.8%
Cambodia					23.5%
Cameroon	76.1%	61.8%	88.8%		59.5%
Canada	39.8%	66.7%	63.6%		32.2%
Chile	72.6%	88%	90.3%	87.2%	55.7%
Colombia	87.1%	85.8%	90.6%	94.2%	57.5%
Congo Brazzaville	67%	52.1%	81.7%		69.4%
Costa Rica	56.5%	76.1%	88.6%	67.2%	24.8%

(continued)

(continued)

Country	Low confidence in elections	Low confidence in government	Corruption	No free speech	No free media
Croatia	67.7%	88.8%	97%		51%
Cyprus	58.5%	84%	95.5%		46.8%
Czech Republic	54.3%	84.1%	93.5%		37.2%
Denmark	57.1%	62.1%	36.1%		14.3%
Dominican Republic	64.5%	50.2%	70.2%	81.4%	27.8%
Ecuador	72.2%	62.1%	81.2%	90.8%	39.3%
Egypt	63%	35.7%			43.7%
El Salvador	60.6%	34.1%	67.1%	84.6%	32.5%
Estonia	43.4%	57.8%	59.6%		26%
Finland	15.9%	50%	46.2%		10.1%
France	43.6%	63.4%	69.9%		17.4%
Gabon	82.9%	65.8%	83.1%		80%
Georgia	82.2%	71.6%	85.4%		50.3%
Germany	28.7%	51.3%	52.2%		14.9%
Ghana	60.2%	50.8%	92%		32.8%
Greece	46%	75.2%	82.5%		55.6%
Guinea	73.3%				46.2%
Honduras	87.7%	84.9%	88.3%	89.9%	48.2%
Hong Kong	90%	85.8%	53.4%		88.2%
Hungary	78.3%	86%	94.3%		79.1%
Iceland	26.5%	53.2%	76.1%		17.5%
India	45.8%	31.9%	80.3%		28.9%
Indonesia	60.6%	43.8%	93.9%		46.9%
Iran	57.5%	74.2%			
Iraq	80%	71%	95.2%		63.4%
Ireland	19%	45.7%	54.9%		8.5%
Israel	41.5%	65.8%	91.7%		28.8%
Italy	47%	67.6%	81.6%		34.8%
Ivory Coast	66.5%	43.3%	77%		54.4%
Jamaica	70.3%	66.9%	92.5%	83.3%	34.6%
Japan	54.8%	84.1%	82.1%		50%
Jordan	71.1%	30.1%	81.2%		48.7%
Kazakhstan	80.5%	52.4%	89.1%		61.3%
Kenya	70.8%	58.8%	87.3%		40.9%
Kosovo	53.7%	44.5%	90.9%		22.8%
Kyrgyzstan	82.4%	57.8%	94.5%		37.1%
Laos					17.4%
Latvia	52.3%	74.2%	88.7%		45%
Lebanon	91.1%	89%	97%		44.5%
Lithuania	61.6%	68.3%	92.4%		56.6%
Malawi	72%	63.2%	82%		30.9%

(continued)

Country	Low confidence in elections	Low confidence in government	Corruption	No free speech	No free media
Malaysia	64.3%	59.7%	85.5%		46.7%
Mali	63.9%	55.8%	93.2%		26.4%
Malta	47.2%	54.4%	85.6%		36.1%
Mauritius	76.1%	66.5%	88.9%		61.3%
Mexico	69.5%	66.2%	82.4%	90.5%	48.2%
Moldova	61.1%	62.5%	84.3%		52%
Mongolia	93.1%	89.8%	88.5%		41.2%
Morocco					42.5%
Mozambique	58.6%	40.1%	78.4%		44.5%
Myanmar	53.1%	87.5%	82.4%		83.2%
Namibia	65.5%	52.9%	85.2%		30.9%
Nepal	56.7%	43.4%	78%		27.4%
Netherlands	46.7%	64.5%	54.1%		21.3%
New Zealand	20%	54%	34.4%		17.7%
Nicaragua	71.2%	56.9%	76.9%	87.3%	53.3%
Nigeria	90.2%	85.1%	92.9%		55.5%
North Macedonia	79.6%	72.1%	91%		50.5%
Norway	16%	32.6%	28%		11.5%
Pakistan	65.4%				25%
Panama	78.6%	78.6%	93.5%	88.3%	37.2%
Paraguay	84%	80%	94.2%	88.4%	24.1%
Peru	79.1%	80.9%	92.5%	92.9%	35.4%
Philippines	76.1%	53.9%	78.9%		45.9%
Poland	61%	93.5%	91%		70.7%
Portugal	43.5%	54.9%	89.1%		21.7%
Romania	74.2%	84.9%	94.4%		23.9%
Russia	88.9%	86.7%	93.3%		84.5%
Saudi Arabia					
Senegal	65.2%	61%	88.8%		33.4%
Serbia	75.1%	70%	92.4%		61.3%
Sierra Leone	39.9%	22.1%	84.3%		29.2%
Singapore	28.5%	18.6%	26.4%		57.4%
Slovakia	47%	87.6%	94.5%		31.3%
Slovenia	37.9%	82.2%	89.5%		56.2%
South Africa	68.9%	60.4%	90.9%		34.2%
South Korea	51.3%	77.4%	79.3%		41%
Spain	42.2%	67.8%	80.2%		28.9%
Sri Lanka	65.8%	71.5%	93.9%		37.9%
Sweden	24.3%	56%	24.1%		17.2%
Switzerland	17.5%	17.5%	50.9%		7%
Taiwan	73.4%	70.2%	84.1%		36.4%

(continued)

(continued)

Country	Low confidence in elections	Low confidence in government	Corruption	No free speech	No free media
Tajikistan					
Tanzania	36.8%	18.4%	75.5%		37%
Thailand	91%	96.5%	97.3%		72.4%
Togo	74.3%	55.1%	87.7%		52.5%
Tunisia	74.1%	68.5%	94.8%		33.9%
Turkey	84.8%	80.5%	92%		86.6%
Uganda	62.6%	50.8%	86.3%		66.4%
Ukraine	72.3%	85.6%	97.8%		64%
United Arab Emirates					
United Kingdom	26%	68.1%	49.5%		9.2%
United States	51.7%	80.3%	81.4%		16.1%
Uruguay	47.6%	60.3%	71.8%	77.8%	37.8%
Uzbekistan		24.4%			35.5%
Venezuela	91.9%	93.2%	94.3%	93.2%	86.8%
Vietnam					
Zambia	36.1%	19.2%	86.8%		28.8%
Zimbabwe	61.5%	51.1%	83.3%		56.8%

Appendix C: Elections Study Alternative Analyses

To calculate the index of dissatisfaction with liberal democratic protections and institutions, four separate indicators are combined using principal component analysis: The indicators include: whether corruption is widespread throughout the government (yes/no), whether the media has a lot of freedom (yes/no), whether people are afraid to openly express their political views (four-point scale), and whether they have confidence in the national government (yes/no).

For any one respondent, missing values are relatively common in at least one of those indicators. For this reason, prior to calculating the index, and for the index only, multiple imputation is conducted for the indicators relying on the *mice* package in R.[1] With this imputed dataset, we then calculate principal components. The index of dissatisfaction with liberal democracy is based on the first principal component from this analysis, which captures almost 41 percent of the variation in these data (the second component captures 19 percent of variation). The indicators load positively on the first component which, together with the proportion of the variance captured by it, we take as indication that the index provides an appropriate aggregation of the five indicators into a single measure of dissatisfaction.

For the analysis using this index of dissatisfaction with liberal freedoms and institutions, only observations for which, at most, two of the original four indicators are missing are used, so that the analyses rely only to a limited extent on imputed observations. For analyses that rely only on the individual indicators the original data is used, rather than the imputed data.

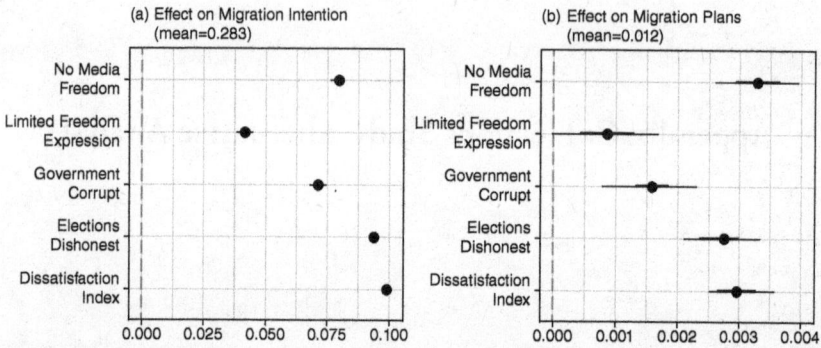

FIGURE C.1 Individual views on democratic quality and migration intentions (panel a) and plans (panel b). Subsample of countries with a Liberal Democracy Index between 0.1 and 0.7.

ALTERNATIVE ANALYSIS RELYING ON SUBSAMPLE OF COUNTRIES

The results presented in Figure 2.2, which study the impact of dissatisfaction with liberal democratic freedoms and institutions, on migration desires and plans rely on the full available sample. Here, an alternative set of results is presented, focusing on countries with a Liberal Democracy Index from Varieties of Democracy (V-Dem) scores between 0.1 and 0.7; this subset thus excludes the most authoritarian countries in the world, as well as the most democratic ones. Overall, this restricts the sample to approximately 630,000 respondents from 107 different countries across 13 years.

Figure C.1 presents the same analysis as in Figure 2.2 but relying on this subsample of countries. The findings are qualitatively similar, although some effect sizes are somewhat different.

ALTERNATIVE ANALYSIS WITHOUT CONTROLS VARIABLES

The results presented in Figure 2.2 control for a variety of factors related to personal economic conditions and exposure to violence. Figure C.2 shows instead an analysis that does not control for these additional factors. Because of fewer observations excluded due to missing values, the sample used in Figure C.2 includes approximately 1.5 million respondents across 157 countries.

Overall, the results presented in Figure C.2 are fairly similar to those of Figure 2.2 in both direction and magnitude. This is partly due to the

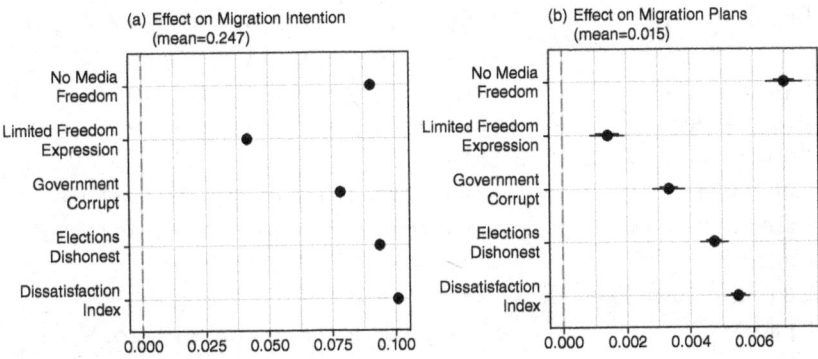

FIGURE C.2 Individual views on democratic quality and migration intentions (panel a) and plans (panel b), without control variables.

fact that while personal economic conditions and exposure to violence and crime are important push and pull factors in migration decisions, they do not seem to correlated very strongly with satisfaction or dissatisfaction with liberal democratic values.

Countries and years used for Figure 2.2 include:

Country	Years covered
Afghanistan	2009, 2010, 2017, 2018, 2021
Albania	2015, 2016, 2017, 2018, 2019, 2021
Algeria	2010, 2017, 2018
Argentina	2009, 2010, 2011, 2012, 2013, 2015, 2016, 2017, 2018, 2019, 2021
Armenia	2009, 2010, 2013, 2015, 2016, 2017, 2018, 2019, 2021
Australia	2010, 2015, 2016, 2017, 2020, 2021
Austria	2010, 2015, 2016, 2017, 2021
Azerbaijan	2013, 2015, 2016, 2017, 2018, 2019
Bangladesh	2009, 2010, 2015, 2016, 2017, 2018, 2022
Belarus	2009, 2010, 2013, 2015, 2016, 2017, 2018, 2019
Belgium	2010, 2015, 2016, 2017, 2021, 2022
Benin	2015, 2016, 2017, 2018, 2021
Bhutan	2015
Bolivia	2009, 2010, 2011, 2012, 2013, 2015, 2016, 2017, 2018, 2020, 2021
Bosnia and Herzegovina	2015, 2016, 2017, 2018, 2019, 2021
Botswana	2015, 2016, 2017, 2018

Brazil	2009, 2010, 2011, 2013, 2015, 2016, 2017, 2018, 2019, 2021
Bulgaria	2010, 2015, 2016, 2017, 2018, 2019, 2021
Burkina Faso	2010, 2015, 2016, 2017, 2018, 2021
Burundi	2009
Cambodia	2010, 2015, 2016, 2017
Cameroon	2010, 2015, 2016, 2017, 2018, 2021
Canada	2009, 2010, 2017, 2018, 2021
Central African Republic	2010, 2016, 2017
Chad	2009, 2010, 2015, 2016, 2017, 2018
Chile	2009, 2010, 2011, 2012, 2013, 2015, 2016, 2017, 2018, 2020, 2021
Colombia	2009, 2010, 2011, 2012, 2013, 2015, 2016, 2017, 2018, 2019, 2021
Comoros	2018
Congo-Brazzaville	2015, 2016, 2017, 2018, 2021
Congo-Kinshasa	2009, 2015, 2016, 2017
Costa Rica	2009, 2010, 2011, 2012, 2013, 2015, 2016, 2017, 2018, 2019, 2021
Croatia	2015, 2016, 2017, 2018, 2019, 2021
Cyprus	2009, 2010, 2015, 2016, 2017, 2021
Czech Republic	2010, 2015, 2016, 2017, 2018, 2021
Denmark	2009, 2010, 2015, 2016, 2017, 2021
Djibouti	2010
Dominican Republic	2009, 2010, 2011, 2012, 2013, 2015, 2016, 2017, 2018, 2019, 2021
Ecuador	2009, 2010, 2012, 2013, 2015, 2016, 2017, 2018, 2019, 2021
Egypt	2010, 2011, 2012, 2016, 2021
El Salvador	2009, 2010, 2011, 2012, 2013, 2015, 2016, 2017, 2018, 2019, 2021
Estonia	2015, 2016, 2017, 2018, 2019, 2021
Eswatini	2018
Ethiopia	2015, 2016, 2017, 2018
Finland	2010, 2015, 2016, 2017, 2020, 2021
France	2009, 2010, 2015, 2016, 2017, 2021
Gabon	2015, 2016, 2017, 2018, 2021
Gambia	2017, 2018
Georgia	2009, 2010, 2015, 2016, 2017, 2018, 2019, 2021

Germany	2009, 2010, 2015, 2016, 2017, 2021
Ghana	2009, 2010, 2015, 2016, 2017, 2018, 2021
Greece	2009, 2010, 2015, 2016, 2017, 2018, 2019, 2021
Guatemala	2009, 2010, 2011, 2012, 2013, 2015, 2016, 2017, 2018, 2019
Guinea	2015, 2016, 2017, 2018, 2021
Haiti	2010, 2011, 2012, 2013, 2015, 2016, 2017, 2018
Honduras	2009, 2010, 2011, 2012, 2013, 2015, 2016, 2017, 2018, 2019, 2021
Hong Kong	2009, 2010, 2016, 2017, 2021
Hungary	2010, 2015, 2016, 2017, 2018, 2019, 2021
Iceland	2016, 2017, 2021
India	2009, 2010, 2015, 2016, 2017, 2018, 2021
Indonesia	2009, 2010, 2015, 2016, 2017, 2018, 2021
Iran	2015, 2016, 2018
Iraq	2015, 2016, 2017, 2019, 2021
Ireland	2009, 2010, 2015, 2016, 2017, 2021
Israel	2009, 2010, 2015, 2016, 2017, 2018, 2020, 2021
Italy	2009, 2010, 2015, 2016, 2017, 2021
Ivory Coast	2015, 2016, 2017, 2018, 2021
Jamaica	2011, 2013, 2017, 2020, 2021
Japan	2009, 2010, 2015, 2016, 2017, 2018, 2021
Jordan	2015, 2016, 2017, 2018, 2021
Kazakhstan	2009, 2010, 2013, 2015, 2016, 2017, 2018, 2019, 2021
Kenya	2010, 2015, 2016, 2017, 2018, 2021
Kosovo	2015, 2016, 2017, 2018, 2019, 2021
Kyrgyzstan	2009, 2010, 2013, 2015, 2016, 2017, 2018, 2019, 2021
Laos	2017
Latvia	2009, 2015, 2016, 2017, 2018, 2019, 2021
Lebanon	2010, 2015, 2016, 2017, 2018, 2021
Lesotho	2016, 2017
Liberia	2010, 2015, 2016, 2017, 2018
Libya	2017, 2018
Lithuania	2009, 2010, 2015, 2016, 2017, 2018, 2019, 2021

Luxembourg	2010, 2015, 2016, 2017
Madagascar	2015, 2016, 2017, 2018
Malawi	2009, 2015, 2016, 2017, 2018, 2021
Malaysia	2009, 2010, 2015, 2018, 2021
Mali	2009, 2010, 2015, 2016, 2017, 2018, 2021
Malta	2010, 2015, 2016, 2017, 2020, 2021
Mauritania	2010, 2015, 2016, 2017, 2018
Mauritius	2016, 2017, 2018, 2021
Mexico	2009, 2010, 2011, 2012, 2013, 2015, 2016, 2017, 2018, 2019, 2021
Moldova	2009, 2010, 2013, 2015, 2016, 2018, 2019, 2021
Mongolia	2010, 2015, 2016, 2017, 2018, 2021
Montenegro	2015, 2016, 2017, 2018, 2019
Mozambique	2015, 2017, 2018, 2021
Myanmar	2015, 2016, 2017, 2018, 2021
Nagorno-Karabakh	2013
Namibia	2017, 2018, 2021
Nepal	2009, 2010, 2015, 2016, 2017, 2018, 2021
Netherlands	2010, 2015, 2016, 2017, 2020, 2021
New Zealand	2010, 2015, 2016, 2017, 2018, 2020, 2021
Nicaragua	2009, 2010, 2011, 2012, 2013, 2015, 2016, 2017, 2018, 2019, 2021
Niger	2009, 2010, 2015, 2016, 2017, 2018
Nigeria	2009, 2010, 2015, 2016, 2017, 2018, 2021
North Macedonia	2009, 2015, 2016, 2017, 2018, 2019, 2021
Northern Cyprus	2015, 2016
Norway	2015, 2016, 2017, 2020, 2021
Pakistan	2009, 2010, 2015, 2016, 2017, 2018, 2021
Palestine	2010, 2015, 2016, 2017, 2018
Panama	2009, 2010, 2011, 2012, 2013, 2015, 2016, 2017, 2018, 2019, 2021
Paraguay	2009, 2010, 2011, 2012, 2013, 2015, 2016, 2018, 2019, 2021
Peru	2009, 2010, 2011, 2012, 2013, 2015, 2016, 2017, 2018, 2019, 2021
Philippines	2009, 2010, 2015, 2016, 2017, 2018, 2021
Poland	2010, 2015, 2016, 2017, 2018, 2019, 2021
Portugal	2010, 2015, 2016, 2017, 2020, 2021
Romania	2010, 2015, 2016, 2017, 2018, 2019, 2021

Russia	2009, 2010, 2013, 2015, 2016, 2017, 2018, 2020, 2021
Rwanda	2009, 2015, 2016, 2017, 2018
Senegal	2009, 2010, 2015, 2016, 2017, 2018, 2021
Serbia	2015, 2016, 2017, 2018, 2019, 2021
Sierra Leone	2010, 2015, 2016, 2017, 2018, 2021
Singapore	2009, 2010, 2015, 2016, 2017, 2018, 2021
Slovakia	2010, 2015, 2016, 2017, 2018, 2019, 2021
Slovenia	2009, 2010, 2015, 2016, 2017, 2020, 2021
Somalia	2015, 2016
Somaliland	2010
South Africa	2010, 2015, 2016, 2017, 2018, 2021
South Korea	2009, 2010, 2015, 2016, 2017, 2018, 2021
South Sudan	2015, 2016, 2017
Spain	2009, 2010, 2016, 2017, 2021
Sri Lanka	2009, 2015, 2017, 2018, 2021
Suriname	2012
Sweden	2009, 2010, 2015, 2016, 2017, 2020, 2021
Switzerland	2009, 2015, 2016, 2017, 2021
Taiwan	2010, 2015, 2016, 2017, 2018, 2021
Tajikistan	2009, 2010, 2013, 2015, 2016, 2017
Tanzania	2009, 2010, 2015, 2016, 2017, 2018, 2021
Thailand	2009, 2010, 2016, 2017, 2018, 2021
Togo	2015, 2016, 2017, 2018, 2021
Trinidad and Tobago	2011, 2013, 2017
Tunisia	2010, 2015, 2016, 2017, 2018, 2021
Turkey	2015, 2016, 2017, 2018, 2021
Uganda	2009, 2010, 2015, 2016, 2017, 2018, 2021
Ukraine	2009, 2010, 2013, 2015, 2016, 2017, 2018, 2019, 2021
United Kingdom	2009, 2010, 2015, 2016, 2017, 2021
United States	2009, 2010, 2017, 2018, 2019, 2020, 2021
Uruguay	2009, 2010, 2011, 2012, 2013, 2015, 2016, 2017, 2018, 2020, 2021
Venezuela	2009, 2010, 2011, 2012, 2013, 2015, 2016, 2017, 2018, 2019, 2021
Vietnam	2009
Yemen	2010, 2015, 2016, 2017, 2018
Zambia	2009, 2015, 2016, 2017, 2018, 2021
Zimbabwe	2010, 2015, 2016, 2017, 2018, 2021

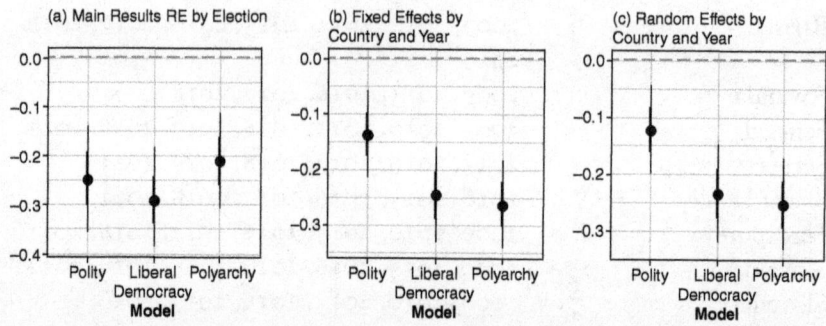

FIGURE C.3 Migration plans within the next twelve months and democratic consolidation and deconsolidation. Panel (a) shows original results from Figure 3.2, panel (b) uses fixed effects by year and by country, and panel (c) uses random effects by country and year.

ALTERNATIVE RANDOM AND FIXED
EFFECTS SPECIFICATIONS

Figure C.3 presents two alternative specifications for the original models. The first model uses fixed effects by country and by year instead of random effects by election. The second specification includes random effects by country and by year, rather than by election. The figure also includes the results from the original specification for comparison. In all cases, the interaction term from the original model is depicted for ease of comparison.

Overall, the two alternative specifications considered here confirm the main findings; in all cases, deconsolidating elections tend to be followed by an increase in migration intentions compared to consolidating elections (a negative interaction term). The results from the fixed effects model is almost identical to that from the random effects model by country and year.[2] The effect sizes for the main specification differ somewhat from the models in panels (b) and (c), but are substantively equivalent.

ALTERNATIVE TIME BANDS AROUND ELECTIONS

Figure C.4 shows estimates from the main specification from the original models, but using alternative time bands around the elections, from 30 days to 210 days, by additions of 15 days. When focusing on the Polity Index and the Polyarchy Index, the findings are robust to timeframes of up to 120 days before and after the election, although polyarchy

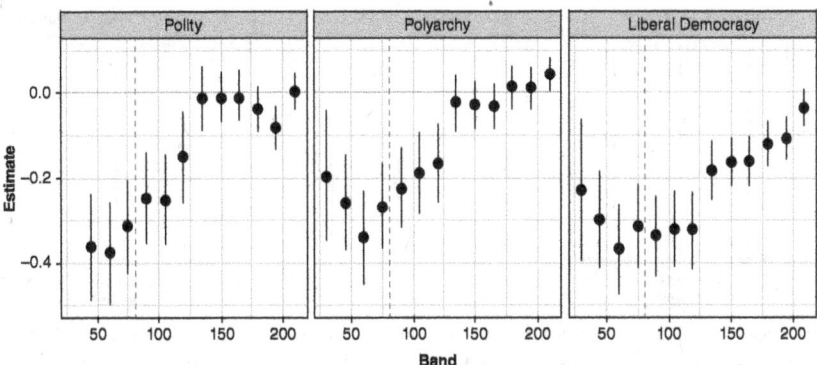

FIGURE C.4 Effect of consolidating/deconsolidating elections using alternative time bands around elections.
Note: The vertical dashed line shows the bandwidth for the main results.

results become marginally nonstatistically significant around the 120-day mark. In the case of the Liberal Democracy Index, the results are robust to even longer timeframes. Overall, these results suggest that the eighty-one-day window around an election selected by optimal Imbens–Kalyanaraman bandwidths are robust to alternative bandwidths. It is important to note here that longer time bands are not advisable, since the salience of the election itself is likely to diminish over time and other upcoming elections (at the national, regional, provincial, or local levels) are likely to overlap, limiting the comparability between the before and after election periods.

ALTERNATIVE SUBSAMPLES

Figure C.5 shows results of the main specification using alternative subsamples, with main results for comparison. The first relies only on Gallup survey ways that were directly intersected by an election, so that there are respondents both before and after the election from the same country – this subsample is significantly smaller than the main sample, with 53,817 respondents from 39 countries in 47 different elections. It is important to note that this is specific subsample of countries that may not be fully representative of the broader group of countries considered elsewhere. The second is similar to the original sample but excludes countries in which respondents are always interviewed before or are always interviewed after an election. Therefore, for every country in this second subsample, there are respondents interviewed before and after elections (although not necessarily the same election). This results in a sample of 168,645

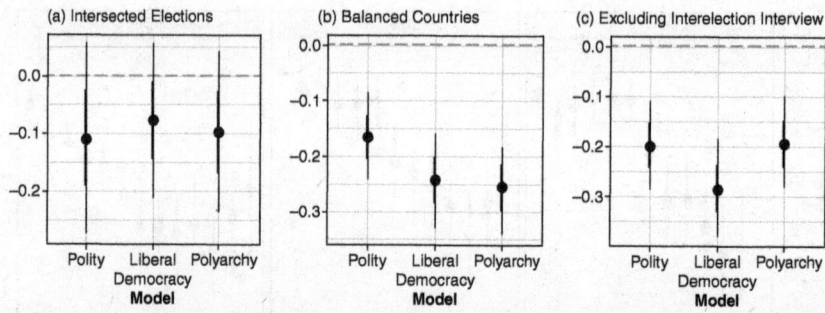

FIGURE C.5 Main specification using alternative subsamples. Panel (a) includes only country-years with respondents interviewed before and after the same election, panel (b) includes only countries that include interviews before and after elections (but not necessarily the same election), and panel (c) excludes respondents that were interviewed between two closely held elections.

respondents across 77 different countries. The third excludes respondents that were interviewed between two closely held elections (as is the case with runoffs), which results in a sample of 193,111 respondents in 120 different countries.

In all three cases the results are consistent with the main results reported in Figure 3.2. The only caveat are elections that directly intersect a survey wave such that respondents in the same survey wave are interviewed both before and after the election. While the point estimates in this case are in the same direction as the main findings, the results are not statistically significant. It is important to note, however, that this analysis relies on a significantly smaller sample.

Countries and years used in Figure 3.2 include:

Country	Years covered
Afghanistan	2008, 2009, 2014
Albania	2008, 2009, 2010, 2011, 2012, 2013, 2014, 2015, 2016, 2017, 2018, 2019, 2020, 2021
Algeria	2010, 2011, 2012
Argentina	2008, 2009, 2010, 2011, 2012, 2013, 2014, 2015, 2017, 2018, 2019, 2020, 2021
Armenia	2010, 2011, 2012, 2015, 2016, 2017, 2018, 2019, 2021
Australia	2015, 2016, 2017
Austria	2010, 2011, 2015, 2016
Azerbaijan	2012, 2013, 2014, 2015, 2016
Bahrain	2011, 2012, 2013, 2014, 2015, 2016

Bangladesh   2011, 2012, 2013, 2016, 2017, 2018
Belarus   2012, 2013, 2016, 2017, 2018, 2019
Belgium   2010, 2011, 2012, 2013, 2014, 2015,
                      2016
Benin   2011, 2012, 2016, 2017
Bhutan   2013, 2014, 2015
Bolivia   2012, 2013, 2014, 2015, 2016, 2017, 2018,
                      2020
Bosnia and Herzegovina 2009, 2010, 2011, 2012, 2013, 2014, 2015,
                      2016, 2017, 2018, 2019, 2020, 2021
Botswana   2012, 2013, 2014, 2015, 2016
Brazil   2008, 2009, 2010, 2013, 2014, 2015, 2016,
                      2017, 2018, 2019, 2020, 2021
Bulgaria   2010, 2011, 2013, 2014, 2015, 2017, 2018,
                      2019, 2020, 2021
Cambodia   2016, 2017, 2018, 2019, 2020, 2021
Cameroon   2013, 2014, 2015, 2016, 2017, 2018
Canada   2010, 2011, 2012, 2013
Central African Republic 2010
Chad   2013, 2014, 2015, 2016, 2017
Chile   2012, 2013
Colombia   2010, 2011, 2012, 2013, 2014, 2015, 2016,
                      2018, 2019, 2020, 2021
Comoros   2011, 2012
Congo-Brazzaville   2012, 2013, 2014, 2015, 2016
Congo-Kinshasa   2009, 2011, 2012, 2013, 2014
Costa Rica   2018, 2019, 2021
Croatia   2016, 2017, 2018, 2019
Cyprus   2010, 2011, 2012, 2013, 2014, 2015, 2016
Czech Republic   2010
Denmark   2014, 2015, 2016, 2017
Dominican Republic   2014, 2015, 2016, 2017
Ecuador   2008, 2009, 2010, 2011, 2012, 2013, 2014,
                      2017, 2018, 2019, 2020, 2021
Egypt   2008, 2009, 2010, 2011, 2012, 2013, 2014,
                      2015
Estonia   2009, 2011, 2012
Ethiopia   2012, 2013, 2014, 2015, 2016, 2017,
                      2018
Finland   2010, 2011, 2014, 2015, 2016

France	2010, 2011, 2012, 2013, 2014, 2017, 2018, 2019, 2020, 2021
Gabon	2014, 2015, 2016, 2017, 2018
Georgia	2013, 2014, 2018
Germany	2009, 2010, 2011, 2012
Greece	2009, 2011, 2012, 2013
Guatemala	2012, 2013, 2016, 2017, 2019
Haiti	2015, 2018
Honduras	2012, 2013, 2014, 2015, 2016, 2017, 2018, 2019, 2021
Hungary	2009, 2010, 2012
Iceland	2012, 2013, 2016
Indonesia	2008, 2009, 2012, 2013, 2014, 2015, 2016
Iran	2011, 2012, 2013, 2014, 2015, 2016, 2017, 2018
Iraq	2008, 2009, 2010, 2011, 2012
Ireland	2009, 2010, 2011, 2014, 2015, 2016, 2017
Israel	2020, 2021
Italy	2011, 2012, 2013, 2014, 2015
Ivory Coast	2014, 2015, 2016
Jamaica	2011, 2013
Japan	2008, 2009, 2010, 2013, 2014, 2015, 2016, 2018, 2019, 2020, 2021
Kazakhstan	2009, 2010, 2011, 2013, 2014, 2016, 2017, 2018, 2019, 2020, 2021
Kenya	2011, 2012, 2013, 2014
Kosovo	2013, 2014, 2015, 2016, 2017, 2018, 2019, 2020, 2021
Kuwait	2013, 2014, 2015
Kyrgyzstan	2009, 2010, 2014, 2015, 2016
Laos	2011, 2012, 2017, 2018, 2019, 2020, 2021
Latvia	2013, 2014, 2015, 2016, 2017, 2018, 2019, 2020, 2021
Lebanon	2013, 2014, 2015, 2016, 2017, 2018, 2020, 2021
Lesotho	2016, 2017, 2019
Lithuania	2009, 2010, 2014, 2015
Malaysia	2018, 2019, 2021
Mali	2013, 2016, 2017, 2018
Malta	2011, 2012, 2013, 2014, 2015, 2016, 2017, 2018, 2019, 2020, 2021

Mauritius	2014, 2016
Mexico	2008, 2009, 2010, 2011, 2012, 2013, 2014, 2015, 2016
Moldova	2009
Mongolia	2011, 2012, 2013, 2014, 2015, 2016, 2017
Montenegro	2013, 2014, 2018, 2019
Namibia	2014, 2017
Nepal	2016, 2017, 2018, 2019, 2020, 2021
Netherlands	2010, 2011, 2012, 2013, 2014, 2015, 2016, 2017, 2018, 2019, 2020, 2021
New Zealand	2011, 2012, 2013, 2014, 2015, 2016, 2017, 2018, 2019
Nicaragua	2009, 2010, 2011, 2012, 2013
Niger	2016, 2017, 2018, 2019
Nigeria	2013, 2014, 2015, 2016
North Macedonia	2010, 2011, 2012, 2014, 2015, 2018, 2019
Norway	2014, 2015, 2016, 2017, 2018, 2019, 2020, 2021
Pakistan	2011, 2012, 2013, 2016, 2017, 2018, 2020, 2021
Panama	2008, 2009, 2010, 2011
Peru	2011, 2012, 2013, 2014, 2015, 2016, 2017
Philippines	2009, 2010, 2011, 2012, 2013, 2014, 2015, 2016, 2017
Poland	2010, 2015, 2016, 2017, 2018, 2019
Portugal	2008, 2010, 2011, 2012, 2013, 2014, 2015, 2016, 2017, 2018, 2019, 2020, 2021
Romania	2018, 2019
Russia	2012, 2013, 2014
Rwanda	2012, 2013, 2014, 2015, 2018, 2019
Senegal	2012, 2013, 2014
Serbia	2010, 2011, 2012, 2015, 2016, 2017, 2018
Singapore	2014, 2015, 2016, 2017, 2018
Slovakia	2010, 2011, 2012, 2015, 2016, 2017
Slovenia	2014, 2015
South Africa	2008, 2009, 2010, 2011
South Korea	2010, 2011, 2012, 2014, 2015, 2016, 2017, 2018
Spain	2016, 2017, 2020, 2021
Sri Lanka	2010, 2011, 2012
Sudan	2009, 2010, 2011, 2012

Sweden	2009, 2010, 2011, 2012, 2013, 2014, 2015, 2016
Switzerland	2009, 2012, 2014, 2015, 2016, 2017, 2018, 2019, 2020, 2021
Syria	2009, 2010, 2011, 2012
Taiwan	2014, 2015, 2016, 2017
Tajikistan	2018, 2019
Tanzania	2013, 2014, 2015, 2016, 2017
Thailand	2009, 2010, 2011, 2012
Togo	2014, 2015, 2016
Tunisia	2009, 2010, 2011, 2012, 2013, 2014, 2020, 2021
Turkey	2009, 2010, 2011, 2012, 2015, 2016, 2017, 2018, 2019, 2020, 2021
Uganda	2014, 2015, 2016, 2017, 2018, 2019, 2020, 2021
Ukraine	2014, 2015, 2016, 2019, 2020, 2021
United Arab Emirates	2009, 2010, 2011, 2012, 2013, 2014, 2015, 2016, 2017, 2018, 2019, 2020, 2021
United Kingdom	2008, 2009, 2010, 2011, 2012, 2013, 2014, 2015, 2016, 2017, 2018
United States	2010, 2011, 2013, 2014, 2015, 2018, 2019
Uruguay	2008, 2009, 2012, 2013, 2014, 2017, 2018, 2020, 2021
Uzbekistan	2018, 2019, 2020, 2021
Venezuela	2009, 2010, 2011, 2012, 2013, 2014, 2015, 2016
Vietnam	2008, 2009, 2010, 2011, 2012, 2013, 2014, 2015, 2016, 2017, 2018, 2019, 2021
Yemen	2009, 2010, 2011, 2012, 2013, 2014, 2015, 2016, 2017, 2018, 2019
Zambia	2011, 2012, 2013, 2014, 2015, 2016, 2017, 2018, 2019, 2020, 2021
Zimbabwe	2016, 2017, 2018, 2019, 2020, 2021

Note: For many countries, data for nonelection years is also used because the pre or post-election year spans into the preceding or following year. For example, Argentine elections are held in late October, which means that the post-election period of eighty-one days used in the analysis extends into the following year.

ALTERNATIVE MEASURES OF DECONSOLIDATION

As additional robustness checks, democratic consolidation can also be measured as a binary variable, depending on whether the main measures of consolidation increase/remain the same (1) or decrease (0) between the year prior and the year after the election.

Additionally, three indices of consolidation/deconsolidation are built, based on the extent of anti-pluralism in the lower chamber of the country's legislature, the party of the head of government, and the parties in government. To measure party anti-pluralism we rely on the Anti-pluralism Index at the party level from the Varieties of Party Identity and Organization (V-Party). The measure of anti-pluralism in the lower chamber is based on the average of party-level anti-pluralism, weighted by each party's seat share. The measure of anti-pluralism in the government parties is the average of party-level anti-pluralism for parties in government, weighted by their seat share in the lower chamber. To measure consolidation and deconsolidation from these data, we calculate the change in the indices of anti-pluralism relative to the previous election. For consistency with previous results, the estimates we present flip the sign of anti-pluralism, so that an increase in this variable represents consolidation.

Figure C.6 shows the results of these analyses. Panel (a) shows that the main results generally hold when using dummy variables for consolidation.

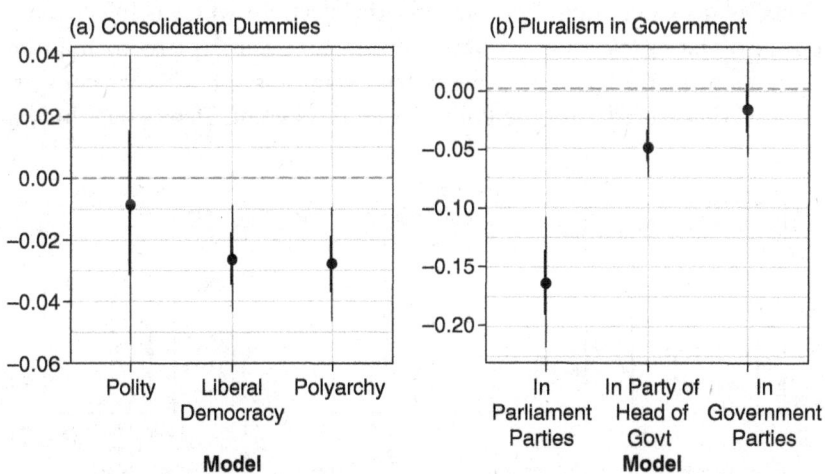

FIGURE C.6 Main specification using alternative measures of deconsolidation. Panel (a) uses consolidation dummies based on the Polity, Liberal Democracy, and Polyarchy Indices, and panel (b) relies on measures of anti-pluralism (rescaled so that higher values mean less anti-pluralism).

For all main measures of deconsolidation, effects are in the same direction as the main results. It should be noted, however, that the dummy measure of consolidation using the Polity score is not statistically significant.

Panel (b) shows the analysis using anti-pluralism, rescaled so that higher values mean less anti-pluralism (and thus democratic consolidation). These results show that elections that lead to increased pluralism among the parties in parliament are associated with a reduced intention to migrate, relative to countries in which pluralism decreased (anti-pluralism increased). Similarly, elections in which the party of the head of government becomes more pluralist are associated with a subsequent reduction in migration intentions. Finally, when considering the pluralism of parties in government, effects are identified in the same direction although not statistically significant.[3]

ALTERNATIVE OUTCOME: PLANS TO MIGRATE

This subsection presents results in which the outcome is whether a respondent has made plans to migrate within the next twelve months, instead of simply expressing a desire to migrate to another country. Beyond the use of a different outcome, the model is exactly the same as the original.

The results, presented in Figure C.7 show similar patterns as those in Figure 3.2. Following a consolidating election (in dark gray) respondents' plans to migrate decrease after the election; whereas following a deconsolidating election (in light gray) respondents' plans to migrate increase after the election. This is true regardless of whether consolidation is measured with the Polity score, the Liberal Democracy Index,

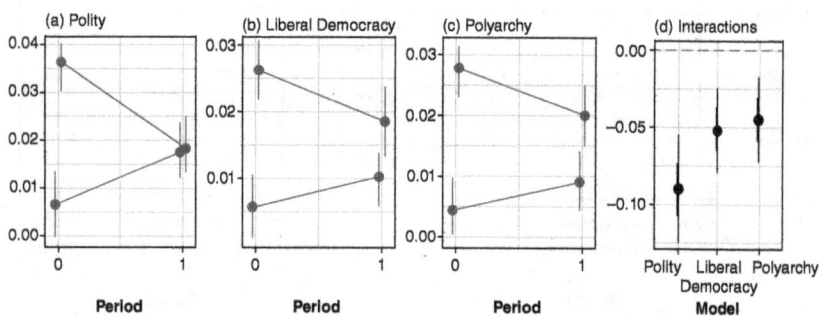

FIGURE C.7 Migration plans within the next twelve months and democratic consolidation and deconsolidation. Panels (a), (b), and (c) show predicted values before and after the election for consolidating countries (solid) and deconsolidating countries (dashed), and panel (d) shows the interaction effect from Equation 2.

or the Polyarchy Index. It should be noted that the predicted values in Figure C.5 are much smaller than those in Figure 3.2 because fewer respondents have made specific plans to migrate in the next twelve months, whereas many more have less defined intentions to migrate. However, the sizes of the effects are comparable to those from Figure 3.2.

ALTERNATIVE OUTCOME: PLACEBO ELECTION DATES

This subsection presents analyses that rely on placebo election dates which help determine whether the results presented in Figure 3.2 can be attributed to the impact of the elections themselves or not.

To construct these placebos, two alternative "fake" election dates were devised, one that occurs two years prior the actual election and another that occurs two years after. The measures of consolidation are synchronized with these "fake" election dates.

The findings are presented in Figure C.8. For all three measures of democratic consolidation, there is no effect of these placebo election dates on migration intentions. This suggests that the findings presented in Figure 3.2 are the result of the consolidating/deconsolidating nature of the election and not other factors.

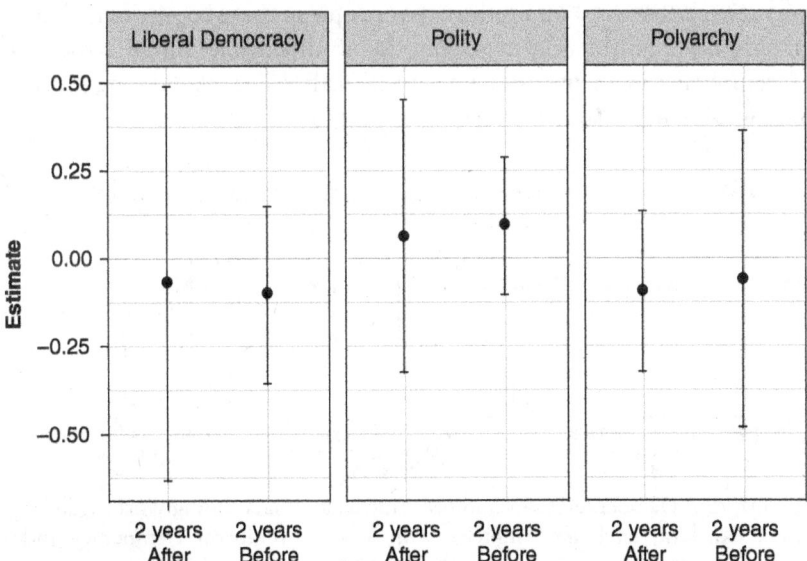

FIGURE C.8 Estimates of the effect of consolidating and deconsolidating elections using placebo dates set two years prior and two years after the corresponding election.

ALTERNATIVE SUBSAMPLES: BY DEMOCRATIC TRENDS

This subsection considers three alternative subsamples. The first one (panel a) considers countries that are neither strong democracies nor strong autocracies, by focusing exclusively on countries with a V-Dem Liberal Democracy Index between 0.1 and 0.7. The second one (panel b) considers countries that, in the five years prior to the election, had seen democratizing trends. The third one (panel c) considers countries that experienced democratic backsliding in the five years prior to the election under consideration. The results for these subsamples are presented in Figure C.9.

The results from panel (a) show that the main findings are not driven by strong democracies or strong autocracies, but that they apply to countries with middling democratic qualities. A comparison of panels (b) and (c) shows that the impact of deconsolidating elections is stronger on countries that were previously democratizing. Additionally, in countries that were already experiencing democratic backsliding, the impact of elections is in the same direction as the main results, but they are not statistically significant for any of the measures of consolidation. While part of this has to do with smaller sample sizes involved in any subsample, the effect sizes are smaller, indicating that deconsolidating elections in already deconsolidating nations have a more limited impact on migration decisions. Put another way, people in these countries may have already been considering migrating due to dissatisfaction with the state of democracy in their countries and a further deconsolidating election only weakly increases the impetus to leave.

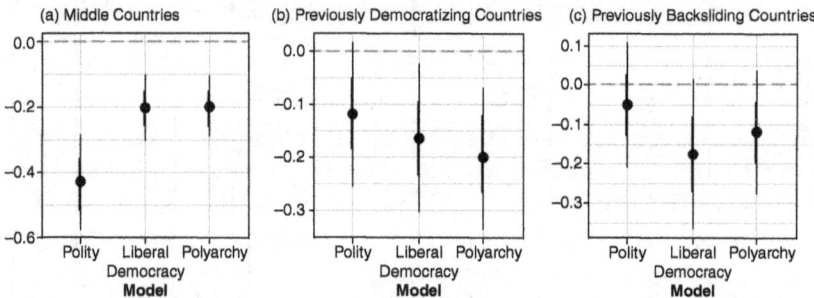

FIGURE C.9 Democracy scores: improvements and backsliding worldwide.
Note: Panel (a) excludes countries with a V-Dem Liberal Democracy Index below 0.1 (strong autocracies) and higher than 0.7 (strong democracies), panel (b) includes only countries that experienced democratic improvements in the five years preceding the election, and panel (c) includes only countries that experienced democratic backsliding in the five years prior to the election.

TABLES FOR MODELS IN FIGURES 2.2, 3.2, AND 3.3

TABLE C.1 *Models from Figure 2.2(a).*

	Model 1	Model 2	Model 3	Model 4	Model 5
Dissatisfaction	0.099*** (0.001)				
Media no freedom		0.083*** (0.001)			
Limited freedom of expression			0.039*** (0.001)		
Government corrupt				0.073*** (0.001)	
Elections dishonest					0.093*** (0.001)
Unemployed	0.112*** (0.002)	0.112*** (0.002)	0.111*** (0.002)	0.113*** (0.002)	0.112*** (0.002)
Employed part-time, want full	0.057*** (0.002)	0.057*** (0.002)	0.055*** (0.002)	0.056*** (0.002)	0.057*** (0.002)
No money for food	0.005*** (0.001)	0.007*** (0.001)	0.006*** (0.001)	0.005*** (0.001)	0.006*** (0.001)
No money for housing	0.017*** (0.001)	0.016*** (0.001)	0.015*** (0.001)	0.016*** (0.001)	0.016*** (0.001)
Difficulty with income	-0.003*** (0.001)	0.001 (0.001)	-0.0003 (0.001)	-0.001 (0.001)	-0.003*** (0.001)
Living standard bad	0.050*** (0.001)	0.059*** (0.001)	0.060*** (0.001)	0.058*** (0.001)	0.052*** (0.001)

(continued)

TABLE C.1 (continued)

	Model 1	Model 2	Model 3	Model 4	Model 5
Living standard worsening	-0.00000	0.006***	0.006***	0.004***	0.002*
	(0.001)	(0.001)	(0.001)	(0.001)	(0.001)
Victim of theft	0.061***	0.065***	0.066***	0.065***	0.064***
	(0.001)	(0.001)	(0.002)	(0.001)	(0.001)
Victim of assault	0.055***	0.054***	0.061***	0.059***	0.056***
	(0.002)	(0.002)	(0.002)	(0.002)	(0.002)
Constant	0.206***	0.168***	0.190***	0.140***	0.153***
	(0.010)	(0.012)	(0.015)	(0.011)	(0.011)
N	908776	777734	661056	892967	890034
Log likelihood	-481860.300	-417977.600	-358821.500	-477710.400	-473602.900
AIC	963748.700	835983.300	717670.900	955448.900	947233.800
BIC	963912.800	836145.200	717830.500	955612.700	947397.600

*** $p < 0.01$; ** $p < 0.05$; * $p < 0.1$.

Note: AIC (Akaike Information Criterion); BIC (Bayesian Information Criterion).

TABLE C.2 *Models from Figure 2.2(b).*

	Those who have made plans to emigrate				
	Model 1	Model 2	Model 3	Model 4	Model 5
Dissatisfaction	0.003*** (0.0002)				
Media no freedom		0.004*** (0.0003)			
Limited freedom of expression			0.001*** (0.0003)		
Government corrupt				0.002*** (0.0003)	
Elections dishonest					0.003*** (0.0002)
Unemployed	0.010*** (0.0004)	0.011*** (0.0005)	0.011*** (0.001)	0.010*** (0.0004)	0.010*** (0.0004)
Employed part-time want full	0.004*** (0.0004)	0.005*** (0.0004)	0.004*** (0.0004)	0.004*** (0.0004)	0.004*** (0.0004)
No money for food	0.0003 (0.0003)	0.0003 (0.0003)	0.0004 (0.0003)	0.0003 (0.0003)	0.0004 (0.0003)
No money for housing	0.001*** (0.0003)	0.001*** (0.0003)	0.001*** (0.0003)	0.001*** (0.0003)	0.001*** (0.0003)
Difficulty with income	-0.002*** (0.0002)	-0.002*** (0.0003)	-0.001*** (0.0003)	-0.002*** (0.0002)	-0.002*** (0.0002)
Living standard bad	0.001*** (0.0002)	0.001*** (0.0003)	0.001*** (0.0003)	0.001*** (0.0003)	0.001*** (0.0003)

(continued)

TABLE C.2 (continued)

Those who have made plans to emigrate

	Model 1	Model 2	Model 3	Model 4	Model 5
Living standard worsening	0.001***	0.001***	0.001***	0.001***	0.001***
	(0.0003)	(0.0003)	(0.0003)	(0.0003)	(0.0003)
Victim of theft	0.004***	0.005***	0.004***	0.004***	0.004***
	(0.0003)	(0.0004)	(0.0004)	(0.0003)	(0.0003)
Victim of assault	0.008***	0.009***	0.008***	0.008***	0.008***
	(0.0004)	(0.0005)	(0.001)	(0.0004)	(0.0004)
Constant	0.010***	0.010**	0.006	0.009**	0.009**
	(0.004)	(0.004)	(0.005)	(0.004)	(0.004)
N	908776	777734	661056	892967	890034
Log likelihood	837673.600	673236.400	583958.700	820216.600	818025.800
AIC	−1675319.000	−1346445.000	−1167889.000	−1640405.000	−1636024.000
BIC	−1675155.000	−1346283.000	−1167730.000	−1640241.000	−1635860.000

*** $p < 0.01$; ** $p < 0.05$; * $p < 0.1$.

TABLE C.3 *Models from Figure 3.2.*

	Those who have expressed an interest in emigrating		
	Model 1	Model 2	Model 3
After election1	0.025***	0.006	0.006
	(0.005)	(0.004)	(0.004)
After election1:Dd polity	−0.249***		
	(0.054)		
After election1:Dd libdem		−0.292***	
		(0.048)	
After election1:Dd polyarchy			−0.211***
			(0.049)
Dd polity	0.283***		
	(0.030)		
Dd polyarchy			0.257***
			(0.029)
Dd libdem		0.278***	
		(0.031)	
Age	−0.006***	−0.006***	−0.006***
	(0.0003)	(0.0003)	(0.0003)
Age squared	0.00002***	0.00001***	0.00001***
	(0.00000)	(0.00000)	(0.00000)
Female	−0.033***	−0.031***	−0.031***
	(0.002)	(0.002)	(0.002)
Children	−0.003	−0.002	−0.003
	(0.002)	(0.002)	(0.002)
Urban	0.040***	0.040***	0.040***
	(0.002)	(0.002)	(0.002)
Health problems	0.005**	0.008***	0.008***
	(0.003)	(0.002)	(0.002)
Married	−0.037***	−0.038***	−0.038***
	(0.002)	(0.002)	(0.002)
Income 5Second 20%	−0.018***	−0.018***	−0.018***
	(0.004)	(0.003)	(0.003)
Income 5Middle 20%	−0.019***	−0.018***	−0.018***
	(0.003)	(0.003)	(0.003)
Income 5Fourth 20%	−0.015***	−0.015***	−0.015***
	(0.003)	(0.003)	(0.003)
Income 5Richest 20%	−0.008**	−0.009***	−0.009***
	(0.003)	(0.003)	(0.003)
Constant	0.486***	0.506***	0.506***
	(0.011)	(0.010)	(0.010)
N	148821	191591	191591
Log likelihood	−72405.190	−95314.890	−95318.070
AIC	144844.400	190663.800	190670.100
BIC	145012.900	190836.600	190842.900

*** $p < 0.01$; **$p < 0.05$; *$p < 0.1$.

TABLE C.4 *Models from Figure 3.2.*

	Those who have expressed an interest in emigrating		
	Model 1	Model 2	Model 3
After election1	−0.004 (0.006)	−0.004 (0.005)	−0.005 (0.005)
Dd polity	0.066 (0.057)		
Dd libdem		0.165*** (0.054)	
Dd polyarchy			0.135*** (0.050)
Dissatisfaction	0.095*** (0.003)	0.096*** (0.002)	0.096*** (0.002)
After election1:Dd polity	−0.143** (0.069)		
After election1:Dd libdem		−0.132** (0.063)	
After election1:Dd polyarchy			−0.132** (0.060)
After election1: dissatisfaction	0.006 (0.004)	0.011*** (0.003)	0.010*** (0.004)
Dd polity: dissatisfaction	−0.071** (0.029)		
After election1:Dd polity: dissatisfaction	−0.093* (0.051)		
Dd libdem: dissatisfaction		0.015 (0.037)	
After election1:Dd libdem: dissatisfaction		−0.096 (0.061)	
Dd polyarchy: dissatisfaction			0.008 (0.032)
after election1:Dd polyarchy: dissatisfaction			−0.154*** (0.059)
Constant	0.245*** (0.010)	0.246*** (0.010)	0.247*** (0.010)
N	159980	200736	200736
Log likelihood	−81930.050	−105141.300	−105139.100
AIC	163882.100	210304.700	210300.200
BIC	163991.900	210417.000	210412.500

*** $p < 0.01$; **$p < 0.05$; *$p < 0.1$.

Notes

PREFACE

1. Lewis Jackson, "After Trump's Win, Many Despondent Americans Research Moving Abroad," *Reuters*, November 8, 2024.

2. Alex Baker, "1 in 5 US Residents 'More Likely' to Move after Election, According to Redfin," *Yahoo! News*, November 16, 2024. www.yahoo.com/news/1-5-us-residents-more-150052398.html.

3. Laurie Udesky and Jack Leeming, "Exclusive: A *Nature* Analysis Signals the Beginnings of a US Science Brain Drain," *Nature*, April 22, 2025. www.nature.com/articles/d41586-025-01216-7. Also see Alexandra Witze, "75% of US Scientists Who Answered *Nature* Poll Consider Leaving," *Nature*, March 27, 2025. www.nature.com/articles/d41586-025-00938-y.

4. Edward Helmore, "Record Number of Americans Are Seeking Residency in UK, According to Home Office," *The Guardian*, May 24, 2025. www.theguardian.com/us-news/2025/may/24/americans-british-citizenship.

5. Patrick J. Carr and Maria J. Kefalas, *Hollowing Out the Middle: The Rural Brain Drain and What It Means for America* (Boston: Beacon Press, 2009). Also see J. A. Rodden, *Why Cities Lose: The Deep Roots of the Urban-Rural Political Divide* (New York: Basic Books, 2019).

6. Gabriel Trip, "Two Families Got Fed Up with Their State's Politics. So They Moved Out," *The New York Times*, October 7, 2024. www.nytimes.com/2023/10/07/us/politics/politics-states-moving.html. Also see Ronda Kaysen and Ethan Singer, "Millions of Movers Reveal American Polarization in Action," *The New York Times*, October 30, 2024. www.nytimes.com/interactive/2024/10/30/upshot/voters-moving-polarization.html.

I DEMOCRATIC DRAIN

1. Nikolai, as with all emigrants who fled Russia and are interviewed as part of my field research, has been assigned an alias to protect him from being identified and subjected to retribution. I also assign aliases to the pro-democratic, Middle Eastern, and North African activists whom I interview as part of Chapter 6.

2. See "Serbia's Incumbent President Vucic Set to Win Second Term," *Reuters*, April 3, 2022.

3. Inter alia, see Alex Irwin-Hunt, "Brain Drain: Countries with the Greatest Human Capital Flight," *FDI Intelligence*, April 19, 2023. Frédéric Docquier and Hillel Rapoport, "Globalization, Brain Drain, and Development," *Journal of Economic Literature* 50, no. 3 (2012): 681–730. Frédéric Docquier, "The Brain Drain from Developing Countries," IZA World of Labor, 2014, https://doi.org/10.15185/izawol.

4. Note that this was before the Russian government initiated a military draft. See Georgi Kantchev, Evan Gershkovich, and Yuliya Chernova, "Russia's Brain Drain: Hundreds of Thousands of Professionals and Highly Skilled Workers Have Left Country since Putin's Invasion of Ukraine," *MarketWatch*, April 11, 2022. "International Migration in Russia from 1997 to 2021, by Flow," *Statista*, September 2, 2025.

5. Kantchev et al. 2022.

6. "Remarks by President Biden on the United Efforts of the Free World to Support the People of Ukraine," *White House*, March 26, 2022.

7. Georgi Kantchev, Evan Gershkovich, and Yuliya Chernova, "Fleeing Putin, Thousands of Educated Russians Are Moving Abroad," *The Wall Street Journal*, April 10, 2022, https://www.wsj.com/world/russia/fleeing-putin-thousands-of-educated-russians-are-moving-abroad-11649583003?gaa.

8. Still, it is worth noting that some subset of these émigrés work for foreign companies, which would have been constrained by sanctions. See Kantchev et al. 2022.

9. For example, see Aleksandar Vasovic, "A Mini Russia Emerges in Serbia as Thousands Flee War," *Reuters*, September 10, 2024.

10. Anna Boucher, *Gender, Migration and the Global Race for Talent* (Manchester: Manchester University Press, 2016).

11. Peter Huber and Klaus Nowotny, "Risk Aversion and the Willingness to Migrate in 30 Transition Countries," *Journal of Population Economics* 33 (2020): 1463–1498; Mehtap Akgüç, Xingfei Liu, Massmiliano Tani, and Klaus Zimmerman, "Risk Attitudes and Migration," *China Economic Review* 37 (2016): 166–176.

12. Moti Michaeli, Marco Casari, Andrea Ichino, Maria De Paola, Ginevra Marandola, and Vincenzo Scoppa, "Civicness Drain," *The Economic Journal* 133, no. 649 (2023): 323–354.

13. In East Germany during the Cold War, emigration by refugees signaled regime weakness and inspired protest up to a certain level, but when emigration became too extensive, it depleted the "social fabric" that supported citizen mobilization, undermining collective action and attenuating the movement's base. See S. Pfaff and H. Kim, "Exit-Voice Dynamics in Collective Action: An Analysis of Emigration and Protest in the East German Revolution," *American Journal of Sociology* 109, no. 2 (2003): 401–444. Similar dynamics have been identified among voluntary migrants since many Eastern European countries joined the EU's free mobility zone. See R. D. Kelemen, "The European Union's Authoritarian Equilibrium," *Journal of European Public Policy* 27, no. 3 (2020): 481–499; D. Auer

and M. Schaub, "Mass Emigration and the Erosion of Liberal Democracy," *International Studies Quarterly* 68, no. 2 (2024): 1–14; J. Lim, "The Electoral Consequences of International Migration in Sending Countries: Evidence from Central and Eastern Europe," *Comparative Political Studies* 56, no. 1 (2023): 36–64. Domestically in Italy, scholars have found that higher emigration rates resulted in reduced voter turnout and stifled local political change by depleting communities of dynamic and educated youths. See M. Anelli and G. Peri, "Does Emigration Delay Political Change? Evidence from Italy during the Great Recession," *Economic Policy* 32, no. 91 (2017): 551–596. An important predecessor of this work comes from Devesh Kapur's recognition of the effects of Indian emigrants' "absence," as one of four "channels" through which migration affects the origin country. See Devesh Kapur, *Diaspora, Development, and Democracy: The Domestic Impact of International Migration from India* (Princeton, NJ: Princeton University Press, 2010).

14. Today, more people than ever live in a country other than the one in which they were born. According to the Population Division of the United Nations Department of Economic and Social Affairs, as of July 1, 2020 the global number of international migrants was estimated to be 281 million. International migrants comprise some 3.5 percent of the global population, compared to 2.8 percent in 2000 and 2.3 percent in 1980. See "Global Issues: International Migration," United Nations, www.un.org/en/global-issues/migration. And about two-thirds of the world's migrants are voluntary migrants. See "The Future of Migration," Office of the Director of National Intelligence, April 2021.

15. Sheri Berman, *Democracy and Dictatorship in Europe: From the Ancient Régime to the Present Day* (New York: Oxford University Press, 2019).

16. See Natasha Wunsch and Philippe Blanchard, "Patterns of Democratic Backsliding in Third-Wave Democracies: A Sequence Analysis Perspective," *Democratization* 30, no. 2 (2023): 278–301; and also Anna Grzymala-Busse, "The Failure of Europe's Mainstream Parties," *Journal of Democracy* 30, no. 4 (2019): 35–47.

17. Lisa Anderson, "Searching Where the Light Shines: Studying Democratization in the Middle East," *Annual Review of Political Science* 9 (2006): 189–214.

18. Thomas Carothers and Marina Ottaway, *Uncharted Journey: Promoting Democracy in the Middle East* (Washington, DC: Carnegie, 2005).

19. See Seymour Martin Lipset, *Political Man: The Social Bases of Politics* (Garden City, NY: Doubleday, 1960); Robert Jackman, "On the Relations of Economic Development to Democratic Performance," *American Journal of Political Science* 17 (1973): 611–621; Kenneth Bollen, "Political Democracy and the Timing of Development," *American Sociological Review* 44 (1979): 572–587; A. Przeworski and F. Limongi, "Modernization: Theories and Facts," *World Politics* 49 (1997): 155–183.

20. Samuel Huntington, *The Third Wave: Democratization in the Late Twentieth Century* (Norman: University of Oklahoma Press, 1991).

21. Farhad Kazemi and Augustus Richard Norton, "Authoritarianism, Civil Society and Democracy in the Middle East: Mass Media in the Persian Gulf,"

Middle East Studies Bulletin 40, no. 2 (2006): 201–211; Michael Ross, "Will Oil Drown the Arab Spring?," *Foreign Affairs* 90, no. 5 (2001): 2–7; Barbara Geddes, "What Do We Know about Democratization after Twenty Years?," *Annual Review of Political Science* 2 (1999): 115–144, p. 118.

22. Eva Bellin, "The Robustness of Authoritarianism in the Middle East: Exceptionalism in Comparative Perspective," *Comparative Politics* 36, no. 2 (2004): 139–157.

23. E. C. Merem, Y. A. Twumasi, J. Wesley, D. Olagbegi, M. Crisler, C. Romorno, M. Alsarari, P. Isokpehi, M. Alrefai, S. Ochai, E. Nwagboso, S. Fageir, and S. Leggett, "The Assessment of China's Scramble for Natural Resources Extraction in Africa," *World Environment* 11, no. 1 (2021): 9–25.

24. For example, H. G. Betz, *Radical Right-Wing Populism in Western Europe* (New York: St. Martin's Press, 1994); Sarah de Lange, "A New Winning Formula?: The Programmatic Appeal of the Radical Right," *Party Politics* 13, no. 4 (2007): 411–435; Daphne Halikiopoulou and Sofia Vasilopoulou, "Breaching the Social Contract: Crises of Democratic Representation and Patterns of Extreme Right Party Support," *Government and Opposition* 53, no. 1 (2018): 26–50; Tarik Abou-Chadi and Thomas Kurer, "Economic Risk within the Household and Voting for the Radical Right," *World Politics* 73, no. 3 (2021): 482–511; Massimo Anelli, Italo Colantone, and Piero Stanig, "Individual Vulnerability to Industrial Robot Adoption Increases Support for the Radical Right," *Proceedings of the National Academy of Sciences* 118, no. 47 (2021): e2111611118.

25. For example, Elizabeth Ivarsflaten, "What Unites Right-Wing Populists in Western Europe?: Re-examining Grievance Mobilization Models in Seven Successful Cases," *Comparative Political Studies* 41, no. 1 (2008): 3–23; David Cutts, Robert Ford and Matthew Goodwin, "Anti-Immigrant, Politically Disaffected or Still Racist after All? Examining the Attitudinal Drivers of Extreme Right Support in Britain in the 2009 European Elections," *European Journal of Political Research* 50, no. 3 (2011): 418–440; Robert Ford, Matthew Goodwin, and David Cutts, "Strategic Eurosceptics and Polite Xenophobes: Support for the United Kingdom Independence Party (UKIP) in the 2009 European Parliament Elections: Strategic Eurosceptics and Polite Xenophobes," *European Journal of Political Research* 51, no. 2 (2012): 204–234; Lenka Bustikova, "Revenge of the Radical Right," *Comparative Political Studies* 47, no. 12 (2014): 1738–1765; Eelco Harteveld, Joep Schaper, Sarah de Lange, and Wouter Van Der Brug, "Blaming Brussels? The Impact of (News about) the Refugee Crisis on Attitudes towards the EU and National Politics," *JCMS: Journal of Common Market Studies* 56, no. 1 (2018): 157–177; Glenn Kefford and Shaun Ratcliff, "Populists or Nativist Authoritarians? A Cross-National Analysis of the Radical Right," *Australian Journal of Political Science* 56, no. 3 (2021): 261–279.

26. Daniel Ziblatt, *Conservative Parties and the Birth of Democracy* (Cambridge: Cambridge University Press, 2017). See also David Bateman, "The Dilemmas of Democratic Peoplehood," Annual Meeting of the American Political Science Association, September 2020.

27. Joseph Schumpeter, *Das Wesen und der Hauptinhalt der theoretischen Nationalökonomie* (Leipzig: Duncker & Humblot, 1908); Joseph Schumpeter, "On the Concept of Social Value," *Quarterly Journal of Economics*, 23 (1909): 213–232.

28. Max Weber, *Economy and Society*, ed. Guenther Roth and Claus Wittich (Berkeley: University of California Press, 1968), 13.

29. See Friedrich von Hayek, "Scientism and the Study of Society I," *Economica* 9 (1942): 267–291; Friedrich von Hayek, "Scientism and the Study of Society II," *Economica* 10 (1943): 34–63; Friedrich von Hayek, "Scientism and the Study of Society III," *Economica* 11 (1944): 27–39; Friedrich von Hayek, *The Counter-Revolution of Science* (New York: Free Press, 1955).

30. Margaret Peters and Michael Miller, "Emigration and Political Contestation," *International Studies Quarterly*, 66, no. 1 (2022), https://shorturl.at/mcQvS.

31. Jack Goldstone, "Population and Security: How Demographic Change Can Lead to Violent Conflict," *Journal of International Affairs* 56, no. 1 (2002): 3–21, p. 4.

32. See Justin Gest, *Majority Minority* (Oxford: Oxford University Press, 2022).

33. H. Ware, "Demography, Migration and Conflict in the Pacific," *Journal of Peace Research* 42, no. 4 (2005): 435–454.

34. M. Bello and V. Reyes, "Filipino Americans and the Marcos Overthrow: The Transformation of Political Consciousness," *Amerasia Journal* 13, no. 1 (1986): 73–83.

35. D. Roy, "Egyptian Emigrant Labor: Domestic Consequences," *Middle Eastern Studies* 27, no. 4 (1991): 551–582.

36. A qualifying "upgrade" would entail a 10 percent difference on the vDem democracy scoring system.

37. The vDem dataset is by Michael Coppedge, John Gerring, Carl Henrik Knutsen, Staffan I. Lindberg, Jan Teorell, David Altman, Michael Bernhard, Agnes Cornell, M. Steven Fish, Lisa Gastaldi, Haakon Gjerløw, Adam Glynn, Ana Good God, Sandra Grahn, Allen Hicken, Katrin Kinzelbach, Joshua Krusell, Kyle L. Marquardt, Kelly McMann, Valeriya Mechkova, Juraj Medzihorsky, Natalia Natsika, Anja Neundorf, Pamela Paxton, Daniel Pemstein, Josefine Pernes, Oskar Rydén, Johannes von Römer, Brigitte Seim, Rachel Sigman, Svend-Erik Skaaning, Jeffrey Staton, Aksel Sundström, Eitan Tzelgov, Yi-ting Wang, Tore Wig, Steven Wilson, and Daniel Ziblatt, "V-Dem [Country-Year/Country-Date] Dataset v13," Varieties of Democracy (V-Dem) Project, 2023, https://doi.org/10.23696/vdemds23. See also Daniel Pemstein, Kyle L. Marquardt, Eitan Tzelgov, Yi-ting Wang, Juraj Medzihorsky, Joshua Krusell, Farhad Miri, and Johannes von Römer, "The V-Dem Measurement Model: Latent Variable Analysis for Cross-National and Cross-Temporal Expert-Coded Data," V-Dem Working Paper No. 21. 8th ed., University of Gothenburg, Varieties of Democracy Institute, 2023.

38. See Gerasimos Tsourapas, "Why Do States Develop Multi-tier Emigrant Policies? Evidence from Egypt," *Journal of Ethnic and Migration Studies*, preprint (2015).

39. Timothy Hatton, *Seeking Asylum: Trends and Policies in the OECD* (London: Centre for Economic Policy Research, 2011).

40. See J. Dunlevy, "On the Settlement Patterns of Recent Caribbean and Latin Immigrants to the United States," *Growth and Change* 22 (1991): 54–67; Douglas Massey, Joaquin Arango, Graeme Hugo, Ali Kouanouci, Adela Pellegrino, and Edward Taylor, "An Evaluation of International Migration Theory: The North American Case," *Population and Development Review* 20, no. 4 (1994): 699–751; Douglas Massey and K. E. Espinosa, "What's Driving Mexico–U.S. Migration? A Theoretical, Empirical, and Policy Analysis," *American Journal of Sociology* 102, no. 4 (1997): 939–999; Douglas Massey and Rene Zenteno, "A Validation of the Ethnosurvey: The Case of Mexico–U.S. Migration," *International Migration Review* 34, no. 3 (2000): 766–793; P. Winters, A. D. Janvry, and E. Sadoulet, "Family and Community Networks in Mexico–U.S. Migration," *Journal of Human Resources* 36, no. 1 (2001): 159–184; E. Fussell and D. Massey, "The Limits to Cumulative Causation: International Migration from Mexican Urban Areas," *Demography* 41, no. 1 (2004): 151–171; F. Garip and S. R. Curran, "Increasing Migration, Diverging Communities: Changing Character of Migrant Streams in Rural Thailand," *Population Research and Policy Review* 29, no. 5 (2010): 685–695.

41. For example, see A. Lichtenheld, *Guilt by Location: Forced Displacement and Population Sorting in Civil Wars* (Cambridge: Cambridge University Press, 2024). The author explores the strategic use of forced displacement by armed groups during civil wars, highlighting its role as a weapon for sorting the civilian population based on loyalty and affiliation, making communities more "legible" for the combatants, who can then extract resources, recruit fighters, and signal legitimacy.

42. Jennifer Fitzgerald, David Leblang, and Jessica Teets, "Defying the Law of Gravity: The Political Economy of International Migration," *World Politics* 66, no. 3 (2014): 151–171.

43. A. Schachar, "The Race for Talent: Highly Skilled Migrants and Competitive Immigration Regimes," *New York University Law Review* 81 (2006): 148–206; J. Doomernik, R. Koslowski, L. Laurence, R. Maxwell, I. Michalowski, and D. Thraenhardt, *No Shortcuts: Selective Migration and Integration* (Washington, DC: Transatlantic Academy, 2009); Michel Beine, Anna Boucher, Brian Burgoon, Mary Crock, Justin Gest, Michael Hiscox, Patrick McGovern, Hillil Rapoport, Joep Schaper, and Eiko Theilemann, "Comparing Immigration Policies: An Overview from the IMPALA Database," *International Migration Review* 50, no. 4 (2016): 827–863; Michael A. Clemens, "Economics and Emigration: Trillion-Dollar Bills on the Sidewalk?" *Journal of Economic Perspectives* 25, no. 3 (2011): 83–106; Anna Boucher and Justin Gest, *Crossroads: Comparative Immigration Regimes in a World of Demographic Change* (Cambridge: Cambridge University Press, 2018).

44. See Edward Gonzalez-Acosta, "Dominican Republic: Building Trans-migrant Citizenship," *Alterinfos*, 2007; Michel Beine, Frederic Docquier, and Hillel Rapoport, "Brain Drain and Human Capital Formation in Developing Countries: Winners and Losers," *Economic Journal* 188 (2008): 631–652; Michel Beine, Frederic Docquier, and Maurice Schiff, "Brain Drain and Its Determinants: A Major Issue for Small States," IZA Discussion Papers No. 3398, Institute for the Study of Labor, 2008; Christian Dustmann and Oliver Kirchkamp, "The Optimal Migration Duration and Activity Choice after

Re-migration," *Journal of Development Economics* 67, no. 2 (2002): 361–372; Beata Javorcik, Çağlar Özden, Mariana Spatareanu, and Cristina Neagu, "Migrant Networks and Foreign Direct Investment," World Bank Policy Research Working Paper No. 4046, 2006; Elisabetta Lodigliani, "Diaspora Externalities as a Cornerstone of the New Brain Drain Literature," Universit catholique de Louvain, Institut de Recherches Economiques et Sociales, Discussion Paper No. 2009-36, 2009; Jean-Baptiste Meyer and Mercy Brown, "Scientific Diasporas: A New Approach to Brain Drain," World Conference on Science, UNESCO-ICSU, 2009; J. E. Rauch, "Diasporas and Development: Theory, Evidence, and Programmatic Implications," Department of Economics, University of California at San Diego, 2003; J. E. Rauch and V. Trindade, "Ethnic Chinese Networks in International Trade," *Review of Economics and Statistics* 84, no. 1 (2002): 116–130; Annalee Saxenian, *Silicon Valley's New Immigrant Entrepreneurs* (San Francisco: Public Policy Institute of California, 1999); C. Woodruff and R. Zenteno, "Remittances and Microenterprises in Mexico," UCSD, Graduate School of International Relations and Pacific Studies Working Paper, 2021; Dean Yang and Claudia Martinez, "Home Areas: Evidence from the Philippines," in *International Migration, Remittances, and the Brain Drain*, ed. Çaglar Özden and Maurice W. Schiff, 81–122 (Washington, DC, Basingstoke, New York: The World Bank and Palgrave Macmillan, 2006).

45. "Personal Remittances, Received (% of GDP)," World Bank, 2014.
46. Peggy Levitt, "Social Remittances: Migration Driven Local-Level Forms of Cultural Diffusion," *International Migration Review* 32, no. 4 (1998): 926–948.
47. Paul Collier, *Exodus: How Migration Is Changing Our World* (Oxford, New York: Oxford University Press, 2013). Jackline Wahba, "The Economics of Return Migration," in *Handbook of Return Migration*, ed. Russell King and Katie Kuschminder, 24–37, Elgar Handbooks in Migration Series (Northampton: Edward Elgar Publishing, 2022).
48. Félix Krawatzek and Lea Müller-Funk, "Two Centuries of Flows between 'Here' and 'There': Political Remittances and Their Transformative Potential," *Journal of Ethnic and Migration Studies* 46, no. 6 (2019): 1003–1024.
49. Walter Connor, "Homelands in a World of States," in *Understanding Nationalism*, ed. Montserrat Guidernau and John Hutchinson, 53–73 (Cambridge: Polity Press, 2001); Mary Kaldor, *New and Old Wars: Organised Violence in a Global Era* (Cambridge: Polity Press, 1999); Mary Kaldor and Diego Muro, "Nationalist and Religious Militant Networks," in *Global Civil Society*, ed. Mary Kaldor, Helmut Anheier, and Marlies Glasius, 154–160 (Oxford: Oxford University Press, 2003); Peggy Levitt and Rafael de la Dehesa, "Transnational Migration and the Redefinition of the State: Variations and Explanations," *Ethnic and Racial Studies* 26, no. 4 (2003): 587–611; Denisa Kostovicova and Albert Prestreshi, "Education, Gender and Religion: Identity Transformations among Kosovo Albanians in London," *Journal of Ethnic and Migration Studies* 29, no. 6 (2010): 1079–1096; Terrence Lyons and Peter Mandaville, *Politics from Afar: Transnational Diasporas and Networks* (New York: Columbia University Press, 2012).
50. Kapur 2010.
51. Antonio Spillembergo, "Democracy and Foreign Education," *American Economic Review* 99, no. 1 (2009): 528–543.

52. Frederic Docquier and Hillel Rapoport, "Ethnic Discrimination and the Migration of Skilled Labor," *Journal of Development Economics* 70, no. 1 (2003): 159–172; F. Mariani, "Migration as an Antidote to Rent-Seeking?," *Journal of Development Economics* 84, no. 2 (2007): 609–630.
53. Jose Alemán and Dwayne Woods, "No Way Out: Travel Restrictions and Authoritarian Regimes," *Migration and Development* 3, no. 2 (2014): 285–305.
54. Tsourapas 2015, p. 16.
55. Eva Østergaard-Nielsen, "The Democratic Deficit of Diaspora Politics: Turkish Cypriots in Britain and the Cyprus Issue," *Journal of Ethnic and Migration Studies* 29, no. 4 (2003): 683–700. Recent research on remittances also demonstrates that the money emigrants return to their families and friends tends not to promote democratic values. G. L. Goodman and J. T. Hiskey, "Exit without Leaving: Political Disengagement in High Migration Municipalities in Mexico," *Comparative Politics* 40, no. 2 (2008): 169–188 report a decrease in political engagement in Mexican cities with high level of emigrants. R. Germano, "Migrants' Remittances and Economic Voting in the Mexican Countryside," *Electoral Studies* 32, no. 4 (2013): 875–885 finds that remittance recipients are less likely to pressure and oppose politicians because they are more optimistic about their economic conditions. A. Berdiev, N. Y. Kim, and C. Chang, "Remittances and Corruption," *Economics Letters* 118, no. 1 (2013): 182–185 and Y. Abdih, R. Chami, and J. Dagher, "Remittances and Institutions: Are Remittances a Curse?" *World Development* 40, no. 4 (2012): 657–666 find that remittances increases the likelihood that the government will spend more time in rent-seeking behavior and invest less in public goods because recipients may procure such goods on their own. See Maty Konte, "The Effects of Remittances on Support for Democracy in Africa: Are Remittances a Curse of a Blessing?" Working Paper, 2015.
56. Elizabeth Iams Wellman, Nathan W. Allen, and Benjamin Nyblade, "The Extraterritorial Voting Rights and Restrictions Dataset (1950–2020)," *Comparative Political Studies* 56, no. 6 (2023): 897–929.
57. See Kacper Szulecki, Davide Bertelli, Marta Bivand Erdal, Anatolie Coșciug, Angelina Kussy, Gabriella Mikiewicz, and Corina Tulbure, "To Vote or Not to Vote? Migrant Electoral (Dis)engagement in an Enlarged Europe," *Migration Studies* 9, no. 3 (2021): 989–1010; Michael Ahn Paarlberg, "Transnational Militancy: Diaspora Influence over Electoral Activity in Latin America," *Comparative Politics* 49, no. 4 (2017): 541–559.
58. Albert Hirschman, *Exit, Voice, and Loyalty: Responses to Decline in Firms, Organizations, and States* (Cambridge, MA: Harvard University Press, 1970).
59. See I. Somin, *Free to Move: Foot Voting, Migration, and Political Freedom* (New York: Oxford University Press, 2020).

2 DEMOCRACY'S CARRIERS

1. This account is drawn from Alex Larzelere, *Castro's Ploy, America's Dilemma: The 1980 Cuban Boatlift* (Washington, DC: National Defense University Press, 1988).
2. J. M. Colomer, "Exit, Voice, and Hostility in Cuba," *International Migration Review* 34, no. 2 (2000): 423–442.

3. See B. Hoffmann, "Emigration and Regime Stability: The Persistence of Cuban Socialism," *Journal of Communist Studies and Transition Politics* 21, no. 4 (2005): 436–461. According to Hoffmann, part of the reason that the Castro government survived for so long was because of its ability to maintain its role as the "gatekeeper state." In other words, the access gates to emigration were consistently under firm state control, defining when and how emigration would take place. Emigration was made into a "once and for all" decision. The government would confiscate an emigrant's property before leaving and reentry was only possible with a state-issued entry permit. The exit option was therefore easily available but also costly. Those who were willing to assume the costs could be assumed by the state to be the most fervent dissidents. Hoffmann, however, argues that factors other than the level of dissent were more important, such as income expectation in the target country or whether family members abroad could bear some of the cost.

4. Because most receiving countries gave priority to victims of political persecution, immigrants might deliberately use dissidence to "move up the visa queue" (Hoffmann, 2005, p. 442). This makes it is difficult to ascertain how sincere dissident activities were, so it may be that the most fervent dissidents are those who incur the high cost of staying rather than the costs of leaving. Nonetheless, the regime takes advantage of this by framing dissidents as being motivated by personal interests rather than political conviction, further turning the domestic population against both dissidents and émigrés. By turning what is usually a private phenomenon into a public event, the state broadcasts images of emigrants to show the defeat of the old elite and the success of the regime while also making it clear that the government always has a watchful eye on emigration. The publicity is a show of force demonstrating the regime's ability to withstand the pressure of its opponents over a long period of time without giving in. It also allows the state to paint emigrants as traitors, calling for supporters to demonstrate their loyalty through acts of rejection of emigrants.

5. Larry Nackerud, Alyson Springer, Christopher Larrison, and Alicia Issac, "The End of the Cuban Contradiction in U.S. Refugee Policy," *International Migration Review* 33, no. 1 (1999): 176–192, https://doi.org/10.2307/2547327.

6. Throughout this book, references to prospective migrants as reported in survey data are based on responses to the question "If you had the opportunity, would you like to move permanently to another country?" This question is derived from the Gallup World Poll indicator, but applied in my original survey research as well. Like Gallup, I also asked respondents if they plan to migrate within the next twelve months and whether they have taken any actions in preparation for such a move such as applied for work, purchased plane tickets, or searched for housing.

7. Anita Pugliese and Julie Ray, "Nearly 900 Million Worldwide Wanted to Migrate in 2021," *Gallup*, January 24, 2023.

8. Neli Esipova, Julie Ray, and Anita Pugliese, "Gallup World Poll: The Many Faces of Global Migration," International Organization for Migration (IOM) Migration Research Series No. 43, 2011. For Gallup, Inc. visualizations of these data, please see Appendix A.

9. Research suggestions that self-reporting about emigration intentions are good predictors of future emigration. See Hendrik P. van Dalen and Kène Henkens,

"Emigration Intentions: Mere Words or True Plans? Explaining International Migration Intentions and Behavior," Social Science Research Network, 2008.

10. Esipova et al. 2023, p. 35, but also Boucher 2016. Beyond this gender dynamic, it is possible that there are latent factors in women's emigration decisions in relation to their political values. However, I did not observe any evidence of gender effects in my subsequent statistical analysis or my fieldwork. When focusing on elite dissidents in particular, one challenge is that political leaders and activists in Eastern Europe, the Middle East, and North Africa are disproportionately men. (In the case of the Syrian diaspora leaders interviewed in Chapter 5, they were nearly exclusively men.) While I nevertheless pursued a more balanced sample of interviewees for Chapter 6, female respondents pointed to similar trends and considerations as their male peers.

11. But also see Michael A. Clemens and Hannah M. Postel, "Deterring Emigration with Foreign Aid: An Overview of Evidence from Low-Income Countries," *Population and Development Review* 44, no. 4 (2018), 667–693.

12. For examples, consider E. Georges, *The Making of a Transnational Community: Migration, Development and Cultural Change in the Dominican Republic* (New York: Columbia University Press, 1990); Peggy Levitt and Mary Waters, *The Changing Face of Home: The Transnational Lives of the Second Generation* (New York: Russell Sage, 2002), 221–241; Alejandro Portes, "The Debates and Significance of Immigrant Transnationalism," *Global Networks* 1, no. 3 (2001): 181–193; Alejandro Portes, L. E. Guarnizo, and P. Landolt, "The Study of Transnationalism: Pitfalls and Promises of an Emergent Research Field," *Ethnic and Racial Studies* 22, no. 2 (1999): 217–237; Michael Smith and Luis Guarnizo, *Transnationalism from Below* (New Brunswick: Transaction, 1998); Steven Vertovec, "Trends and Impacts of Migrant Transnationalism," Centre on Migration, Policy and Society WP-04-03, Working Paper No. 3, University of Oxford, 2004.

13. Alberto Alesina and Paola Giuliano, "Preferences for Redistribution," National Bureau of Economic Research Working Paper No. 14825, 2010; Erzo Luttmer and Monica Singhal, "Culture, Context and the Taste for Redistribution," National Bureau of Economic Research Working Paper No. 14268, 2011.

14. Alberto Alesina and Paola Giuliano, "Family Ties and Political Participation," *Journal of the European Economic Association* 9, no. 5 (2011): 817–839.

15. A. Becker, T. Deckers, T. Dohmen, A. Falk, and F. Kosse, "The Relationship between Economic Preferences and Psychological Personality Measures," *Annual Review of Economics* 4, no. 1 (2012): 453–478, cited by Didier Fouarge, Merve Bezihe Ozer, and Philipp Seegers, "Personality Traits, Migration Intentions, and Cultural Distance," *Papers in Regional Science* 98, no. 6 (2019): 2425–2454.

16. Peter Vandor, "Are Voluntary International Migrants Self-Selected for Entrepreneurship? An Analysis of Entrepreneurial Personality Traits," *Journal of World Business* 56, no. 2 (2021): 101142. See also Jonathan Levie, "Immigration, In-Migration, Ethnicity and Entrepreneurship in the United Kingdom," *Small Business Economics* 28, nos. 2/3 (2007): 143–169. However, there are some conflicting results from Nonna Kushnirovich, Sibylle Heilbrunn, and Liema Davidovich, "Diversity of Entrepreneurial

Perceptions: Immigrants vs. Native Population," *European Management Review* 15, no. 3 (2018): 341–355; and Stefan Remhof, Marjaana Gunkel, and Christopher Schlaegel, "Goodbye Germany! The Influence of Personality and Cognitive Factors on the Intention to Work Abroad," *International Journal of Human Resource Management* 25, no. 16 (2014): 2319–2343.

17. S. Ayhan, K. Gatskova and H. Lehmann, "The Impact of Non-cognitive skills and Risk Preferences on Rural-to-Urban Migration: Evidence from Ukraine," IZA Discussion Paper Series No. 10982, 2017. See also A. S. Camperio Ciani, C. Capiluppi, A. Veronese, and G. Sartori, "The Adaptive Value of Personality Differences Revealed By Small Island Population Dynamics," *European Journal of Personality* 21, no. 1 (2017): 3–22; D. Canache, M. Hayes, J. J. Mondak, and S. C. Wals, "Openness, Extraversion and the Intention to Emigrate," *Journal of Research in Personality* 47, no. 4 (2013): 351–355; M. Jokela, "Personality Predicts Migration within and between U.S. States," *Journal of Research in Personality* 43, no. 1 (2009): 79–83; M. Jokela, M. Elovainio, M. Kivimäki, and L. Keltikangas-Järvinen, "Temperament and Migration Patterns in Finland," *Psychological Science* 19, no. 9 (2008): 831–837; E. Paulauskaitė, L. Šeibokaitė, and A. Endriulaitienė, "Big Five Personality Traits Linked with Migratory Intentions in Lithuanian Student Sample," *International Journal of Psychology: A Biopsychosocial Approach* 7 (2010): 41–58; K. Silventoinen, N. Hammar, E. Hedlund, M. Koskenvuo, T. Rönnemaa, and J. Kaprio, "Selective International Migration by Social Position, Health Behaviour and Personality," *European Journal of Public Health* 18, no. 2 (2008): 150–155. Also see G. Pop-Eleches and J. A. Tucker, *Communism's Shadow: Historical Legacies and Contemporary Political Attitudes* (Princeton, NJ: Princeton University Press, 2017).

18. A. Bütikofer and G. Peri, "Cognitive and Noncognitive Skills and the Selection and Sorting of Migrants," National Bureau of Economic Research Working Paper No. 23877, 2017.

19. Prior to creating weights, IPSOS removed responses flagged as violating data quality standards and removed those respondents who are ineligible to vote. The final sample consists of 19,296 respondents. The poll collected a variety of information about respondents' demographic attributes, political and electoral preferences, and social and economic attitudes.

20. Authoritarian attitudes is an additive index of the following items each ranging from strongly disagree (1) to strongly agree (4) – rescaled between 0 and 1, where 0 indicates the lowest observed value and 1 the highest: "Please indicate the extent to which you agree or disagree with each of the following statements? (1) Young people should be taught to respect authority; (2) Censorship of films and magazines is necessary to uphold moral standards; (3) People who break the law should be given stiffer sentences; (4) The law should be obeyed, even if a specific law is wrong."

21. Those without migration plans score on average 66.56 percent versus 59.84 for prospective migrants. The model includes fixed effects by country.

22. Jonathan Hiskey, Jorge Daniel Montalvo, and Diana Orcés, "Democracy, Governance, and Emigration Intentions in Latin America and the Caribbean," *Studies in Comparative International Development* 49 (2014): 89–111.

23. Van Dalen and Henkens 2008.
24. Alexi Gugushvili, "Democratic Discontent and Emigration: Do Political Attitudes Explain Emigration Intentions?" Mimeo, European University Institute, 2011.
25. Joel S. Fetzer and Brandon Alexander Millan, "The Causes of Emigration from Singapore: How Much Is Still Political?" *Critical Asian Studies* 45, no. 3 (2015): 462–476.
26. Jennifer H. Lundquist and Douglas S. Massey, "Politics or Economics? International Migration during the Nicaraguan Contra War," *Journal of Latin American Studies* 37, no. 1 (2005): 29–53.
27. Susanne Bygnes and Aurore Flipo, "Political Motivations for Intra-European Migration," *Acta Sociologica* 60, no. 3 (2017): 199–212.
28. Rafaela Dancygier, Sirus H. Dehdari, David D. Laitin, Moritz Marbach, and Kåre Vernby, "Emigration and Radical Right Populism," *American Journal of Political Science* 69, no. 1 (2025): 252–267, https://onlinelibrary.wiley.com/doi/10.1111/ajps.12852.
29. Marie Poprawe, "On the Relationship between Corruption and Migration: Empirical Evidence from a Gravity Model of Migration," *Public Choice* 163, nos. 3/4 (2015): 337–354.
30. Christian Dustmann and Anna Okatenko, "Out-Migration, Wealth Constraints, and the Quality of Local Amenities," *Journal of Development Economics* 110 (2014): 52–63.
31. This research component is based on my co-authored article, Jeremy Ferwerda and Justin Gest, "Pull Factors and Migration Preferences: Evidence from the Middle East and North Africa," *International Migration Review* 55, no. 2 (2021): 431–459.
32. The Palestinian Territories is a self-governing territory. Since 1995, the Palestinian National Authority has issued passports that permit residents to travel abroad. However, visa barriers and/or nonrecognition of passports imply that barriers to international movement may be higher for Palestinian prospective migrants relative to other prospective migrants in the sample.
33. Working with national polling companies in each country, I implemented a standardized questionnaire translated into the local dialect. Surveys were translated by dual-language nationals accustomed to working within each country and pretested to ensure comprehension. These questions were appended to public opinion surveys unrelated to migration that had been designed and implemented by the nongovernmental organization (NGO). Sample size varied across countries, according to prior arrangements between the polling firm and the NGO. In total, I surveyed 1,000 people in Jordan (April 2016), 3,111 people in Libya (May 2016), 1,225 people in Tunisia (May 2016), 1,200 people in the Palestinian Territories (July 2016), and 2,055 people in Lebanon (September 2016) – for a total of 8,591 respondents across the region. Further information on the survey samples is available in Ferwerda and Gest 2021.

In Tunisia and the Palestinian Territories, surveys were conducted using tablets. In Jordan and Lebanon, surveys were fielded in paper format. To conduct the randomization in these latter cases, I developed a web script that randomly generated individual questionnaires for printing. In Libya, due to ongoing conflict, the survey was administered over the phone. While the phone questionnaire's content was identical to in-person fielding, to ensure comprehension, I instructed enumerators to summarize the list of similarities and differences between the two countries after discussing each country's characteristics.

Enumerators were nationals from each respective country, employed by polling companies but trained by the research team, either in-person or via conference call, to implement the conjoint design. When administering hypothetical questions, enumerators were instructed to offer only the information provided and nothing further. Enumerators were instructed to clarify the differences between the country choices by presenting subjects with a table that made discrepancies visually apparent. If subjects felt equally displeased or equally pleased by both country options or did not want to respond, enumerators urged them to select the better of the two and to reserve their impressions for the following question, which rated their interest in the countries as described. They were also instructed to ensure comprehension by readministering the question if respondents' binary choice did not correspond to their country ratings. Response rates to the conjoint question among prospective migrants varied across contexts in a manner unrelated to fielding method. However, I observed lower rates of response among older and female respondents.

The survey asked three questions to ascertain respondents' migration intentions. First, respondents were asked whether they were considering migrating to another state within the next twelve months. This measure was derived from Gallup, Inc. and has been previously validated on cross-national samples (e.g., S. Migali and M. Scipioni, "A Global Analysis of Intentions to Migrate," European Commission, 2018, https://shorturl.at/bvEyd). Second, respondents were asked the name of the state to which they were considering migrating (intended destination). Finally, as a behavioral measure, respondents were asked whether they had made concrete preparations for a move, such as applying for a residency permit or visa or purchasing a ticket.

34. This was also true before the 2015–2016 asylum seeker crisis in Europe, according to 2013 data.

35. Prospective migrants were identified as those respondents who selected "yes" or "maybe," when asked whether they were considering moving to a different country in the next twelve months. Conclusions remain unchanged when excluding respondents who answered "maybe" from the analysis.

36. Due to the nature of the population I study, the prospective migrants I surveyed were neither transient migrants nor likely asylum seekers. For an analysis of asylum-seeker preferences, see A. Holland, M. Peters, and T. Sanchez, "Migrants' Destination Choices," Working Paper, 2018.

37. For the main analysis, I focus on all respondents who indicated that they were considering moving in the next twelve months. In the robustness checks, I limit the sample to those who indicated that they had made concrete plans, with similar results.

38. The Gallup World Poll is a large and globally representative survey administered annually across numerous countries.

39. Some analyses will have fewer observations due to missing values on certain indicators. The minimum number of observations is 108,204.

40. Recoded to 1/0, with 1 being most, many, or some are afraid, and 0 no one is afraid.

41. For economic well-being, I use respondents' self-reported employment status, whether they report having enough money to buy food in the last twelve months and to pay for their housing, whether they are getting by with their current income, whether they are satisfied with their standard of living, and whether their standard of living is getting better or worse. For exposure to crime or violence, I use whether respondents have been robbed of money or other property in the last twelve months and whether they have been assaulted or mugged.

42. These effects control for random effects by country, so differences are within-country.

43. This corresponds to a 10.4 percentage point increase in the *desire* to migrate to a foreign country.

44. This corresponds to a 0.37 percentage point increase in people reporting that they have *made plans* to migrate to a foreign country within the next twelve months.

45. Gallup asks: "Have you done any of the following in the past month? How about donated money to a charity? How about volunteered your time to an organization? How about helped a stranger or someone you didn't know who needed help?" If I scale these three indicators (0 to 1) across 120 countries, people considering their departure to another country score, on average, 0.02 points higher. Nonmigrants report a 0.41 score, while those prospective migrants report a 0.43 score. This civic engagement index is virtually uncorrelated with people's views of democracy.

46. R. King, "Theories and Typologies of Migration: An Overview and a Primer," *Willy Brandt Series of Working Papers in International Migration and Ethnic Relations* 3, no. 12 (2012): 1–43; E. Thielemann, "The Effectiveness of Governments' Attempts to Control Unwanted Migration," in *Immigration and the Transformation of Europe*, ed. C. A. Parsons and T. M. Smeeding, 442–472 (Cambridge: Cambridge University Press, 2008); A. Mayda, "International Migration: A Panel Data Analysis of the Determinants of Bilateral Flows," *Journal of Population Economics* 23, no. 4 (2010): 1249–1274; S. Castles, H. de Haas, and M. Miller, *The Age of Migration: International Population Movements in the Modern World*, 5th ed. (New York: Guilford Press, 2013); M. Van Der Velde and T. Van Naerssen, *Mobility and Migration Choices: Threshold to Crossing Borders* (London: Routledge, 2015); P. James and L. Mayblin, "Factors Influencing Asylum Destination Choice: A Review of the Evidence," University of Sheffield Working Papers No. 04/16.1, 2016.

47. Larry Sjaastad, "The Costs and Returns on Human Migration," *Journal of Political Economy* 70, no. 5 (1962): 80–93; John Harris and Michael Todaro, "Migration, Unemployment and Development: A Two-Sector Analysis," *American Economic Review* 60, no. 1 (1970): 126–142.

48. Oded Stark and David Bloom, "The New Economics of Labor Migration," *American Economic Review* 75, no. 2 (1985): 173–178; J. E. Taylor,

"Undocumented Mexico–U.S. Migration and the Returns to Households in Rural Mexico," *American Journal of Agricultural Economics* 69, no. 3 (1987): 616–638; Giacomo De Giorgi and Michele Pellizzari, "Welfare Migration in Europe," *Labour Economics* 16, no. 4 (2008): 353–363; W. Geis, S. Uebelmesser, and M. Werding, "How Do Migrants Choose Their Destination Country? An Analysis of Institutional Determinants," *Review of International Economics* 21, no. 5 (2013): 825–840.

49. A. Abreu, "The New Economics of Labor Migration: Beware of Neoclassicals Bearing Gifts," *Forum for Social Economics* 41, no. 1 (2012): 46–67.

50. For the US see: George Borjas, "Immigration and Welfare Magnets," *Journal of Labour Economics* 17, no. 4 (1999): 607–637. But more recently see T. Boeri, "Immigration to the Land of Redistribution," *Economica* 77, no. 308 (2010): 651–687; O. Agersnap, A. S. Jensen, and H. Kleven, "The Welfare Magnet Hypothesis: Evidence from an Immigrant Welfare Scheme in Denmark," Report No. w26454, National Bureau of Economic Research, 2019. For Europe see: G. P. Freeman, "Migration and the Political Economy of the Welfare State," *Annals of the American Academy of Political and Social Science* 485 (1986): 51–63; Nicolas Péridy, "Welfare Magnets, Border Effects or Policy Regulations: What Determinants Drive Migration Flows into the EU," *Global Economy Journal* 6, no. 4 (2006): 1–35; Thierry Warin and Pavel Svaton, "European Migration: Welfare Migration or Economic Migration," *Global Economy Journal* 8, no. 3 (2008): 1–30; De Giorgi and Pellizzari 2008.

51. P. B. Levine and D. J. Zimmerman, "An Empirical Analysis of the Welfare Magnet Debate Using the NLSY," *Journal of Population Economics* 12, no. 3 (1999): 391–409; S. W. Allard and S. Danziger, "Welfare Magnets: Myth or Reality?" *Journal of Politics* 62, no. 2 (2000): 350–368.

52. H. Brücker, G. S. Epstein, B. McCormick, G. Saint-Paul, A. Venturini, and C. Zimermann, "Managing Migration in the European Welfare State," in *Immigration Policy and the Welfare System*, ed. T. Boeri, G. Hanson, and B. McCormick, 1–167 (Oxford: Oxford University Press, 2002); P. J. Pedersen, M. Pytlikova, and N. Smith, "Selection and Network Effects: Migration Flows into OECD Countries 1990–2000," *European Economic Review* 52, no. 7 (2008): 1160–1186.

53. Douglas Massey, "Social Structure, Household Strategies, and the Cumulative Causation of Migration," *Population Index* 56, no. 1 (1990): 3–26; Douglas Massey and Felipe Garcia España, "The Social Process of International Migration," *Science* 237, no. 4816 (1987): 733–738.

54. M. B. Aguilera and Douglas Massey, "Social Capital and the Wages of Mexican Migrants: New Hypotheses and Tests," *Social Forces* 82, no. 2 (2003): 671–701; Kavian Munshi, "Networks in the Modern Economy: Mexican Migrants in the U.S. Labor Market," *Quarterly Journal of Economics* 118, no. 2 (2003): 549–599; Anita Drever and Onno Hoffmeister, "Immigrants and Social Networks in a Job-Scarce Environment: The Case of Germany," *International Migration Review* 42, no. 2 (2008): 425–448.

55. Alejandro Portes and M. Zhou, "The New Second Generation: Segmented Assimilation and Its Variants," *The Annals of the American Academy*

of Political and Social Science 530, no. 1 (1993): 74–96; K. Korinek, B. Entwisle, and A. Jampaklay, "Through Thick and Thin: Layers of Social Ties and Urban Settlement among Thai Migrants," *American Sociological Review* 70, no. 5 (2005): 779–800.

56. Fitzgerald et al. 2014.
57. H. Crawley, *Chance or Choice? Understanding Why Asylum Seekers Come to the UK* (London: Refugee Council, 2010); Albert O. Hirschman, "Exit, Voice, and the State," *World Politics* 31, no. 1 (1978): 90–107.
58. Imran Arif, "The Determinants of International Migration: Unbundling the Role of Economic, Political and Social Institutions," *World Economy* 43, no. 6 (2020): 1699–1729.
59. For corruption see: Poprawe 2015; Hiskey et al. 2014. Andreas Etling, Leonie Backeberg, and Jochen Tholen, "The Political Dimension of Young People's Migration Intentions: Evidence from the Arab Mediterranean Region," *Journal of Ethnic and Migration Studies* 46, no. 7 (2020): 1388–1404. For discrimination see: T. Iosifides, M. Lavrentiadou, E. Petracou, and A. Kontis, "Forms of Social Capital and the Incorporation of Albanian Immigrants in Greece," *Journal of Ethnic and Migration Studies* 33, no. 8 (2007): 1343–1361; R. Henry, "Does Racism Affect a Migrant's Choice of Destination? A Case Study of African Americans, 1995–2000," Paper presented at 10th European Summer Symposium in Labour Economics, IZA, Buch, Germany, October 8–12, 2008. Nabamita Dutta and Sanjukta Roy, "Do Potential Skilled Emigrants Care about Political Stability at Home?" *Review of Development Economics* 15, no. 3 (2011): 442–457.
60. J. Carling, "Migration in the Age of Involuntary Immobility: Theoretical Reflections and Cape Verdean Experiences," *Journal of Ethnic and Migration Studies* 28, no. 1 (2002): 5–42; J. Carling, "Emigration, Return and Development in Cape Verde: The Impact of Closing Borders," *Population, Space and Place* 10, no. 2 (2004): 113–132; H. De Haas, "Migration and Development: A Theoretical Perspective," *International Migration Review* 44, no. 1 (2010): 227–264.
61. V. Guiraudon and C. Joppke, "Controlling a New Migration World," in *Controlling a New Migration World*, ed. V. Guiraudon and C. Joppke, 13–40 (London: Routledge, 2003); Boucher and Gest 2018.
62. J. Carling and K. Schewel, "Revisiting Aspiration and Ability in International Migration," *Journal of Ethnic and Migration Studies*, 44, no. 6 (2018): 945–963. Recently, several studies have sought to address this issue by surveying prospective migrants prior to their departure. Although not all individuals surveyed within the sending state will successfully complete a move, measuring these initial preferences more accurately indicates the considerations that *motivate* prospective migrants. Following this logic, in the studies cited earlier, Gallup, Inc. solicits interest in emigration and respondents' preferred destination across their international polls (Esipova et al. 2011). A similar effort motivated the EUMAGINE project (K. Hemmerechts, H. M. De Clerck, R. Willems, and C. Timmerman, "Project Paper 14: Eumagine Final Report with Policy Considerations," EUMAGINE, 2014), which triangulated qualitative and quantitative evidence among prospective migrants in Morocco, Senegal,

Turkey, and Ukraine to ascertain their relative appraisals of conditions in home states versus perceptions of life in the European Union.

63. James and Mayblin 2016; J. Gest and A. Boucher, "A Segmented Theory of Immigration Regimes," *Polity* 53, no. 3 (2021), 439–468.

64. Daron Acemoglu, Suresh Naidu, Pascual Restrepo, and James A. Robinson, "Democracy Does Cause Growth," *Journal of Political Economy* 127, no. 1 (2019): 47–100; Quan-Jing Wang, Gen-Fu Feng, Hai-Jie Wang, and Chun-Ping Chang, "The Impacts of Democracy on Innovation: Revisited Evidence," *Technovation* 108 (2021): 102333; Thierry Baudassé, Rémi Bazillier, and Ismaël Issifou, "Migration and Institutions: Exit and Voice (from Abroad)?" *Journal of Economic Surveys* 32, no. 3 (2018): 727–766.

65. A compounding issue is that not all possible configurations of pull factors are visible within observational data. As a result, it is difficult to separate correlated national characteristics within a standard regression framework.

66. J. Hainmueller, D. J. Hopkins, and T. Yamamoto, "Causal Inference in Conjoint Analysis: Understanding Multidimensional Choices via Stated Preference Experiments," *Political Analysis* 22, no. 1 (2014): 1–30.

67. Y. Horiuchi, Z. D. Markovich, and T. Yamamoto, "Can Conjoint Analysis Mitigate Social Desirability Bias?" Working Paper, 2018.

68. J. Hainmueller, D. Hangartner, and T. Yamamoto, "Validating Vignette and Conjoint Survey Experiments against Real-World Behavior," *Proceedings of the National Academy of Sciences* 112, no. 8 (2015): 2395–2400.

69. J. Hainmueller and D. Hopkins, "Public Attitudes toward Immigration," *Annual Review of Political Science* 17, no. 1 (2014): 225–249; K. Clayton, J. Ferwerda, and Y. Horiuchi, "Exposure to Immigration and Admission Preferences: Evidence from France," *Political Behavior* 43 (2018): 1–26.

70. K. Bansak, J. Hainmueller, and D. Hangartner, "How Economic, Humanitarian, and Religious Concerns Shape European Attitudes toward Asylum Seekers," *Science* 354, no. 6309 (2016): 217–222; C. L. Adida, A. Lo, and M. Platas, "Engendering Empathy, Begetting Backlash: American Attitudes towards Syrian Refugees," Working Paper, 2017.

71. M. Wright, M. Levy, and J. Citrin, "Public Attitudes toward Immigration Policy across the Legal/Illegal Divide: The Role of Categorical and Attribute-Based Decision-Making," *Political Behavior* 38 (2016): 229–253.

72. The number of conjoint tables respondents viewed varied across countries, due to constraints on survey length. Respondents were asked to complete three conjoint tasks in Jordan, the Palestinian Territories, and Tunisia, and two in Lebanon and Libya.

73. See Hainmueller et al. 2014. In conjoint analysis, the marginal effect is referred to as the AMCE (average marginal component effect) and is averaged across the joint distribution of other attributes. In the design here, the R package *cjoint* estimates AMCEs. However, in cases where the conjoint design is unconstrained (attribute levels are fully independent), the coefficients can be estimated by regressing the outcome on a set of dummy variables for each characteristic.

I focus on the period after arrival, given observed variation in welfare rights across receiving states (see "Migrant Access to Social Security and Healthcare:

Policies and Practice," European Migration Network, 2014). The majority of states in the Organisation for Economic Co-operation and Development extend welfare benefits shortly after migrant arrival or upon receiving permanent residency; a smaller subset condition welfare rights on citizenship (S. W. Goodman, *Immigration and Membership Politics in Western Europe* (New York: Cambridge University Press, 2014)); S. W. Goodman and G. C. Baldi, "Migrants into Members: Social Rights Civic Requirements, and Citizenship in Western Europe," *West European Politics* 38, no. 6 (2015): 1152–1173. Given that eventual welfare access remains a possibility within the universe of destination states, I do not query whether respondents would migrate to a country in which such rights were permanently withheld.

This measure proxies the presence of communities that could ease transition within a destination country. However, it does not directly account for a personal relationship between the respondent and someone in the destination country. Pretesting a personal relationship measure revealed confusion among the set of respondents who indicated they did not have relatives abroad.

74. The survey design varies five characteristics for each country, each of which randomly takes one of two values. I limit variation to binary options for two reasons. First, since the number of prospective migrants within each country was unknown a priori, a conservative design was necessary to maximize statistical power. Second, given the diversity across my cross-national sample, mapping responses to binary extremes (i.e., liberal democracy versus autocracy) increases the probability that the design will be evaluated consistently across national samples. More subtle gradations, such as the relative strength of democracy or the difference between a "high" and "medium" unemployment rate, would likely be interpreted differently depending on respondents' context-specific experiences.

75. Although potential destinations vary along additional dimensions than those tested here, my design intentionally restricts the scope of such variation. Since the pool of real-world countries is limited, over-specificity would encourage respondents to link hypothetical countries with a single real-world example or, alternately, present an implausible combination of country characteristics. Either possibility would undermine the comparability of estimates across country pairs. In addition, constraining the number of characteristics limits the cognitive demands imposed on survey respondents, who may be unfamiliar with conjoint survey tasks.

76. Interestingly, these pull factors were stronger among nonmigrants within the larger national samples. Compared to prospective migrants, nonmigrants rated hypothetical profiles with co-ethnics higher by 0.12 points ($t = 2.34$) and profiles that were geographically proximate higher by 0.15 points ($t = 2.91$) on the 7-point rating scale.

77. G. Fagiolo and G. Santoni, "Revisiting the Role of Migrant Social Networks as Determinants of International Migration Flows," *Applied Economics Letters* 23, no. 3 (2016): 188–193.

78. For overviews of rights regimes, see Michael Fix and Jeffrey Passel, "The Scope and Impact of Welfare Reform's Immigrant Provisions," Urban Institute,

2002; E. Koning, "The Real and Perceived Economics of Immigration: Welfare Chauvinism and Immigrants' Use of Government Transfers in Twelve Countries," Working Paper, 2011; D. Sainsbury, *Welfare States and Immigrant Rights: The Politics of Inclusion and Exclusion* (Oxford: Oxford University Press, 2012).

79. The inclusion of these additional items was not possible in other surveys due to space constraints imposed by my institutional partner. Due to similar constraints, questions concerning other conjoint attributes were not asked.

80. US Department of Health and Human Services Office of the Assistant Secretary for Planning and Evaluation, "Overview of Immigrants' Eligibility for SNAP, TANF, Medicaid, and CHIP," March 26, 2012.

3 OUTVOTED, VOTING OUT

1. "Basic Law Chapter I – General Principles," Government of the Hong Kong Special Administrative Region of the People's Republic of China, www .basiclaw.gov.hk/en/basiclaw/chapter1.html.

2. "Hong Kong National Security Law: What Is It and Is It Worrying?", *BBC*, June 28, 2022, www.bbc.com/news/world-asia-china-52765838.

3. James Griffiths, "The Return of Hong Kong's Umbrella Movement," *CNN*, June 12, 2019, www.cnn.com/2019/06/12/asia/hong-kong-umbrella-extradition-intl-hnk/index.html.

4. This and the following quotes were reported by Griffiths 2019.

5. "Hong Kong National Security Law" 2022.

6. Sum Lok-kei, "Fighting an Exodus, Hong Kong Faces a Tough Task to Lure Back Young People," *The Guardian*, November 23, 2022.

7. Gao Feng and Liam Scott, "Hong Kong Exodus May Threaten City's Global Financial Status," *Voice of America News*, August 19, 2022.

8. "Hong Kong: UK Makes Citizenship Offer to Residents," *BBC*, July 1, 2020, www.bbc.com/news/uk-politics-53246899.

9. Lok-kei 2022.

10. Kanis Leung and Zen Soo, "Hong Kong Offers New Visa to Woo Talent amid Brain Drain," Associated Press, October 19, 2022.

11. Cheng Yut Yiu, "State Media Calls on Hong Kong to Compensate for Tide of Emigration," *Radio Free Asia*, August 30, 2021, www.rfa.org/english/news/ china/emigrate-08302021135106.html.

12. Kelly Ho, "Hong Kong Security Chief Hails 100% Conviction Rate in National Security Cases," *Hong Kong Free Press*, April 14, 2023.

13. Vivian Wang and Joy Dong, "Hong Kong Is Holding Elections: It Wants Them to Look Real," *New York Times*, September 24, 2021, www.nytimes .com/2021/09/24/world/asia/hong-kong-elections.html.

14. Ronald Skeldon, "Emigration and the Future of Hong Kong," *Pacific Affairs* 63, no. 4 (1990): 500–523.

15. Wong Siu-lun, "Emigration and Stability in Hong Kong," *Asian Survey* 32, no. 10 (1992): 918–33.

16. All data in this paragraph is reported by Siu-lun 1992.

17. Joseph Cheng, "The Tiananmen Incident and the Pro-democracy Movement in Hong Kong," *China Perspectives* 2, no. 78 (2009): 91–100.
18. All data in this paragraph is reported by ibid.
19. Skeldon 1990.
20. Cheng 2009.
21. Brian Hook, "Political Change in Hong Kong," *The China Quarterly* 136 (1993): 840–863.
22. Siu-lun 1992.
23. The politicized nature of Hong Kongers is further corroborated by Pei-te Lien, "Pre-emigration Socialization, Transnational Ties, and Political Participation across the Pacific: A Comparison among Immigrants from China, Taiwan, and Hong Kong," *Journal of East Asian Studies* 10, no. 3 (2010): 453–482.
24. Siu-lun 1992.
25. Anton Troianovski, "Putin Assails Russians Who Back the West, Signaling More Repression," *New York Times*, March 16, 2022, www.nytimes .com/2022/03/16/world/europe/putin-russia-ukraine-protests.html.
26. Ibid.
27. Anton Troianovski, "Spurred by Putin, Russians Turn on One Another over the War," *New York Times*, April 10, 2022.
28. Ibid.
29. "Russians Have Emigrated in Huge Numbers since the War in Ukraine," *The Economist*, August 23, 2023.
30. Dimitar Bechev, "Hedging Its Bets: Serbia between Russia and the EU," Carnegie Europe, January 19, 2023.
31. Christopher Jasper and Misha Savic, "Russians Have a Secret Escape Hatch to Europe – Serbia," *Fortune*, March 11, 2022, https://fortune .com/2022/03/11/russia-secret-escape-hatch-to-europe-air-serbia/.
32. Ibid.
33. Milica Stojanovic, "Russian Flights Tickets to Serbia, Turkey, Sell Out after Mobilization," Balkan Insight, September 21, 2022.
34. Marko Lopušina and Dušan Lopušina, eds., *Hotel MOSKVA – prvih 100 godina* (Belgrade: Hotel Moskva, 2008).
35. P. Robinson, "The White Russian Army in Exile, 1920–1941," PhD thesis, University of Oxford, 1999; Jovana Babović, "Political, Social, and Personal: The Encounters of the Russian Emigration in Yugoslavia, 1921–1941," *Serbian Studies: Journal of the North American Society for Serbian Studies* 21, no. 1 (2007): 1–36.
36. "Russians Founded More than 300 Companies in Serbia since the Beginning of the War in Ukraine," Maj Novsitad, April 2, 2022.
37. Colin Barry, K. Chad Clay, Michael E. Flynn, and Gregory Robinson, "Freedom of Foreign Movement, Economic Opportunities Abroad, and Protest in Non-Democratic Regimes," *Journal of Peace Research* 51, no. 5 (2014): 574–588, p. 575.
38. Alan Dowty, "Emigration and Expulsion in the Third World," *Third World Quarterly* 8, no. 1 (1986): 155–165; Sigrid Faath and Hanspeter Mattes, "Political Conflicts and Migration in the MENA States," in *Migration from the Middle East and North Africa to Europe: Past Developments, Current*

Status, and Future Potentials, ed. Michael Bommes, Heinz Fassmann, and Wiebke Sievers, 159–190 (Amsterdam University Press, 2014), 180; Eghosa Osaghae, "Exiting from the State in Nigeria," *African Journal of Political Science/Revue Africaine de Science Politique* 4, no. 1 (1999): 83–98, p. 84.

39. Jonathan Hiskey and Diana Orces, "Transition Shocks and Emigration Profiles in Latin America," *The Annals of the American Academy of Political and Social Science* 630 (2010): 116–136, p. 120.
40. Ibid., p. 122.
41. This research component is based on my co-authored working paper, Justin Gest, Lucas Núñez, and Jeremy Ferwerda, "Democratic Drain: Migration and Democratic Deconsolidation," Working Paper, 2025.
42. To select a bandwidth of time around each election for our analysis, I relied on the Imbens–Kalyanaraman optimal bandwidth, which equals 81 days for our data. Guido Imbens and Karthik Kalyanaraman, "Optimal Bandwidth Choice for the Regression Discontinuity Estimator," *The Review of Economic Studies* 79, no. 3 (2012): 933–959.

    Figure C.4 shows estimates from the main specification, but using alternative time bands around the elections, from 30 days to 210 days, by additions of 15 days. When focusing on the Polity Index and the Polyarchy Index, my findings are robust to timeframes of up to 120 days before and after the election, although polyarchy results become marginally nonstatistically significant around the 120-day mark. In the case of the Liberal Democracy Index, the results are robust to even longer timeframes. Overall, these results suggest that our 81-day window around an election selected by optimal Imbens–Kalyanaraman bandwidths are robust to alternative bandwidths. It is important to note here that longer time bands are not advisable, since the salience of the election itself is likely to diminish over time and other upcoming elections (at the national, regional, provincial, or local levels) are likely to overlap, limiting the comparability between the before and after election periods.

43. To determine whether the 305 elections under consideration shift governments in a democratic or authoritarian direction, I consult three alternative measures of democracy, the Polyarchy Index and the Liberal Democracy Index from the Varieties of Democracy (V-Dem) dataset, and the Polity score. Measures of democratic consolidation from these data are built as a "donut hole" change in the corresponding variable over time:

$$Consol_{c,t} = Dem_{c,t+1} - Dem_{c,t-1}$$

Where $Consol_{c,t}$ is the measure of consolidation/deconsolidation for country c in year t (an election year); $Dem_{c,t+1}$ is a measure of democracy in country c in year $t + 1$ (the year after the election); and $Dem_{c,t-1}$ is a measure of democracy in country c in year $t - 1$ (the year before the election). I use this "donut hole" change measure rather than year-on-year change in democracy measures because: (1) it is not clear, in general, whether the year of the election can be appropriately considered as a measure of "before" or "after"; and (2) it may take at least a few months for any democratic consolidating or deconsolidating measures to take effect following an election. Examining the

resulting changes in scores, I can discern when countries become more democratic (consolidate) or less democratic (deconsolidate).

As an additional robustness check, I also build three indices of consoli-
dation/deconsolidation based on the extent of anti-pluralism in the lower
chamber of the country's legislature, the party of the head of government,
and the government parties. To measure party anti-pluralism I rely on the
anti-pluralism index at the party level from the Varieties of Party Identity
and Organization (V-Party). The measure of anti-pluralism in the lower
chamber is based on the average of party-level anti-pluralism weighted by
each party's seat share. The measure of anti-pluralism in the government
parties is the average of party-level anti-pluralism for parties in government,
weighted by their seat share in the lower chamber. To measure consolidation
and deconsolidation from these data, I calculate the change in the indices of
anti-pluralism relative to the previous election.

44. The pre-election baseline for consolidating and deconsolidating countries differ depending on the measure of consolidation being used. This is
because the three measures of democracy differ from each other and thus
there are some differences in which countries each measure considers to be
consolidating or deconsolidating.

45. To produce estimates, the deconsolidating value was set to a −0.3-point
drop and consolidating at a 0.3-point rise. The main estimates are based in
the following model:

$$Migrate_{i,i[t]} = \alpha + \beta_1 Post_{c[i],t} + \beta_2 Consol_{c[i],t} + \delta Post_{c[i],t} \times Consol_{c[i],t}$$
$$+ \tau_t + \alpha_{c[i]} + \varepsilon_{i[t]}.$$

Where *Migrate* is a binary indicator for respondents' desire to migrate, *Post*
is an indicator for the post-election period, *Consol* is a measure of democratic consolidation/deconsolidation, τ_t are random effects by year, and $\alpha_{c[i]}$
are random effects by country. The main coefficient of interest is δ, which
measures the extent to which changes in migration desires between before
and after the election are related to the extent of democratic consolidation or
deconsolidation around said election.

A large variety of robustness checks are present in the results, including
fixed effects rather than random effects; random effects by election rather
than by country and year; longer and smaller time bands around the elections; samples limited to countries and elections in which respondents in the
same Gallup wave were interviewed both before and after the election; samples excluding respondents interviewed between rounds of an election.

46. As shown in Appendix C, the results hold if using alternative time bands
around the election both shorter and longer than ninety days; when studying plans to migrate rather than desire to migrate; when using a dummy
variable that indicates whether a country is consolidating or not; when limiting the sample exclusively to elections in which respondents were interviewed both before and after the election; when excluding respondents who
are interviewed in between two elections held within three months of each
other; when utilizing fixed effects by country and year rather than random
effects; and when utilizing random effects by election. Additionally, these

results are also robust to measuring consolidation and deconsolidation based on the level of anti-pluralism in the lower chamber of the legislature, the parties in government, and the party of the head of government.

47. Barry et al. 2014, p. 584.

4 THE SLIDING SCALE

1. See Lasse Skytt, *Orbánland: Why Viktor Orbán's Hungary Matters* (Williamstown, MA: New Europe Books, 2021); Paul Lendvai, *Orbán: Europe's New Strongman* (London: Hurst, 2019).

2. I interviewed eighteen prospective emigrants from Hungary (seven women, five men) and Serbia (four women, two men) between April 10 and 14, 2022. Subjects were encountered on the street or recruited via social media outreach in advance. In all interviews, I used a standardized topic guide and an unstandardized, conversational approach in order to reassure respondents during discussions that lasted between forty minutes and two hours. Questions included:

   Are you planning to emigrate? Have you made any preparations, did you buy any tickets? Did you start to look at jobs abroad? What are your next steps? Where do you want to move? Why do you want to leave?

   When did you decide that you want to leave? What changed after the elections? Why didn't you decide before? Do you think if the elections went in another direction than you would stay in Hungary? Are you politically active?

   What do you think about the state of democracy in Hungary? Who else do you think will move abroad?

   What happens to the people who are left behind?

3. For full details, see Dominic Spadacene, "Orban Has Begun Taking Steps to Preserve His Power," *EURACTIV*, May 5, 2021.

4. "World Population Prospects 2019," United Nations Department of Economic and Social Affairs Population Division, 2019.

5. Mark Rice-Oxley and Jennifer Rankin, "Europe's South and East Worry More about Emigration than Immigration – Poll," *The Guardian*, March 31, 2019.

6. For example, Romania's population dropped by almost 10 percent in the decade after its accession by the European Union. The main reasons these principally working-age Romanians depart relate to poor living standards and few job opportunities, but also frustrations with corruption. See Rice-Oxley and Rankin 2019; see also Justina Alexandra Sava, "Main Reasons Why Young People Decide to Leave Romania in 2019," Statista Research Department, 2019, www.statista.com/statistics/1103824/reasons-to-leave-romania/.

7. This is also true in a number of Western European states including Austria, Denmark, Germany, Italy, the Netherlands, Spain, and Sweden.

8. After the sample was obtained, respondent characteristics were statistically calibrated to be representative of national populations using standard survey adjustment procedures based on each country's population distribution on gender, age, occupation, region, and population density.

9. An additive scale was constructed of the following items which were reverse coded so that higher levels of agreement (strongly agree) were coded as 4 and lower levels of agreement (strongly disagree) as 1. The entire scale was then rescaled between 0 and 1, where 0 indicates the lowest observed value and 1 the highest: (1) Before making decisions, the government of [country] should consult religious leaders. (2) It is better to have a strong, unelected leader than a weak leader who is elected by the people. (3) The government of [country] should comply with the interests of the majority, even if this comes at the expense of ethnic and religious minority groups' civil rights. (4) The government of [country] should be empowered to prosecute members of the news media who make offensive or unpatriotic statements. (5) The government of [country] should be empowered to remove judges when their decisions go against the national interest.

10. To be clear, unlike vote shares – which are limited to people who report voting – I measure favorability among nonvoters as well. These scores are less predictable. While in some cases ruling parties are viewed favorably in a manner that reflects their vote share, in other cases ruling parties' favorability scores are lower than their counterparts in the opposition. This may reflect the burden of being in government, but also local subjectivities.

11. Kelemen 2020; Lim 2023; Y. Giesing and F. Schikora, "Emigrants' Missing Votes," *European Journal of Political Economy* 78 (2023): 102398; Auer and Schaub 2024; Dancygier et al. 2025.

12. L. Chauvet and M. Mercier, "Do Return Migrants Transfer Political Norms to their Origin Country? Evidence from Mali," *Journal of Comparative Economics* 42, no. 3 (2014): 630–651. Also see C. Pérez-Armendáriz and D. Crow, "Do Migrants Remit Democracy? International Migration, Political Beliefs, and Behavior in Mexico," *Comparative Political Studies* 43, no. 1 (2010): 119–148.

13. However, no significant differences were found regarding trust in domestic institutions, domestic political engagement, or national voting behaviors. See R. Careja and P. Emmenegger, "Making Democratic Citizens: The Effects of Migration Experience on Political Attitudes in Central and Eastern Europe," *Comparative Political Studies* 45, no. 7 (2012): 875–902.

14. And according to the World Bank post, four situations account for over two thirds of these returns – Afghanistan following the withdrawal of Soviet troops in 1989 and the collapse of the Taliban regime in 2001; Rwanda immediately after the 1994 genocide and following the entry of Rwandan troops in Zaire; Iraq after the 1991 Gulf War; and Mozambique after peace was concluded in the early 1990s. See Kara Ross Camarena, "Repatriation during Conflict: A Signaling Analysis," *World Development* 158 (2022): 105960; Xavier Devictor, "Toward a Path to Sustainable Refugee Return," World Bank Blog, November 13, 2023, https://blogs.worldbank.org/en/dev4peace/toward-path-sustainable-refugee-return.

15. "Figures at a Glance: 117.3 Million People Worldwide were Forcibly Displaced," UNHCR, 2024, www.unhcr.org/about-unhcr/who-we-are/figures-glance.

16. European Commission, "A Humane and Effective Return and Readmission Policy," Migration and Home Affairs, n.d.

17. J. J. Azose and A. E. Raftery, "Estimation of Emigration, Return Migration, and Transit Migration between All Pairs of Countries," *Proceedings of the National Academy of Sciences* 116, no. 1 (2019): 116–122. But also see OECD Directorate for Employment, Labour and Social Affairs, Employment, Labour and Social Affairs Committee, "Return Migration: A New Perspective," September 17, 2008, https://one.oecd.org/document/ DELSA/ELSA/MI(2008)6/en/pdf.

18. C. Chen, A. Bernard, R. Rylee, and G. Abel, "Brain Circulation: The Educational Profile of Return Migrants," *Population Research and Policy Review* 41, no. 1 (2022): 387–399.

19. J. Wahba, "Return Migration and Economic Development," in *International Handbook on Migration and Economic Development*, ed. Robert E. B. Lucas, 327–349 (Northampton: Edward Elgar Publishing, 2014).

5 DEMOCRATIC GAIN

1. "Report of the Independent International Commission of Inquiry on the Syrian Arab Republic," United Nations Human Rights Council, August 9, 2018; Jessica Brandt and Robert L. McKenzie, "Addressing the Syrian Refugee Crisis," Brookings Institution, December 16, 2016.

2. By diaspora, I mean "a social collectivity that exists across state borders and that has succeeded over time to (1) sustain a collective national, cultural, or religious identity through a sense of internal cohesion and sustain ties with a real or imagined homeland and (2) display an ability to address the collective interests of members of the social collectivity through a developed internal organizational framework and transactional links." Fiona Adamson and Madeline Demetriou, "Remapping the Boundaries of 'State' and 'National Identity,'" *European Journal of International Relations* 13, no. 4 (2007): 489–526.

3. Georges 1990; Smith and Guarnizo 1998; Portes et al. 1999; Peggy Levitt, *The Transnational Villagers* (Berkeley: University of California Press, 2001); Nina Glick Schiller and Georges Eugene Fouron, *Georges Woke Up Laughing: Long Distance Nationalism and the Search for Home* (Durham, NC: Duke University Press, 2001); Michael Jones-Correa, *Between Two Nations: The Political Predicament of Latinos in New York City* (Cornell, NY: Cornell University Press, 1998); Luis Eduardo Guarnizo, Alejandro Portes, and William Haller, "Assimilation and Transnationalism: Determinants of Transnational Political Action among Contemporary Migrants," *American Journal of Sociology* 108, no. 6 (2003): 1211–1248.

4. For example, Connor 2001; Kaldor 1999; Kaldor and Muro 2003; Levitt and de la Dehesa 2003; Kostovicova and Prestreshi 2010; Lyons and Mandaville 2012; Østergaard-Nielsen 2012.

5. Benedict Anderson, *The Spectre of Comparisons: Nationalism, Southeast Asia, and the World* (New York: Verso, 1998); Margaret E. Keck and Kathryn Sikkink, *Activists beyond Borders: Advocacy Networks in International Politics* (Ithaca, NY: Cornell University Press, 1998); Gabriel Sheffer,

Diaspora Politics: At Home Abroad (New York: Cambridge University Press, 2003); Paul Hockenos, *Homeland Calling: Exile Patriotism and the Balkan Wars* (Ithaca, NY: Cornell University Press, 2003); Roger Waldinger and David Fitzgerald, "Transnationalism in Question," *American Journal of Sociology* 109, no. 5 (2004): 1177–1195; Sidney Tarrow, *The New Transnational Activism* (New York: Cambridge University Press, 2005); Anderson 2006.

6. C. Pérez-Armendáriz and D. Crow, "Do Migrants Remit Democracy? International Migration, Political Beliefs, and Behavior in Mexico," *Comparative Political Studies* 43, no. 1 (2010): 119–148, p. 120. Also see A. Escribà-Folch, C. Meseguer, and J. Wright, *Migration and Democracy: How Remittances Undermine Dictatorships* (Princeton, NJ: Princeton University Press, 2020).

7. Keck and Sikkink 1998; Tarrow 2005.

8. Hazel Smith and Paul Stares, *Diasporas in Conflict: Peace-Makers or Peace-Wreckers?* (New York: United Nations University Press, 2007); Camilla Orjuela, "Distant Warriors, Distant Peace Workers? Multiple Diaspora Roles in Sri Lanka's Violent Conflict," *Global Networks* 8, no. 4 (2008): 436–452.

9. N. Van Hear, *New Diasporas: The Mass Exodus, Dispersal and Regrouping of Migrant Communities* (London: UCL Press, 1998); N. Van Hear, "Sustaining Societies under Strain: Remittances as a Form of Transnational Exchange in Sri Lanka and Ghana," in *New Approaches to Migration? Transnational Communities and the Transformation of Home*, ed. Nadje al-Ali and Khalid Koser, 202–223 (London: Routledge, 2002); Y. Shain, *Marketing the American Creed Abroad: Diasporas in the US and Their Homelands* (New York: Cambridge University Press, 1999); Spillembergo 2009; Maria Koinova, "Diasporas and Democratization in the Post-Communist World," *Communist & Post-Communist Studies* 42, no. 1 (2009): 41–64; Maria Koinova, "Can Conflict-Generated Diasporas Be Moderate Actors during Episodes of Contested Sovereignty? Lebanese and Albanian Diasporas Compared," *Review of International Studies* 37, no. 1 (2011b): 437–462.

10. N. Nyberg-Sørensen, N. Van Hear, and P. Engberg-Pedersen, "The Migration–Development Nexus: Evidence and Policy Options," *International Migration* 40, no. 5 (2002): 49–73; D. Kapur, "Remittances: The New Development Mantra?" United Nations Conference on Trade and Development, April 2004, https://unctad.org/system/files/official-document/gdsmdpbg2420045_en.pdf; Jennifer Brinkerhoff, ed., *Diasporas and Development* (Boulder, CO: Lynne Rienner, 2008); A. Escribà-Folch, C. Meseguer, and J. Wright, "Remittances and Democratization," *International Studies Quarterly* 59, no. 3 (2015): 571–586.

11. Y. Shain, "The Role of Diasporas in Conflict Perpetuation and Resolution," *SAIS Review* 22, no. 2 (2002): 115–144; Y. Shain and Ravinatha P. Aryasinha, "Spoilers or Catalysts? The Role of Diasporas in Peace Processes," in *Challenges to Peacebuilding: Managing Spoilers during Conflict Resolution*, ed. Edward Newman and Oliver Richmond, 105–133 (Tokyo: United Nations University Press, 2006); B. Baser and A. Swain, "Diasporas as Peace-Makers: Third Party Mediation in Home-Land Politics," *International*

Journal on World Peace 25, no. 3 (2008): 7–28; F. Cochrane, B. Baser, and A. Swain, "Home Thoughts from Abroad: Diasporas and Peace-Building in Northern Ireland and Sri Lanka," *Studies in Conflict and Terrorism* 32, no. 8 (2009): 681–704; Maria Koinova, "Diasporas and Secessionist Conflicts: the Mobilization of the Armenian, Albanian and Chechen Diasporas," *Ethnic and Racial Studies* 34, no. 2 (2011): 333–356.

12. Sanjeev Khagram, James V. Riker and Kathryn Sikkink, eds., *Restructuring World Politics: Transnational Social Movements, Networks, and Norms* (Minneapolis: University of Minnesota Press, 2002); Donatella della Porta and Sidney Tarrow, "Transnational Processes and Social Activism: An Introduction," in *Transnational Protest and Global Activism*, ed. Sidney Tarrow and Donatella della Porta, 1–17 (Lanham: Rowman & Littlefield, 2004); Clifford Bob, *The Marketing of Rebellion: Insurgents, Media and International Activism* (New York: Cambridge University Press, 2005); Lyons and Mandaville 2012.

13. Levitt 1998, p. 941.

14. Østergaard-Nielsen 2003; Spillembergo 2009, p. 35.

15. Goodman and Hiskey 2008. A contradictory finding emerges from Brazil, however. See Alexandre Gori Maia and Yao Lu, "Migration and Democratization in Brazil: The Case of Electoral Participation and Competition," *Demography* 58, no. 1 (2021): 191–217.

16. J. Itzigsohn and D. Villacrés, "Migrant Political Transnationalism and the Practice of Democracy: Dominican External Voting Rights and Salvadoran Home Town Associations," *Ethnic & Racial Studies* 31, no. 4 (2008): 664–686.

17. P. Tabar, "'Political Remittances': The Case of Lebanese Expatriates Voting in National Elections," *Journal of Intercultural Studies* 35, no. 4 (2014): 442–460.

18. Patrick J. Haney and Walt Vanderbush, "The Role of Ethnic Interest Groups in U.S. Foreign Policy: The Case of the Cuban American National Foundation," *International Studies Quarterly* 43, no. 2 (1999): 341–361; Koinova 2011; Fiona Adamson, "Mechanisms of Diaspora Mobilization and the Transnationalization of Civil War," in *Transnational Dynamics of Civil War*, ed. Jeffrey Checkel, 63–88 (Cambridge: Cambridge University Press, 2013); Sarah Wayland, "Ethnonationalist Networks and Transnational Opportunities: The Sri Lankan Tamil Diaspora," *Review of International Studies* 30, no. 3 (2004): 405–426; Fiona Adamson, "Globalization, Transnational Political Mobilization, and Networks of Violence," *Cambridge Review of International Affairs* 18, no. 1 (2005): 35–53; Koinova 2009; R. Bauböck and T. Faist, eds., *Diaspora and Transnationalism: Concepts, Theories and Methods* (Amsterdam: Amsterdam University Press, 2010).

19. Espen Stokke and Eric Wieselhaus-Brahm, "Syrian Diaspora Mobilization: Vertical Coordination, Patronage Relations, and the Challenges of Fragmentation in the Pursuit of Transitional Justice," *Ethnic and Racial Studies* 42, no. 11 (2019): 1930–1949.

20. Shain 2002; Nadejda Marinova, *Ask What You Can Do For Your (New) Country: How Host States Use Diasporas* (Oxford, New York: Oxford University Press, 2017).

21. Elizabeth Mavroudi, "Deconstructing Diasporic Mobilisation at a Time of Crisis: Perspectives from the Palestinian and Greek Diasporas," *Journal of Ethnic and Migration Studies* 44, no. 13 (2017): 1–16.

22. C. Pérez-Armendáriz, "Cross-Border Discussions and Political Behavior in Migrant-Sending Countries," *Studies in Comparative International Development* 49, no. 1 (2014): 67–88.

23. Eva Østergaard-Nielsen, "Diasporas in World Politics," in *Non-State Actors in World Politics*, ed. D. Josselin and W. Wallace, 217–235 (New York: Palgrave, 2001); Laurie A. Brand, *Citizens Abroad: Emigration and the State in the Middle East and North Africa* (New York: Cambridge University Press, 2006).

24. Dana Moss, "Transnational Repression, Diaspora Mobilization, and the Case of the Arab Spring," *Social Problems* 63, no. 4 (2016): 480–498.

25. Eric Tucker, Didi Tang, and Nathan Ellgren, "As China and Iran Hunt for Dissidents in the US, the FBI is Racing to Counter the Threat," The Associated Press, May 6, 2024.

26. Ibid.

27. Ibid.

28. Al Jazeera Staff, "US Charges Indian Government Employee in Foiled Sikh Separatist Murder Plot," *Al Jazeera*, October 18, 2024.

29. Hank Johnston, "Talking the Walk: Speech Acts and Resistance in Authoritarian Regimes," in *Repression and Mobilization*, ed. C. Davenport, H. Johnston, and C. Mueller, 108–137 (Minneapolis: University of Minnesota Press, 2005); Steven Pfaff, "The Limits of Coercive Surveillance: Social and Penal Control in the German Democratic Republic," *Punishment & Society* 3, no. 3 (2001): 381–407.

30. Brand 2006.

31. Rowena Xiaoqing He, *Tiananmen Exiles: Voices of the Struggle for Democracy in China* (New York: Palgrave Macmillan, 2014); Waldinger and Fitzgerald 2004.

32. Moss 2016.

33. See Lilia Tapparova, "Putin Is Doing Something Almost Nobody Is Noticing," *The New York Times*, September 23, 2024.

34. R. Deibert, "Cyberspace under Siege," *Journal of Democracy* 26 no. 3 (2015): 64–78; M. Michaelsen and M. Glasius, "Authoritarian Practices in the Digital Age: Introduction," *International Journal of Communication* 12 (2018): 3788–3794.

35. C. Nyst and N. Monaco, "State-Sponsored Trolling: How Governments Are Deploying Disinformation as Part of Broader Digital Harassment Campaigns," Institute for the Future, Palo Alto, CA, July 19, 2018.

36. "'We Will Find You': A Global Look at How Governments Repress Nationals Abroad," Human Rights Watch, February 22, 2024.

37. K. Tertytchnaya, C. De Vries, H. Solaz, and D. Doyle, "When the Money Stops: Fluctuations in Financial Remittances and Incumbent Approval in Central Eastern Europe, the Caucasus and Central Asia," *American Political Science Review* 112, no. 4 (2018): 758–774.

38. T. Pfutze, "Does Migration Promote Democratization? Evidence from the Mexican Transition," *Journal of Comparative Economic* 40, no. 2 (2012): 159–175; F. Ahmed, "Remittances and Incumbency: Theory and Evidence," *Economics & Politics* 29, no. 1 (2017): 22–47; Escribà-Folch et al. 2015; Escribà-Folch et al. 2020.

39. Michael Miller and Margaret Peters, "Restraining the Huddled Masses: Migration Policy and Autocratic Survival," *British Journal of Political Science* 50, no. 2 (2020): 403–433.

40. Ahmed 2017; Germano 2013.

41. F. Ahmed, "The Perils of Unearned Foreign Income: Aid, Remittances, and Government Survival," *American Political Science Review* 106, no. 1 (2012): 146–165.

42. Ahmed 2012.

43. Amal Stefanos, "Eritrea's 'Diaspora Tax' is Funding Violence and Oppression," *Al Jazeera*, February 20, 2023.

44. Ibid.

45. E. Karakoç, T. Köse, and M. Özcan, "Emigration and the Diffusion of Political Salafism: Religious Remittances and Support for Salafi Parties in Egypt during the Arab Spring," *Party Politics* 23, no. 6 (2017): 731–745.

46. Y. Shain and A. Barth, "Diasporas and International Relations Theory," *International Organization* 57, no. 3 (2003): 449–479.

47. Sharon M. Quinsaat, *Insurgent Communities: How Protests Create a Filipino Diaspora* (Chicago: University of Chicago Press, 2024).

48. Shain 2002; Anderson 2006; Martin Sökefeld, "Mobilizing in Transnational Space," *Global Networks* 6, no. 3 (2006): 265–284; Smith and Stares 2007; Orjuela 2008; Maria Koinova, "Why Do Conflict-Generated Diasporas Pursue Sovereignty-Based Claims through State-Based or Transnational Channels? Armenian, Albanian and Palestinian Diasporas in the UK Compared," *European Journal of International Relations* 20, no. 4 (2014): 1043–1071.

49. Maria de la Luz Inclan, "From the ¡Ya Basta! to the Caracoles: Zapatista Mobilization under Transitional Conditions," *American Journal of Sociology* 113, no. 5 (2008): 1316–1350; Dana Moss, "Repression, Response, and Contained Escalation under 'Liberalized' Authoritarianism in Jordan," *Mobilization: An International Quarterly* 19, no. 3 (2014): 489–514.

50. Kaldor 1999; Ann Hironaka, *Neverending Wars: The International Community, Weak States, and the Perpetuation of Civil War* (Cambridge, MA: Harvard University Press, 2005); Erin Jenne, *Ethnic Bargaining: The Paradox of Minority Empowerment* (Ithaca, NY: Cornell University Press, 2007); Kristian Skrede Gleditsch, "Transnational Dimensions of Civil War," *Journal of Peace Research* 44, no. 3 (2007): 293–309; Idean Salehyan, *Rebels without Borders: Transnational Insurgencies in World Politics* (Ithaca, NY: Cornell University Press, 2009); Adamson 2013; B. Baser, *Diasporas and Homeland Conflicts: A Comparative Perspective* (Farnham: Ashgate, 2015); F. Cochrane, *Migration and Security in the Global Age: Diaspora Communities and Conflict* (London: Routledge, 2015); N. Van Hear and

R. Cohen, "Diasporas in Conflict: Distance, Contiguity and Spheres of Engagement," *Oxford Development Studies* 45, no. 2 (2017): 171–184.

51. Terrence Lyons, "Diasporas and Homeland Conflict," in *Territoriality and Conflict in an Era of Globalization*, ed. Miles Kahler and Barbara Walter, 111–131 (New York: Cambridge University Press, 2006); Orjuela 2008; Maria Koinova, "Four Types of Diaspora Mobilization: Albanian Diaspora Activism for Kosovo Independence in the US and the UK," *Foreign Policy Analysis* 9, no. 4 (2013): 433–453.

52. Jennifer Brinkerhoff, "Diasporas and Conflict Societies: Conflict Entrepreneurs, Competing Interests or Contributors to Stability and Development?" *Conflict, Security & Development* 11, no. 2 (2011): 115–143.

53. Hockenos 2003.

54. Koinova 2013; Maria Koinova, "Diaspora Mobilisation for Conflict and Post-Conflict Reconstruction: Contextual and Comparative Dimensions," *Journal of Ethnic and Migration Studies* 44, no. 8 (2018): 1251–1269.

55. J. Rovny, "Circumstantial Liberals: Czech Germans in Interwar Czechoslovakia," HAL Open Science, 2020, https://sciencespo.hal.science/hal-02459013v1/document.

56. Tsourapas 2015, p. 16.

57. Østergaard-Nielsen 2003. Recent research on remittances also demonstrates that the money emigrants return to their families and friends tends not to promote democratic values. Goodman and Hiskey (2008) report a decrease in political engagement in Mexican cities with high level of emigrants. Germano (2013) finds that remittance recipients are less likely to pressure and oppose politicians because they are more optimistic about their economic conditions. Berdiev et al. 2013 and Abdih et al. 2012 find that remittances increases the likelihood that the government will spend more time in rent-seeking behavior and invest less in public goods because recipients may procure such goods on their own. See Konte 2015.

58. Shain and Barth 2003, p. 451.

59. Tarrow 2005, p. 190.

60. Moss 2016; D. Parvaz, "Expats Join Syrian Revolution from Afar," *Al-Jazeera English*, September 8, 2011, www.aljazeera.com/indepth/features/2011/09/201195123037726408.html; Sharmila Devi, "Syrian Diaspora Laments Opposition's Disunity," The National, October 14, 2012; Rob Hastings, "Neighbors from Hell: How Syria's War Hit an Acton Street," *The Independent*, March 18, 2012; Wiebke Hollersen, "Syrian in Berlin Channels Aid to Embattled Countrymen," Spiegel Online, March 16, 2012; "Are Syrian Spies Keeping Tabs on Opposition Activists in U.S.?" Public Broadcasting Service (PBS) News Hour, January 3, 2012, www.pbs.org/newshour/bb/world-jan-june12-syria_01–03/.

61. Barrington Moore, Jr., *Injustice: The Social Bases of Obedience and Revolt* (White Plains, NY: M.E. Sharpe, 1978); Douglas Heckathorn, "Collective Sanctions and the Creation of Prisoner's Dilemma Norms," *American Journal of Sociology* 94, no. 3 (1988): 535–562; Marwan Khawaja, "Repression and Popular Collective Action: Evidence from the West Bank," *Sociological Forum* 8 (1993): 47–71; Golfo Alexopoulos, "Stalin and the Politics of Kinship:

Practices of Collective Punishment, 1920s–1940s," *Comparative Studies in History and Society* 50, no. 1 (2008): 91–117; D. Moss, "The Ties That Bind: Internet Communication Technologies, Networked Authoritarianism, and 'Voice' in the Syrian Diaspora," *Globalizations* 15, no. 2 (2018): 265–282.

62. "Syrian Malware, the Ever Evolving Threat," Kaspersky Lab Global Research and Analysis Team, 2014; J. Scott-Railton, B. Abdulrazzak, A. Hulcoop, M. Brooks, and K. Kleemola, "Group5: Syria and the Iranian Connection," Toronto: The Citizen Lab Report, Munk School of Global Affairs, University of Toronto, 2016.

63. Wendy Pearlman, "Narratives of Fear in Syria," *Perspectives on Politics* 14, no. 1 (2016): 21–37, p. 25.

64. "Statement Issued by Syrian Organizations Working in the Fields of Documentation, Accountability and Transitional Justice in Support of the Work of the International, Impartial and Independent Mechanism (IIIM)," Syria Justice & Accountability Centre, 2018, https://stj-sy.org/uploads/pdf_files/IIIM%20Statement%20Final_%20Signed.pdf; Stokke and Wiebelhaus-Brahm 2019.

65. S. Khamis, P. B. Gold, and K. Vaughn, "Beyond Egypt's 'Facebook Revolution' and Syria's 'YouTube Uprising': Comparing Political Contexts, Actors and Communication Strategies," *Arab Media & Society*, March 28, 2012; P. N. Howard and M. M. Hussain, *Democracy's Fourth Wave? Digital Media and the Arab Spring* (Oxford: Oxford University Press, 2013); Z. Tufekci, *Twitter and Tear Gas: The Power and Fragility of Networked Protest* (New Haven, CT: Yale University Press, 2017).

66. Moss 2016.

67. See F. E. Oppenheimer, "Governments and Authorities in Exile," *American Journal of International Law* 36, no. 4 (1942): 568–595.

68. V. J. Bunce and S. L. Wolchik, *Defeating Authoritarian Leaders in Postcommunist Countries* (Cambridge: Cambridge University Press, 2011).

69. This research component is based on my co-authored working paper, Justin Gest, Jeremy Ferwerda, and Hangyoung Lee, "Citizens under Siege: How Syrians Connect and Disconnect from the Politics of Resistance," Working Paper, 2018.

70. Katarzyna Jasko, David Webber, Erica Molinario, Aerie Kruglanski, and Katharine Touchton-Leonard, "Ideological Extremism among Syrian Refugees Is Negatively Related to Intentions to Migrate to the West," *Psychological Science* 32, no. 9 (2021): 1362–1374. See also M. Motyl, R. Iyer, S. Oishi, S. Trawalter, and B. A. Nosek, "How Ideological Migration Geographically Segregates Groups," *Journal of Experimental Social Psychology* 51 (2014): 1–14.

71. Harris Mylonas and Scott Radnitz, eds., *Enemies Within: The Global Politics of Fifth Columns* (New York: Oxford University Press, 2022).

72. A. Córdova and J. Hiskey, "Shaping Politics at Home: Cross-Border Social Ties and Local-Level Political Engagement," *Comparative Political Studies* 48, no. 11 (2015): 1454–1487.

73. Lauren Duquette-Rury and Zhenxiang Chen, "Does International Migration Affect Political Participation? Evidence from Multiple Data

Sources across Mexican Municipalities, 1990–2013," *International Migration Review* 53, no. 3 (2018): 798–830.

74. Alesina and Giuliano 2011.
75. Ibid.
76. Alesina and Giuliano 2010. Also see Luttmer and Singhal 2011.
77. That is, 17.4 percent of respondents without diaspora ties are mulling their departure, while 26.4 percent of people with such ties do consider emigrating.
78. The effects are too small to be statistically significant at the national level, except in Hungary. So Hungarian expats appear to sway their family and friends to come back home more than others.
79. Levitt 1998; F. Krawatzek and L. Müller-Funk, "Two Centuries of Flows between 'Here' and 'There': Political Remittances and their Transformative Potential," *Journal of Ethnic and Migration Studies* 46, no. 6 (2020): 1003–1024.
80. M. Beine, F. Docquier, and M. Schiff, "International Migration, Transfer of Norms and Home Country Fertility," *Canadian Journal of Economics/ Revue canadienne d'économique*, 46, no. 4 (2013): 1406–1430; M. Karadja and E. Prawitz, "Exit, Voice, and Political Change: Evidence from Swedish Mass Migration to the United States," *Journal of Political Economy* 127, no. 4 (2019): 1864–1925; A. White and I. Grabowska, "Social Remittances and Social Change in Central and Eastern Europe: Embedding Migration in the Study of Society," *Central and Eastern European Migration Review* 8, no. 1 (2019): 33–50.
81. F. Docquier, E. Lodigiani, H. Rapoport, and M. Schiff, "Emigration and Democracy," *Journal of Development Economics* 120 (2016): 209–223; C. Batista and P. C. Vicente, "Do Migrants Improve Governance at Home? Evidence from a Voting Experiment," *The World Bank Economic Review* 25, no. 1 (2011): 77–104.
82. Artjoms Ivlevs and Roswitha King, "Does Emigration Reduce Corruption?" *Public Choice* 171, nos. 3/4 (2017): 389–408. Also see Mariani 2007.
83. Levitt 1998. See also Paarlberg 2017.
84. Kapur 2010.
85. Pérez-Armendáriz and Crow 2010.
86. T. Barsbai, H. Rapoport, A, Steinmayr, and C. Trebesch, "The Effect of Labor Migration on the Diffusion of Democracy: Evidence from a Former Soviet Republic," *American Economic Journal: Applied Economics* 9, no. 3 (2017): 36–69.

6 A HUMAN BASE

1. Samer S. Shehata, "In Egypt, Democrats vs. Liberals," *New York Times*, July 2, 2013, www.nytimes.com/2013/07/03/opinion/in-egypt-democrats-vs-liberals.html.
2. I interviewed twenty-four elite political activists from Egypt, Libya, Morocco, Syria, Tunisia, and Yemen – principal venues of the Arab Spring. I interviewed eight women and fifteen men, between the ages of twenty-three

and seventy-four. All subjects had at some point led or contributed to the leadership of pro-democracy agendas in nondemocratic spaces. Nearly all have completed a bachelor's or graduate degree. Nearly all described encounters with national police officials, time spent in prison, and threats of extradition, execution, and reprisals against family members. Many previously or currently lead opposition parties, movements or organizations, or work as journalists – some overtly, but many covertly – in the limited space their countries of origin provide for activism. Most of these activists now reside in North America or Europe. Ten of my respondents left their countries of origin before the Arab Spring; another seven left after the Arab Spring began in early 2011. Six others returned to their countries of origin after time spent in North America or Europe. Respondents outside the Middle East were interviewed in person, while those who repatriated were interviewed via web conference. Each subject was granted full anonymity. For this reason, my descriptions of subjects' previous roles in the democracy movements of the countries of origin are necessarily vague and sparse. Given the elite group from which these subjects emerge, they could be identified with only a few details. Accordingly, I make use of aliases for all respondents.

3. In all interviews, I use standardized topic guide and an unstandardized, conversational approach in order to reassure respondents during discussions that lasted between one and three hours. Questions included: What is your country of origin? For what organization or movement or cause did or do you work? What was its mission? What roles have you held and for how long? Why are you now abroad and in the United States? How long have you been abroad and away from your country of origin? In your estimation, how many of your countrymen and countrywomen are abroad now? Are you tempted to return? Why? What is the likelihood that you will return? Why? Do many of your fellow expatriates have democratic values? Why do you think your fellow expatriates first moved abroad? Why do your fellow expatriates stay abroad? How would you describe your country of origin's form of government? How close is your country of origin to qualifying as a liberal democracy? To what do you attribute its democratic shortcomings? To what do you attribute your country of origin's struggle to democratize? What difficulties and challenges did you encounter in your advocacy when you lived in your country of origin?

4. Schachar 2006; Doomernik et al. 2009; Beine et al. 2016; Boucher and Gest 2018.

5. See Tsourapas 2015.

6. Amira Mikhail, "The Obliteration of Civil Society in Egypt," *Open Democracy*, October 6, 2014.

7. Dunlevy 1991; Massey et al. 1994; Massey and Espinosa 1997; Massey and Zenteno 2000; Winters et al. 2001; Fussell and Massey 2004; Garip and Curran 2010.

8. Raymond Hinnebusch, "Authoritarian Persistence, Democratization Theory and the Middle East: An Overview and Critique," *Democratization* 13, no. 3 (2006): 373–395; Peter Mandaville, *Global Political Islam* (New York,

London: Routledge, 2007); Ross 2001; Alfred Stepan and Juan J. Linz, "Democratization Theory and the 'Arab Spring,'" *Journal of Democracy* 24, no. 2 (2013): 15–30; Jason Brownlee, Tarek Masoud, and Andrew Reynolds, "Why the Modest Harvest?" *Journal of Democracy* 24, no. 4 (2013): 29–44.

9. S. Levitsky and L. A. Way, *Competitive Authoritarianism: Hybrid Regimes after the Cold War* (Cambridge: Cambridge University Press, 2010).

10. On a positive note, after years of democratic backsliding, countries like Brazil, Guatemala, and Poland have strengthened their democratic institutions recently.

11. Noam Gidron, "Why Israeli Democracy Is in Crisis," *Journal of Democracy* 34, no. 3 (2023): 33–45.

12. Adrian Filut, "A 25% Surge in the Number of Israelis Staying Abroad More Than Two Years," *Calcalist*, July 22, 2024, www.calcalist.co.il/local_news/article/b1kuoorcdr.

13. Israel Young Academy, "The Potential Effects of the Political Crisis in Israel on Human Capital in Academic Institutions Survey," March 20, 2023, https://young.academy.ac.il/News/NewsItem.aspx?nodeId=955&id=622.

14. Sharon Wrobel, "War Spurs Brain Drain, Outflow of Israeli High-Tech Employees, Report Finds," *The Times of Israel*, April 7, 2025.

15. Demet Lüküslü, "The Desire of Young People in Turkey to Live Abroad: An Analysis of Recent Surveys on Youth in Turkey," IPC-Mercator Analysis, Istanbul Policy Center, 2024.

16. Zeliha Ozdogan, "The Effects of Democratic Regression on Turkish Economy and the Brain Drain," in *Human Rights in Turkey: Assaults on Human Dignity*, ed. Hasan Aydın and Winston Langley, 365–382 (Cham: Springer International Publishing, 2021).

17. Ali Çağlar and Türken Çağlar, "Turkish Youth Research 2021," Konrad Adenauer Stiftung, 2022, www.kas.de/en/web/tuerkei/single-title/-/content/turkish-youth-2021-1.

18. Elif Aktaş and Barış Ertürk, "CHP Altogether: Brain Drain Workshop Report," 2021, https://chp.org.tr/yayin/beyn-gocu-raporu.

19. For example, a forensic analysis of the 2023 election results have identified statistical anomalies suggestive of electoral manipulation. Studies indicate that certain regions exhibited unusually high voter turnouts and vote shares favoring Erdoğan, especially in smaller polling stations. These patterns are consistent with ballot-stuffing practices, although the estimated impact – approximately 342,000 excess votes – was not sufficient to alter the overall election outcome. See P. Klimek, A. Aykac, and S. Thurner, "Forensic Analysis of the Turkey 2023 Presidential Election Reveals Extreme Vote Swings in Remote Areas," *PLoS ONE* 18, no. 11 (2023): e0293239, https://doi.org/10.1371/journal.pone.0293239.

20. For my own work on this subject matter, please see: Justin Gest, Tyler Reny, and Jeremy Mayer, "Roots of the Radical Right: Nostalgic Deprivation in the United States and Britain," *Comparative Political Studies* 51, no. 13 (2018): 1694–1719; J. Ferwerda, J. Gest, and T. Reny, "Nostalgic Deprivation and Populism: Evidence from 19 European Countries," *European Journal of Political Research*, 2024, https://doi.org/10.1111/1475-6765.12738;

Gest 2022; Justin Gest, *The New Minority: White Working Class Politics in an Age of Immigration and Inequality* (Oxford: Oxford University Press, 2016).

21. For example, see Morris Levy and Matthew Wright, *Immigration and the American Ethos* (Cambridge: Cambridge University Press, 2020); Tyler Reny and Justin Gest, "Viewers Like You: The Effect of Elite Co-identity Reinforcement on US Immigration Attitudes," *Politics, Groups, and Identities* 12, no. 5 (2023): 969–985; Alexander Kustov, *In Our Interest: How Democracies Can Make Immigration Popular* (New York: Columbia University Press, 2025).

22. This presumes that the world's democracies truly want to promote democracies in sending countries. A critical, neo-Marxist perspective – particularly in Europe – questions whether European powers even prefer democracies to North Africa's autocracies, which are ostensibly more easily leveraged to constrain the flows of people into the Mediterranean. This view has roots in the US government's support for anti-communist authoritarians worldwide during the Cold War. Today, it is a more debatable geopolitical proposition, but it further supports my grander point that any deleterious effects on democracy promotion will not (and should not) outweigh the massive benefits that immigrants provide to their destination states.

23. For an example from the United States, see J. A. Rodden, *Why Cities Lose: The Deep Roots of the Urban–Rural Political Divide* (New York: Basic Books, 2019). However, similar trends are taking place worldwide.

24. Anne Applebaum, *Autocracy, Inc.: The Dictators Who Want to Run the World* (New York: Random House, 2024), 184.

25. Ibid.

APPENDIX C

1. Stef van Buuren and Karin Groothuis-Oudshoorn, "Mice: Multivariate Imputation by Chained Equations in R," *Journal of Statistical Software* 45, no. 3 (2011): 1–67.

2. The random effects model included also has slightly larger standard errors.

3. It is possible that the lack of significance of effects for anti-pluralism in parties in government may be partly drive by coalition governments. For parties to join in a coalition it is necessary for them to not have high levels of anti-pluralism.

Bibliography

Abdih, Y., R. Chami, and J. Dagher. "Remittances and Institutions: Are Remittances a Curse?" *World Development* 40 no. 4 (2012): 657–666.

Abel, Guy and Joel Cohen. "Bilateral International Migration Flow Estimates for 200 Countries." *Scientific Data* 6 no. 82 (2019).

Abou-Chadi, Tarik and Thomas Kurer. "Economic Risk within the Household and Voting for the Radical Right." *World Politics* 73 no. 3 (2021): 482–511.

Abreu, A. "The New Economics of Labor Migration: Beware of Neoclassicals Bearing Gifts." *Forum for Social Economics* 41 no. 1 (2012): 46–67.

Acemoglu, Daron, Suresh Naidu, Pascual Restrepo, and James A. Robinson. "Democracy Does Cause Growth." *Journal of Political Economy* 127 no. 1 (2019): 47–100.

Adamson, Fiona. "Globalization, Transnational Political Mobilization, and Networks of Violence." *Cambridge Review of International Affairs* 18 no. 1 (2005): 35–53.

Adamson, Fiona. "Mechanisms of Diaspora Mobilization and the Transnationalization of Civil War." In *Transnational Dynamics of Civil War*, ed. Jeffrey Checkel, 63–88. Cambridge: Cambridge University Press. 2013.

Adamson, Fiona and Madeline Demetriou. "Remapping the Boundaries of 'State' and 'National Identity.'" *European Journal of International Relations* 13 no. 4 (2007): 489–526.

Adida, C. L., A. Lo, and M. Platas. "Engendering Empathy, Begetting Backlash: American Attitudes towards Syrian Refugees." Working Paper. 2017.

Agersnap, O., A. S. Jensen, and H. Kleven. "The Welfare Magnet Hypothesis: Evidence from an Immigrant Welfare Scheme in Denmark." Report No. w26454, National Bureau of Economic Research. 2019.

Aguilera, M. B. and Douglas Massey. "Social Capital and the Wages of Mexican Migrants: New Hypotheses and Tests." *Social Forces* 82 no. 2 (2003): 671–701.

Ahmed, F. "The Perils of Unearned Foreign Income: Aid, Remittances, and Government Survival." *American Political Science Review* 106 no. 1 (2012): 146–165.

Ahmed, F. "Remittances and Incumbency: Theory and Evidence." *Economics & Politics* 29 no. 1 (2017): 22–47.

Akgüç, Mehtap, Xingfei Liu, Massmiliano Tani, and Klaus Zimmerman. "Risk Attitudes and Migration." *China Economic Review* 37 (2016): 166–176.

Aktaş, Elif and Barış Ertürk. "CHP Altogether: Brain Drain Workshop Report." 2021. https://chp.org.tr/yayin/beyn-gocu-raporu.

Alemán, Jose and Dwayne Woods. "No Way Out: Travel Restrictions and Authoritarian Regimes." *Migration and Development* 3 no. 2 (2014): 285–305.

Alesina, Alberto and Paola Giuliano. "Family Ties and Political Participation." *Journal of the European Economic Association* 9 no. 5 (2011): 817–839.

Alesina, Alberto and Paola Giuliano. "Preferences for Redistribution." National Bureau of Economic Research Working Paper 14825. 2010.

Alexopoulos, Golfo. "Stalin and the Politics of Kinship: Practices of Collective Punishment, 1920s–1940s." *Comparative Studies in History and Society* 50 no. 1 (2008): 91–117.

Allard, S. W. and S. Danziger. "Welfare Magnets: Myth or Reality?" *Journal of Politics* 62 no. 2 (2000): 350–368.

Anderson, Benedict. *The Spectre of Comparisons: Nationalism, Southeast Asia, and the World*. New York: Verso. 1998.

Anderson, Lisa. "Searching Where the Light Shines: Studying Democratization in the Middle East." *Annual Review of Political Science* 9 (2006): 189–214.

Anelli, Massimo, Italo Colantone, and Piero Stanig. "Individual Vulnerability to Industrial Robot Adoption Increases Support for the Radical Right." *Proceedings of the National Academy of Sciences* 118 no. 47 (2021): e2111611118.

Anelli, Massimo and G. Peri. "Does Emigration Delay Political Change? Evidence from Italy during the Great Recession." *Economic Policy* 32 no. 91 (2017): 551–596.

Applebaum, Anne. *Autocracy, Inc.: The Dictators Who Want to Run the World*. New York: Random House. 2024.

"Are Syrian Spies Keeping Tabs on Opposition Activists in U.S.?" *Public Broadcasting Service (PBS) News Hour*. January 3, 2012. www.pbs.org/.

Arif, Imran. "The Determinants of International Migration: Unbundling the Role of Economic, Political and Social Institutions." *World Economy* 43 no. 6 (2020): 1699–1729.

Auer, D. and M. Schaub. "Mass Emigration and the Erosion of Liberal Democracy." *International Studies Quarterly* 68 no. 2 (2024).

Ayhan, S., K. Gatskova, and H. Lehmann. "The Impact of Non-cognitive Skills and Risk Preferences on Rural-to-urban Migration: Evidence from Ukraine." IZA Discussion Paper Series No. 10982. 2017.

Azose, J. J. and A. E. Raftery. "Estimation of Emigration, Return Migration, and Transit Migration between All Pairs of Countries." *Proceedings of the National Academy of Sciences* 116 no. 1 (2019): 116–122.

Babović, Jovana. "Political, Social, and Personal: The Encounters of the Russian Emigration in Yugoslavia, 1921–1941." *Serbian Studies: Journal of the North American Society for Serbian Studies* 21 no. 1 (2007): 1–36.

Baker, Alex. "1 in 5 US Residents 'More Likely' to Move After Election, According to Redfin," *Yahoo! News*, November 16, 2024. https://yahoo.com/news/1-5-us-residents-more-150052398.html.

Bansak, K., J. Hainmueller, and D. Hangartner. "How Economic, Humanitarian, and Religious Concerns Shape European Attitudes toward Asylum Seekers." *Science* 354 no. 6309 (2016): 217–222.

Barry, Colin, K. Chad Clay, Michael E. Flynn, and Gregory Robinson. "Freedom of Foreign Movement, Economic Opportunities Abroad, and Protest in Non-Democratic Regimes." *Journal of Peace Research* 51 no. 5 (2014): 574–588.

Barsbai, T., H. Rapoport, A. Steinmayr, and C. Trebesch. "The Effect of Labor Migration on the Diffusion of Democracy: Evidence from a Former Soviet Republic." *American Economic Journal: Applied Economics* 9 no. 3 (2017): 36–69.

Baser, B. *Diasporas and Homeland Conflicts: A Comparative Perspective.* Farnham, UK: Ashgate. 2015.

Baser, B. and A. Swain. "Diasporas as Peace-Makers: Third Party Mediation in Home-land Politics." *International Journal on World Peace* 25 no. 3 (2008): 7–28.

"Basic Law Chapter I – General Principles." Government of the Hong Kong Special Administrative Region of the People's Republic of China. https://basiclaw.gov.hk/en/basiclaw/chapter1.html.

Bateman, David. "The Dilemmas of Democratic Peoplehood." Annual Meeting of the American Political Science Association. September 2020.

Batista, C. and P. C. Vicente. "Do Migrants Improve Governance at Aome? Evidence from a Voting Experiment." *The World Bank Economic Review* 25 no. 1 (2011): 77–104.

Bauböck, R. and T. Faist, eds. *Diaspora and Transnationalism: Concepts, Theories and Methods.* Amsterdam University Press. 2010.

Baudassé, Thierry, Rémi Bazillier, and Ismaël Issifou. "Migration and Institutions: Exit and Voice (from Abroad)?" *Journal of Economic Surveys* 32 no. 3 (2018): 727–766.

Bechev, Dimitar. "Hedging Its Bets: Serbia between Russia and the EU." *Carnegie Europe.* January 19, 2023. https://carnegieeurope.eu/.

Becker, A., T. Deckers, T. Dohmen, A. Falk, and F. Kosse. "The Relationship between Economic Preferences and Psychological Personality Measures." *Annual Review of Economics* 4 no. 1 (2012): 453–478.

Beine, Michel, Anna Boucher, Brian Burgoon, Mary Crock, Justin Gest, Michael Hiscox, Patrick McGovern, Hillil Rapoport, Joep Schaper, and Eiko Theilemann. "Comparing Immigration Policies: An Overview from the IMPALA Database." *International Migration Review* 50 no. 4 (2016): 827–863.

Beine, Michel, Frederic Docquier, and Hillel Rapoport. "Brain Drain and Human Capital Formation in Developing Countries: Winners and Losers." *Economic Journal* 188 (2008): 631–652.

Beine, Michel, Frederic Docquier, and Maurice Schiff. "Brain Drain and Its Determinants: A Major Issue for Small States." *IZA Discussion Papers 3398,* Institute for the Study of Labor (IZA). 2008.

Beine, Michel, Frederic Docquier, and Maurice Schiff. "International Migration, Transfer of Norms and Home Country Fertility." *Canadian Journal of Economics/ Revue canadienne d'économique* 46 no. 4 (2013): 1406–1430.

Bellin, Eva. "The Robustness of Authoritarianism in the Middle East: Exceptionalism in Comparative Perspective." *Comparative Politics* 36 no. 2 (2004): 139–157.

Bello, M. and V. Reyes. "Filipino Americans and the Marcos Overthrow: The Transformation of Political Consciousness." *Amerasia Journal* 13 no. 1 (1986): 73–83.

Berdiev, A., N. Y. Kim, and C. Chang. "Remittances and Corruption." *Economics Letters* 118 no. 1 (2013): 182–185.

Berman, Sheri. *Democracy and Dictatorship in Europe: From the Ancien Régime to the Present Day.* New York: Oxford University Press. 2019.

Betz, H. G. *Radical Right-Wing Populism in Western Europe.* New York: St. Martin's Press. 1994.

Bob, Clifford. *The Marketing of Rebellion: Insurgents, Media and International Activism.* New York: Cambridge University Press. 2005.

Boeri, T. "Immigration to the Land of Redistribution." *Economica* 77 no. 308 (2010): 651–687.

Bollen, Kenneth. "Political Democracy and the Timing of Development." *American Sociological Review* 44 (1979): 572–587.

Borjas, George. "Immigration and Welfare Magnets." *Journal of Labour Economics* 17 no. 4 (1999): 607–637.

Boucher, Anna. *Gender, Migration and the Global Race for Talent.* Manchester: Manchester University Press. 2016.

Boucher, Anna and Justin Gest. *Crossroads: Comparative Immigration Regimes in a World of Demographic Change.* Cambridge: Cambridge University Press. 2018.

Brand, Laurie A. *Citizens Abroad: Emigration and the State in the Middle East and North Africa.* New York: Cambridge University Press. 2006.

Brandt, Jessica and Robert L. McKenzie. "Addressing the Syrian refugee crisis." Brookings Institution. December 16, 2016. https://brookings.edu/.

Brinkerhoff, Jennifer. "Diasporas and Conflict Societies: Conflict Entrepreneurs, Competing Interests or Contributors to Stability and Development?" *Conflict, Security & Development* 11 no. 2 (2011): 115–143.

Brinkerhoff, Jennifer. ed. *Diasporas and Development.* Boulder, CO: Lynne Rienner. 2008.

Brownlee, Jason, Tarek Masoud, and Andrew Reynolds. "Why the Modest Harvest?" *Journal of Democracy* 24 no. 4 (2013): 29–44.

Brücker, H., G. S. Epstein, B. McCormick, G. Saint-Paul, A. Venturini, and C. Zimermann. "Managing Migration in the European Welfare State." In *Immigration Policy and the Welfare System*, eds. T. Boeri, G. Hanson, and B. McCormick, 1–167. Oxford: Oxford University Press. 2002.

Bunce, V. J. and S. L. Wolchik. *Defeating Authoritarian Leaders in Postcommunist Countries.* Cambridge: Cambridge University Press. 2011.

Bustikova, Lenka. "Revenge of the Radical Right." *Comparative Political Studies* 47 no. 12 (2014): 1738–1765.

Bütikofer, A. and G. Peri. "Cognitive and Noncognitive Skills and the Selection and Sorting of Migrants." National Bureau of Economic Research Working Paper No. 23877. 2017.

Bygnes, Susanne and Aurore Flipo. "Political Motivations for Intra-European Migration." *Acta Sociologica* 60 no. 3 (2017): 199–212.

Çağlar, Ali and Türken Çağlar. *Turkish Youth Research* 2021. Konrad Adenauer Stiftung 2022. https://kas.de/en/web/tuerkei/single-title/-/content/turkish-youth-2021-1.

Camarena, Kara Ross. "Repatriation during Conflict: A Signaling Analysis." *World Development* 158 (2022): 105960.

Camperio, A. S., C. Ciani, A. V. Capiluppi, and G. Sartori. "The Adaptive Value of Personality Differences Revealed by Small Island Population Dynamics." *European Journal of Personality* 21 no. 1 (2017): 3–22.

Canache, D., M. Hayes, J. J. Mondak, and S. C. Wals. "Openness, Extraversion and the Intention to Emigrate." *Journal of Research in Personality* 47 no. 4 (2013): 351–355.

Careja, R. and P. Emmenegger. "Making Democratic Citizens: The Effects of Migration Experience on Political Attitudes in Central and Eastern Europe." *Comparative Political Studies* 45 no. 7 (2012): 875–902.

Carling, J. "Emigration, Return and Development in Cape Verde: The Impact of Closing Borders." *Population, Space and Place* 10 no. 2 (2004): 113–132.

Carling, J. "Migration in the Age of Involuntary Immobility: Theoretical Reflections and Cape Verdean Experiences." *Journal of Ethnic and Migration Studies* 28 no. 1 (2002): 5–42.

Carling, J. and K. Schewel. "Revisiting Aspiration and Ability in International Migration." *Journal of Ethnic and Migration Studies* 44 no. 6 (2018): 945–963.

Carothers, Thomas and Marina Ottaway. *Uncharted Journey: Promoting Democracy in the Middle East*. Washington, DC: Carnegie. 2005.

Carr, Patrick J. and Maria J. Kefalas. *Hollowing Out the Middle: The Rural Brain Drain and What it Means for America*. Boston: Beacon Press. 2009.

Castles, S., H. de Haas, and M. Miller. *The Age of Migration: International Population Movements in the Modern World*, 5th ed. New York: Guilford Press. 2013.

Chauvet, L. and M. Mercier. "Do Return Migrants Transfer Political Norms to their Origin Country? Evidence from Mali." *Journal of Comparative Economics* 42 no. 3 (2014): 630–651.

Chen, C., A. Bernard, R. Rylee, and G. Abel. "Brain Circulation: The Educational Profile of Return Migrants." *Population Research and Policy Review* 41 no. 1 (2022): 387–399.

Cheng, Joseph. "The Tiananmen Incident and the Pro-Democracy Movement in Hong Kong." *China Perspectives* 2 no. 78 (2009): 91–100.

Clayton, K., J. Ferwerda, and Y. Horiuchi. "Exposure to Immigration and Admission Preferences: Evidence from France." *Political Behavior* 43 (2018): 1–26.

Clemens, Michael A. "Economics and Emigration: Trillion-Dollar Bills on the Sidewalk?" *Journal of Economic Perspectives* 25 no. 3 (2011): 83–106.

Clemens, Michael A. and Hannah M. Postel. "Deterring Emigration with Foreign Aid: An Overview of Evidence from Low-Income Countries." *Population and Development Review* 44 no. 4 (2018).

Cochrane, F. *Migration and Security in the Global Age: Diaspora Communities and Conflict*. London, UK: Routledge. 2015.

Cochrane, F., B. Baser, and A. Swain. "Home Thoughts from Abroad: Diasporas and Peace-Building in Northern Ireland and Sri Lanka." *Studies in Conflict and Terrorism* 32 no. 8 (2009): 681–704.

Collier, Paul. *Exodus: How Migration Is Changing Our World*. New York: Oxford University Press. 2013.

Colomer, J. M. "Exit, Voice, and Hostility in Cuba." *International Migration Review* 34 no. 2 (2000): 423–442.

Connor, Walter. "Homelands in a World of States." In *Understanding Nationalism*, eds. Montserrat Guidernau and John Hutchinson, 53–73. Cambridge: Polity Press. 2001.

Coppedge, Michael, et al. "V-Dem [Country-Year/Country-Date] Dataset v13." Varieties of Democracy (V-Dem) Project. 2023. https://doi.org/10.23696/vdemds23.

Córdova, Abby and Jonathan Hiskey. "Shaping Politics at Home: Cross-Border Social Ties and Local-Level Political Engagement." *Comparative Political Studies* 48 no. 11 (2015): 1454–1487.

Crawley, H. *Chance or Choice? Understanding Why Asylum Seekers Come to the UK*. London: Refugee Council. 2010.

Cutts, David, Robert Ford, and Matthew Goodwin. "Anti-Immigrant, Politically Disaffected or Still Racist after All? Examining the Attitudinal Drivers of Extreme Right Support in Britain in the 2009 European Elections: Anti-Immigrant, Politically Disaffected or Still Racist after All?" *European Journal of Political Research* 50 no. 3 (2011): 418–440.

Dancygier, Rafaela, Sirus H. Dehdari, David D. Laitin, Moritz Marbach, and Kåre Vernby. "Emigration and Radical Right Populism." *American Journal of Political Science* (2024). https://onlinelibrary.wiley.com/doi/10.1111/ajps.12852.

De Giorgi, Giacomo and Michele Pellizzari. "Welfare migration in Europe." *Labour Economics* 16 no. 4 (2008): 353–363.

De Haas, H. "Migration and Development: A Theoretical Perspective." *International Migration Review* 44 no. 1 (2010): 227–264.

de la Luz Inclan, Maria. "From the ¡Ya Basta! to the Caracoles: Zapatista Mobilization under Transitional Conditions." *American Journal of Sociology* 113 no. 5 (2008): 1316–1350.

de Lange, Sarah. "A New Winning Formula?: The Programmatic Appeal of the Radical Right." *Party Politics* 13 no. 4 (2007): 411–435.

Deibert, R. "Cyberspace Under Siege." *Journal of Democracy* 26 no. 3 (2015): 64–78.

della Porta, Donatella and Sidney Tarrow. "Transnational Processes and Social Activism: An Introduction." In *Transnational Protest and Global Activism*, eds. Sidney Tarrow and Donnatella della Porta, 1–17. Lanham: Rowman and Littlefield. 2004.

Devi, Sharmila. "Syrian Diaspora Laments Opposition's Disunity." *The National*. October 14, 2012. www.thenational.ae/.

Devictor, Xavier. "Toward a Path to Sustainable Refugee Return." *World Bank Blog*. November 13, 2023. https://blogs.worldbank.org/en/dev4peace/toward-path-sustainable-refugee-return.

Docquier, Frédéric. "The Brain Drain from Developing Countries." IZA World of Labor. https://doi.org/10.15185/izawol.

Docquier, Frédéric and Hillel Rapoport. "Ethnic Discrimination and the Migration of Skilled Labor." *Journal of Development Economics* 70 no. 1 (2003): 159–172.

Docquier, Frédéric and Hillel Rapoport. "Globalization, Brain Drain, and Development." *Journal of Economic Literature* 50 no. 3 (2012): 681–730.

Docquier, Frederic, E. Lodigiani, H. Rapoport, and M. Schiff. "Emigration and democracy." *Journal of Development Economics* 120 (2016): 209–223.

Donato, Katharine M. et al. "Migration in the Americas: Mexico and Latin America in Comparative Context." *The Annals of the American Academy of Political and Social Science* 630 no. 1 (2010): 6–17.

Doomernik, J., R. Koslowski, L. Laurence, R. Maxwell, I. Michalowski, and D. Thraenhardt. *No Shortcuts: Selective Migration and Integration.* Washington, DC: Transatlantic Academy. 2009.

Dowty, Alan. "Emigration and Expulsion in the Third World." *Third World Quarterly* 8 no. 1 (1986): 155–165.

Drever, Anita and Onno Hoffmeister. "Immigrants and Social Networks in a Job-Scarce Environment: The Case of Germany." *International Migration Review* 42 no. 2 (2008): 425–448.

Dunlevy, J. "On the Settlement Patterns of Recent Caribbean and Latin Immigrants to the United States." *Growth and Change* 22 (1991): 54–67.

Duquette-Rury, Lauren and Zhenxiang Chen. "Does International Migration Affect Political Participation? Evidence from Multiple Data Sources across Mexican Municipalities, 1990–2013." *International Migration Review* 53 no. 3 (2018): 798–830.

Dustmann, Christian and Oliver Kirchkamp. "The Optimal Migration Duration and Activity Choice After Re-migration." *Journal of Development Economics* 67 no. 2 (2002): 361–372.

Dustmann, Christian and Anna Okatenko. "Out-migration, Wealth Constraints, and the Quality of Local Amenities." *Journal of Development Economics* 110 (2014): 52–63.

Dutta, Nabamita and Sanjukta Roy. "Do Potential Skilled Emigrants Care about Political Stability at Home?" *Review of Development Economics* 15 no. 3 (2011): 442–457.

Escribà-Folch, A., C. Meseguer, and J. Wright. *Migration and Democracy: How Remittances Undermine Dictatorships.* Princeton, NJ: Princeton University Press. 2020.

Escribà-Folch, A., C. Meseguer, and J. Wright. "Remittances and Democratization." *International Studies Quarterly* 59 no. 3 (2015): 571–586.

Esipova, Neli, Julie Ray, and Anita Pugliese. "Gallup World Poll: The Many Faces of Global Migration." International Organization for Migration (IOM) Migration Research Series No. 43. 2011. https://news.gallup.com/.

Etling, Andreas, Leonie Backeberg, and Jochen Tholen. "The Political Dimension of Young People's Migration Intentions: Evidence from the Arab Mediterranean Region." *Journal of Ethnic and Migration Studies* 46 (7) (2020): 1388–1404.

European Commission, "A Humane and Effective Return and Readmission Policy." Migration and Home Affairs. Undated. https://home-affairs.ec.europa.eu/policies/migration-and-asylum/irregular-migration-and-return/humane-and-effective-return-and-readmission-policy_en.

Faath, Sigrid and Hanspeter Mattes. "Political Conflicts and Migration in the MENA States." In *Migration from the Middle East and North Africa to Europe: Past Developments, Current Status, and Future Potentials*, eds. Michael Bommes, Heinz Fassmann, and Wiebke Sievers, 159–190. Amsterdam: Amsterdam University Press. 2014.

Fagiolo, G. and G. Santoni. "Revisiting the Role of Migrant Social Networks as Determinants of International Migration Flows." *Applied Economics Letters* 23 no. 3 (2016): 188–193.

Feng, Gao and Liam Scott. "Hong Kong Exodus May Threaten City's Global Financial Status." *Voice of America News*. August 19, 2022. https://voanews.com/a/hong-kong-exodus-may-threaten-city-s-global-financial-status-/6709210.html.

Ferwerda, Jeremy and Justin Gest. "Pull Factors and Migration Preferences: Evidence from the Middle East and North Africa." *International Migration Review* 55 no. 2 (2021): 431–459.

Ferwerda, Jeremy, Justin Gest, and T. Reny. "Nostalgic Deprivation and Populism: Evidence from 19 European Countries." *European Journal of Political Research*. 2024. https://doi.org/10.1111/1475-6765.12738.

Fetzer, Joel S. and Brandon Alexander Millan. "The Causes of Emigration from Singapore: How Much Is Still Political?" *Critical Asian Studies* 45 no. 3 (2015): 462–476.

"Figures at a Glance: 117.3 Million People Worldwide Were Forcibly Displaced." UNHCR. 2024. https://unhcr.org/about-unhcr/who-we-are/figures-glance.

Filut, Adrian. "A 25% Surge in the Number of Israelis Staying Abroad More Than Two Years." *Calcalist*, July 22, 2024. https://calcalist.co.il/local_news/article/b1kuoorcdr.

Fitzgerald, Jennifer, David Leblang, and Jessica Teets. "Defying the Law of Gravity: The Political Economy of International Migration." *World Politics* 66 no. 3 (2014): 151–171.

Fix, Michael and Jeffrey Passel. "The Scope and Impact of Welfare Reform's Immigrant Provisions." Urban Institute. 2002. https://urban.org/.

Ford, Robert, Matthew Goodwin, and David Cutts. "Strategic Eurosceptics and Polite Xenophobes: Support for the United Kingdom Independence Party (UKIP) in the 2009 European Parliament Elections: Strategic Eurosceptics and Polite Xenophobes." *European Journal of Political Research* 51 no. 2 (2012): 204–234.

Fouarge, Didier, Merve Bezihe Ozer, and Philipp Seegers. "Personality Traits, Migration Intentions, and Cultural Distance." *Papers in Regional Science* 98 no. 6 (2019): 2425–2454.

Freeman, G. P. "Migration and the Political Economy of the Welfare State." *Annals of the American Academy of Political and Social Science* 485 (1986): 51–63.

Fussell, E. and D. Massey. "The Limits to Cumulative Causation: International Migration from Mexican Urban Areas." *Demography* 41 no. 1 (2004): 151–171.

"The Future of Migration." Office of the Director of National Intelligence. April 2021. https://dni.gov/.

Gabriel, Trip. "Two Families Got Fed Up with Their State's Politics. So They Moved Out," *The New York Times*, October 7, 2024. https://nytimes.com/2023/10/07/us/politics/politics-states-moving.html.

Garip, F. and S. R. Curran. "Increasing Migration, Diverging Communities: Changing Character of Migrant Streams in Rural Thailand." *Population Research and Policy Review* 29 no. 5 (2010): 685–695.

Geddes, Barbara. "What Do We Know About Democratization After Twenty Years." *Annual Review of Political Science* 2 (1999): 115–144.

Geis, W., S. Uebelmesser, and M. Werding. "How Do Migrants Choose Their Destination Country? An Analysis of Institutional Determinants." *Review of International Economics* 21 no. 5 (2013): 825–840.

Georges, E. *The Making of a Transnational Community: Migration, Development and Cultural Change in the Dominican Republic.* New York: Columbia University Press. 1990.

Germano, R. "Migrants' Remittances and Economic Voting in the Mexican Countryside." *Electoral Studies* 32 no. 4 (2013): 875–885.

Gest, Justin. *Majority Minority.* Oxford: Oxford University Press. 2022.

Gest, Justin. *The New Minority: White Working Class Politics in an Age of Immigration and Inequality.* Oxford: Oxford University Press. 2016.

Gest, Justin and Anna Boucher. "A Segmented Theory of Immigration Regimes." *Polity* 53 no. 3 (2020): 439–468

Gest, Justin, Tyler Reny, and Jeremy Mayer. "Roots of the Radical Right: Nostalgic Deprivation in the United States and Britain." *Comparative Political Studies* 51 no. 13 (2018): 1694–1719.

Giesing, Y. and F. Schikora. "Emigrants' Missing Votes." *European Journal of Political Economy* 78 (2023): 102398.

Gleditsch, Kristian Skrede. "Transnational Dimensions of Civil War." *Journal of Peace Research* 44 no. 3 (2007): 293–309.

Glick Schiller, Nina and Georges Eugene Fouron. *Georges Woke Up Laughing: Long Distance Nationalism and the Search for Home.* Durham, NC: Duke University Press. 2001.

"Global Issues: International Migration." United Nations. https://un.org/en/global-issues/migration.

Goldstone, Jack. "Population and Security: How Demographic Change Can Lead to Violent Conflict." *Journal of International Affairs* 56 no. 1 (2002): 3–21.

Gonzalez-Acosta, Edward. "Dominican Republic – Building Trans-Migrant Citizenship." *Alterinfos.* 2007. https://alterinfos.org/.

Goodman, G. L. and J. T. Hiskey. "Exit without Leaving: Political Disengagement in High Migration Municipalities in Mexico." *Comparative Politics* 40 no. 2 (2008): 169–188.

Goodman, S. W. *Immigration and Membership Politics in Western Europe.* New York: Cambridge University Press. 2014.

Goodman, S. W. and G. C. Baldi. "Migrants into Members: Social Rights Civic Requirements, and Citizenship in Western Europe." *West European Politics* 38 no. 6 (2015): 1152–1173.

Gori Maia, Alexandre and Yao Lu. "Migration and Democratization in Brazil: The Case of Electoral Participation and Competition." *Demography* 58 no. 1 (2021): 191–217.

Griffiths, James. "The Return of Hong Kong's Umbrella Movement." *CNN*. June 12, 2019. https://cnn.com.

Grzymala-Busse, Anna. "The Failure of Europe's Mainstream Parties." *Journal of Democracy* 30 no. 4 (2019): 35–47.

Guarnizo, Luis Eduardo, Alejandro Portes, and William Haller. "Assimilation and Transnationalism: Determinants of Transnational Political Action among Contemporary Migrants." *American Journal of Sociology* 108 no. 6 (2003): 1211–1248.

Gugushvili, Alexi. "Democratic Discontent and Emigration: Do Political Attitudes Explain Emigration Intentions?" Mimeo, European University Institute. 2011.

Guiraudon, V. and C. Joppke. "Controlling a New Migration World." In *Controlling a New Migration World*, eds. V. Guiraudon and C. Joppke, 13–40. London: Routledge. 2003.

Hainmueller, J. and D. Hopkins. "Attitudes Toward Immigration." *Annual Review of Political Science* 17 no. 1 (2014): 225–249.

Hainmueller, J., D. Hangartner, and T. Yamamoto. "Validating Vignette and Conjoint Survey Experiments against Real-world Behavior." *Proceedings of the National Academy of Sciences* 112 no. 8 (2015): 2395–2400.

Hainmueller, J., D. J. Hopkins, and T. Yamamoto. "Causal Inference in Conjoint Analysis: Understanding Multidimensional Choices via Stated Preference Experiments." *Political Analysis* 22 no. 1 (2014): 1–30.

Halikiopoulou, Daphne and Sofia Vasilopoulou. "Breaching the Social Contract: Crises of Democratic Representation and Patterns of Extreme Right Party Support." *Government and Opposition* 53 no. 1 (2018): 26–50.

Haney, Patrick J. and Walt Vanderbush. "The Role of Ethnic Interest Groups in U.S. Foreign Policy: The Case of the Cuban American National Foundation." *International Studies Quarterly* 43 no. 2 (1999): 341–361.

Harris, John and Michael Todaro. "Migration, Unemployment and Development: A Two-Sector Analysis." *American Economic Review* 60 no. 1 (1970): 126–142.

Harteveld, Eelco, Joep Schaper, darah de Lange, and Wouter Van Der Brug. "Blaming Brussels? The Impact of (News about) the Refugee Crisis on Attitudes towards the EU and National Politics." *JCMS: Journal of Common Market Studies* 56 no. 1 (2018): 157–177.

Hastings, Rob. "Neighbors from Hell: How Syria's War Hit an Acton Street." *The Independent*. March 18, 2012. www.independent.co.uk/.

Hatton, Timothy. *Seeking Asylum: Trends and policies in the OECD*. London: Centre for Economic Policy Research. 2011.

Hayek, Friedrich von. "Scientism and the Study of Society I." *Economica* 9 (1942): 267–291.

Hayek, Friedrich von. "Scientism and the Study of Society II." *Economica* 10 (1944): 34–63.

Hayek, Friedrich von. "Scientism and the Study of Society III." *Economica* 11 (1955): 27–39.

Hayek, Friedrich von. *The Counter-Revolution of Science.* New York: Free Press. 1955.

He, Rowena Xiaoqing. *Tiananmen Exiles: Voices of the Struggle for Democracy in China.* New York: Palgrave Macmillan. 2014.

Heckathorn, Douglas. "Collective Sanctions and the Creation of Prisoner's Dilemma Norms." *American Journal of Sociology* 94 no. 3 (1988): 535–562.

Hemmerechts, K., H. M. De Clerck, R. Willems, and C. Timmerman. "Project Paper 14: Eumagine Final Report with Policy Considerations." *EUMAGINE.* 2014. http://eumagine.org/.

Henry, R. "Does Racism Affect a Migrant's Choice of Destination? A Case Study of African Americans, 1995–2000." Paper presented at 10th European Summer Symposium in Labour Economics, IZA, Buch, Germany. October 8–12, 2008.

Hinnebusch, Raymond. "Authoritarian Persistence, Democratization Theory and the Middle East: An Overview and Critique." *Democratization* 13 no. 3 (2006): 373–395.

Hironaka, Ann. *Neverending Wars: The International Community, Weak States, and the Perpetuation of Civil War.* Cambridge, MA: Harvard University Press. 2005.

Hirschman, Albert. *Exit, Voice, and Loyalty: Responses to Decline in Firms, Organizations, and States.* Cambridge, MA: Harvard University Press. 1970.

Hirschman, Albert O. "Exit, Voice, and the State." *World Politics* 31 no. 1 (1978): 90–107.

Hiskey, Jonathan, Jorge Daniel Montalvo, and Diana Orcés. "Democracy, Governance, and Emigration Intention in Latin America and the Caribbean." *Studies in Comparative International Development* 49 (2014): 89–111.

Hiskey, Jonathan and Diana Orces. "Transition Shocks and Emigration Profiles in Latin America." *The Annals of the American Academy of Political and Social Science* 630 (2010): 116–136.

Ho, Kelly. "Hong Kong Security Chief Hails 100% Conviction Rate in National Security Cases." *Hong Kong Free Press.* April 14, 2023. https://hongkongfp.com/.

Hockenos, Paul. *Homeland Calling: Exile Patriotism and the Balkan Wars.* Ithaca, NY: Cornell University Press. 2003.

Hoffmann, B. "Emigration and Regime Stability: The Persistence of Cuban Socialism." *Journal of Communist Studies and Transition Politics* 21 no. 4 (2005): 436–461.

Holland, A., M. Peters, and T. Sanchez. "Migrants' Destination Choices." Working Paper. 2018.

Hollersen, Wiebke. "Syrian in Berlin Channels Aid to Embattled Countrymen." *Spiegel Online.* March 16, 2012. www.spiegel.de/.

"Hong Kong National Security Law: What Is It and Is It worrying?" *BBC.* June 28, 2022. https://bbc.com/news/world-asia-china-52765838.

"Hong Kong: UK Makes Citizenship Offer to Residents." *BBC.* July 1, 2020. https://bbc.com/news/uk-politics-53246899.

Hook, Brian. "Political Change in Hong Kong." *The China Quarterly* no. 136 (1993): 840–863.

Horiuchi, Y., Z. D. Markovich, and T. Yamamoto. "Can Conjoint Analysis Mitigate Social Desirability Bias?" Working Paper. 2018.

Howard, P. N. and M. M. Hussain. *Democracy's Fourth Wave?: Digital Media and the Arab Spring.* Oxford: Oxford University Press. 2013.

Huber, Peter and Klaus Nowotny. "Risk Aversion and the Willingness to Migrate in 30 Transition Countries." *Journal of Population Economics* 33 (2020): 1463–1498.

Huntington, Samuel. *The Third Wave: Democratization in the Late Twentieth Century.* Norman, OK: University of Oklahoma Press. 1991.

Imbens, Guido and Karthik Kalyanaraman. "Optimal Bandwidth Choice for the Regression Discontinuity Estimator." *The Review of Economic Studies* 79 no. 3 (2012): 933–959.

"International migration in Russia from 1997 to 2021, by flow." *Statista.* September 2022. https://statista.com/.

Iosifides, T., M. Lavrentiadou, E. Petracou, and A. Kontis. "Forms of Social Capital and the Incorporation of Albanian Immigrants in Greece." *Journal of Ethnic and Migration Studies* 33 no. 8 (2007): 1343–1361.

Irwin-Hunt, Alex. "Brain Drain: Countries with the Greatest Human Capital Flight." *FDI Intelligence.* April 19, 2023. https://fdiintelligence.com/content/data-trends/brain-drain-countries-with-the-greatest-human-capital-flight-82395.

Israel Young Academy. "The Potential Effects of the Political Crisis in Israel on Human Capital in Academic Institutions Survey." March 20, 2023. https://young.academy.ac.il/News/NewsItem.aspx?nodeId=955&id=622.

Itzigsohn, J., and D. Villacrés. "Migrant Political Transnationalism and the Practice of Democracy: Dominican External Voting Rights and Salvadoran Home Town Associations." *Ethnic & Racial Studies* 31 no. 4 (2008): 664–686.

Ivarsflaten, Elizabeth. "What Unites Right-Wing Populists in Western Europe?: Re-Examining Grievance Mobilization Models in Seven Successful Cases." *Comparative Political Studies* 41 no. 1 (2008): 3–23.

Ivlevs, Artjoms and Roswitha King. "Does Emigration Reduce Corruption?" *Public Choice* 171 no. 3/4 (2017): 389–408.

Jackman, Robert. "On the Relations of Economic Development to Democratic Performance." *American Journal of Political Science* 17 (1973): 611–621.

Jackson, Lewis. "After Trump's Win, Many Despondent Americans Research Moving Abroad," *Reuters.* November 8, 2024. https://reuters.com/world/us/after-trumps-win-many-despondent-americans-research-moving-abroad-2024-11-08/.

James, P., and L. Mayblin. "Factors Influencing Asylum Destination Choice: A Review of the Evidence." University of Sheffield Working Papers No. 04/16.1. 2016.

Jasko, Katarzyna, David Webber, Erica Molinario, Aerie Kruglanski, and Katharine Touchton-Leonard. "Ideological Extremism Among Syrian Refugees Is Negatively Related to Intentions to Migrate to the West." *Psychological Science* 32 no. 9 (2021): 1362–1374.

Jasper, Christopher and Misha Savic. "Russians Have a Secret Escape Hatch to Europe – Serbia." *Fortune.* March 11, 2022. https://fortune.com/.

Javorcik, Beata, Çağlar Özden, Mariana Spatareanu, and Cristina Neagu. "Migrant Networks and Foreign Direct Investment." World Bank Policy Research Working Paper 4046. 2006.

Jenne, Erin. *Ethnic Bargaining: The Paradox of Minority Empowerment*. Ithaca, NY: Cornell University Press. 2007.

Johnston, Hank. "Talking the Walk: Speech Acts and Resistance in Authoritarian Regimes." In *Repression and Mobilization*, eds. C. Davenport, H. Johnston, and C. Mueller, 108–137. Minneapolis: University of Minnesota Press. 2005.

Jokela, M. "Personality Predicts Migration within and between U.S. States." *Journal of Research in Personality* 43 no. 1 (2009): 79–83.

Jokela, M., M. Elovainio, M. Kivimäki and L. Keltikangas-Järvinen. "Temperament and Migration Patterns in Finland." *Psychological Science* 19 no. 9 (2008): 831–837.

Jones-Correa, Michael. *Between Two Nations: The Political Predicament of Latinos in New York City*. Cornell, NY: Cornell University Press. 1998.

Kaldor, Mary. *New and Old Wars: Organised Violence in a Global Era*. Cambridge: Polity Press. 1999.

Kaldor, Mary and Diego Muro. "Nationalist and Religious Militant Networks." In *Global Civil Society*, eds. Mary Kaldor, Helmut Anheier, and Marlies Glasius, 154–160. Oxford: Oxford University Press. 2003.

Kantchev, Georgi, Evan Gershkovich, and Yuliya Chernova. "Russia's Brain Drain: Hundreds of Thousands of Professionals and Highly Skilled Workers Have Left Country Since Putin's Invasion of Ukraine." *MarketWatch*. April 11, 2022. https://marketwatch.com/.

Kapur, Devesh. *Diaspora, Democracy, and Development: The Domestic Impact of International Migration from India*. Princeton, NJ: Princeton University Press. 2010.

Kapur, Devesh. "Remittances: The New Development Mantra?" United Nations Conference on Trade and Development. April 2004. https://unctad.org/system/files/official-document/gdsmdpbg2420045_en.pdf.

Karadja, M. and E. Prawitz. "Exit, Voice, and Political Change: Evidence from Swedish Mass Migration to the United States." *Journal of Political Economy* 127 no. 4 (2019): 1864–1925.

Karakoç, E., T. Köse, and M. Özcan. "Emigration and the Diffusion of Political Salafism: Religious Remittances and Support for Salafi Parties in Egypt during the Arab Spring." *Party Politics* 23 no. 6 (2017): 731–745.

Kaysen, Ronda and Ethan Singer. "Millions of Movers Reveal American Polarization in Action," *The New York Times*, October 30, 2024. Accessed via https://nytimes.com/interactive/2024/10/30/upshot/voters-moving-polarization.html.

Kazemi, Farhad and Augustus Richard Norton. "Authoritarianism, Civil Society and Democracy in the Middle East: Mass Media in the Persian Gulf." *Middle East Studies Bulletin* 40 no. 2 (2006): 201–211.

Keck, Margaret E. and Kathryn Sikkink. *Activists Beyond Borders: Advocacy Networks in International Politics*. Ithaca, NY: Cornell University Press. 1998.

Kefford, Glenn and Shaun Ratcliff. "Populists or Nativist Authoritarians? A Cross-National Analysis of the Radical Right." *Australian Journal of Political Science* 56 no. 3 (2021): 261–279.

Kelemen, R. D. "The European Union's Authoritarian Equilibrium." *Journal of European Public Policy* 27 no. 3 (2020): 481–499.

Khagram, Sanjeev, James V. Riker, and Kathryn Sikkink. eds. *Restructuring World Politics: Transnational Social Movements, Networks, and Norms.* Minneapolis: University of Minnesota Press. 2002.

Khamis, S., P. B. Gold, and K. Vaughn. "Beyond Egypt's 'Facebook Revolution' and Syria's 'Youtube Uprising:' Comparing Political Contexts, Actors and Communication Strategies." *Arab Media & Society.* March 28, 2012. https://arabmediasociety.com.

Khawaja, Marwan. "Repression and Popular Collective Action: Evidence from the West Bank." *Sociological Forum* 8 (1993): 47–71.

King, R. "Theories and Typologies of Migration: An Overview and a Primer." *Willy Brandt Series of Working Papers in International Migration and Ethnic Relations* 3 no. 12 (2012): 1–43.

Klimek, P., A. Aykaç, and S. Thurner. "Forensic Analysis of the Turkey 2023 Presidential Election Reveals Extreme Vote Swings in Remote Areas." *PLoS ONE* 18 no. 11 (2023): e0293239. https://doi.org/10.1371/journal.pone.0293239.

Koinova, Maria. "Can Conflict-Generated Diasporas Be Moderate Actors during Episodes of Contested Sovereignty? Lebanese and Albanian Diasporas Compared." *Review of International Studies* 37 no. 1 (2011b): 437–462.

Koinova, Maria. "Diaspora Mobilisation for Conflict and Post-conflict Reconstruction: Contextual and Comparative Dimensions." *Journal of Ethnic and Migration Studies* 44 no. 8 (2018): 1251–1269.

Koinova, Maria. "Diasporas and Democratization in the Post-communist World." *Communist & Post-Communist Studies* 42 no. 1 (2009): 41–64.

Koinova, Maria. "Diasporas and Secessionist Conflicts: The Mobilization of the Armenian, Albanian and Chechen Diasporas." *Ethnic and Racial Studies* 34 no. 2 (2011): 333–356.

Koinova, Maria. "Four Types of Diaspora Mobilization: Albanian Diaspora Activism for Kosovo Independence in the US and the UK." *Foreign Policy Analysis* 9 no. 4 (2013): 433–453.

Koinova, Maria. "Why Do Conflict-Generated Diasporas Pursue Sovereignty-Based Claims Through State-Based or Transnational Channels? Armenian, Albanian and Palestinian Diasporas in the UK Compared." *European Journal of International Relations* 20 no. 4 (2014): 1043–1071.

Koning, E. The Real and Perceived Economics of Immigration: Welfare Chauvinism and Immigrants' Use of Government Transfers in Twelve Countries. Working Paper. 2011.

Konte, Maty. The Effects of Remittances on Support for Democracy in Africa: Are Remittances a Curse of a Blessing? Working Paper. 2015.

Korinek, K., B. Entwisle, and A. Jampaklay. "Through Thick and Thin: Layers of Social Ties and Urban Settlement among Thai Migrants." *American Sociological Review* 70 no. 5 (2005): 779–800.

Kostovicova, Denisa and Albert Prestreshi. "Education, Gender and Religion: Identity Transformations among Kosovo Albanians in London." *Journal of Ethnic and Migration Studies* 29 no. 6 (2010): 1079–1096.

Krawatzek, F. and L. Müller-Funk. "Two Centuries of Flows between 'Here' and 'There': Political Remittances and Their Transformative Potential." *Journal of Ethnic and Migration Studies* 46 no. 6 (2020): 1003–1024.

Kushnirovich, Nonna, Sibylle Heilbrunn, and Liema Davidovich. "Diversity of Entrepreneurial Perceptions: Immigrants vs. Native Population." *European Management Review* 15 no. 3 (2018): 341–355.

Kustov, Alexander. *In Our Interest: How Democracies Can Make Immigration Popular*. New York: Columbia University Press. 2025.

Larzelere, Alex. *Castro's Ploy, America's Dilemma: The 1980 Cuban Boatlift*. Washington, DC: National Defense University Press. 1988.

Lendvai, Paul. *Orbán: Europe's New Strongman*. London: Hurst. 2019.

Leung, Kanis and Zen Soo. "Hong Kong Offers New Visa to Woo Talent Amid Brain Drain." *Associate Press*. October 19, 2022. https://apnews.com/.

Levie, Jonathan. "Immigration, In-Migration, Ethnicity and Entrepreneurship in the United Kingdom." *Small Business Economics* 28 no. 2/3 (2007): 143–169.

Levine, P. B. and D. J. Zimmerman. "An Empirical Analysis of the Welfare Magnet Debate Using the NLSY." *Journal of Population Economics* 12 no. 3 (1999): 391–409.

Levitsky, S. and L. A. Way *Competitive Authoritarianism: Hybrid Regimes after the Cold War*. Cambridge: Cambridge University Press. 2010.

Levitt, Peggy. "Social Remittances: Migration Driven Local-Level Forms of Cultural Diffusion." *International Migration Review* 32 no. 4 (1998): 926–948.

Levitt, Peggy. *The Transnational Villagers*. Berkeley: University of California Press. 2001.

Levitt, Peggy and Rafael de la Dehesa. "Transnational Migration and the Redefinition of the State: Variations and Explanations." *Ethnic and Racial Studies* 26 no. 4 (2003): 587–611.

Levitt, Peggy and Mary Waters. *The Changing Face of Home: The Transnational Lives of the Second Generation*. New York: Russell Sage. 2002.

Levy, Morris and Matthew Wright. *Immigration and the American Ethos*. Cambridge: Cambridge University Press. 2020.

Lichtenheld, A. *Guilt by Location: Forced Displacement and Population Sorting in Civil Wars*. Cambridge: Cambridge University Press. 2024.

Lien, Pei-te. "Pre-Emigration Socialization, Transnational Ties, and Political Participation Across the Pacific: A Comparison Among Immigrants from China, Taiwan, and Hong Kong." *Journal of East Asian Studies* 10 no. 3 (2010): 453–482.

Lim, J. "The Electoral Consequences of International Migration in Sending Countries: Evidence from Central and Eastern Europe." *Comparative Political Studies* 56 no. 1 (2023): 36–64.

Lipset, Seymour Martin. *Political Man: The Social Bases of Politics*. Garden City, NY: Doubleday. 1960.

Lodigliani, Elisabetta. "Diaspora Externalities as a Cornerstone of the New Brain Drain Literature." Universit catholique de Louvain, Institut de Recherches Economiques et Sociales, Discussion Paper 2009-36. 2009.

Lok-kei, Sum. "Fighting an Exodus, Hong Kong Faces a Tough Task to Lure Back Young People." *The Guardian*. November 23, 2022. https://theguardian.com/.

Lopušina, Marko and Dušan Lopušina, eds. *Hotel MOSKVA – prvih 100 godina*. Belgrade: Hotel Moskva. 2008.

Lüküslü, Demet. "The Desire of Young People in Turkey to Live Abroad: An Analysis of Recent Surveys on Youth in Turkey." IPC-Mercator Analysis. 2024. Istanbul: Istanbul Policy Center.

Lundquist, Jennifer H. and Douglas S. Massey. "Politics or Economics? International Migration during the Nicaraguan Contra War." *Journal of Latin American Studies* 37 no. 1 (2005): 29–53.

Luttmer, Erzo and Monica Singhal. "Culture, Context and the Taste for Redistribution." National Bureau of Economic Research Working Paper 14268. 2011.

Lyons, Terrence. "Diasporas and Homeland Conflict." In *Territoriality and Conflict in an Era of Globalization*, eds. Miles Kahler and Barbara Walter, 111–131. New York: Cambridge University Press. 2006.

Lyons, Terrence and Peter Mandaville. *Politics from Afar: Transnational Diasporas and Networks*. New York: Columbia University Press. 2012.

Mandaville, Peter. *Global Political Islam*. New York/London: Routledge. 2007.

Mariani, F. "Migration as an Antidote to Rent-seeking?" *Journal of Development Economics* 84 no. 2 (2007): 609–630.

Marinova, Nadejda. *Ask What You Can Do For Your (New) Country: How Host States Use Diasporas*. Oxford and New York: Oxford University Press. 2017.

Massey, Douglas. "Social Structure, Household Strategies, and the Cumulative Causation of Migration." *Population Index* 56 no. 1 (1990): 3–26.

Massey, Douglas and K. E. Espinosa. "What's Driving Mexico-U.S. Migration? A Theoretical, Empirical, and Policy Analysis." *American Journal of Sociology* 102 no. 4 (1997): 939–999.

Massey, Douglas and Felipe Garcia España. "The Social Process of International Migration." *Science* 237 no. 4816 (1987): 733–738.

Massey, Douglas and Rene Zenteno. "A Validation of the Ethnosurvey: The Case of Mexico-U.S. Migration." *International Migration Review* 34 no. 3 (2000): 766–793.

Massey, Douglas, Joaquin Arango, Graeme Hugo, Ali Kouanouci, Adela Pellegrino, and Edward Taylor. "An Evaluation of International Migration Theory: The North American Case." *Population and Development Review* 20 no. 4 (1994): 699–751.

Mavroudi, Elizabeth. "Deconstructing Diasporic Mobilisation at a Time of Crisis: Perspectives from the Palestinian and Greek Diasporas." *Journal of Ethnic and Migration Studies* 44 no. 13 (2017): 1–16.

Mayda, A. "International Migration: A Panel Data Analysis of the Determinants of Bilateral Flows." *Journal of Population Economics* 23 no. 4 (2010): 1249–1274.

Merem, E. C., Y. A. Twumasi, J. Wesley, D. Olagbegi, M. Crisler, C. Romorno, M. Alsarari, P. Isokpehi, M. Alrefai, S. Ochai, E. Nwagboso, S. Fageir, and

S. Leggett. "The Assessment of China's Scramble for Natural Resources Extraction in Africa." *World Environment* 11 no. 1 (2021): 9–25.

Meyer, Jean-Baptiste and Mercy Brown. "Scientific Diasporas: A New Approach to Brain Drain." World Conference on Science, UNESCO-ICSU. 2009.

Michaeli, Moti, Marco Casari, Andrea Ichino, Maria De Paola, Ginevra Marandola, and Vincenzo Scoppa. "Civicness Drain." *The Economic Journal* 133 no. 649 (2023): 323–354.

Michaelsen, M. and M. Glasius. "Authoritarian Practices in the Digital Age: Introduction." *International Journal of Communication* 12 (2018): 3788–3794.

Migali, S. and M. Scipioni. "A Gobal Analysis of Intentions to Migrate." European Commission. 2018.

"Migrant Access to Social Security and Healthcare: Policies and Practice." European Migration Network. 2014. https://home-affairs.ec.europa.eu/.

Mikhail, Amira. "The Obliteration of Civil Society in Egypt." Open Democracy. October 6, 2014. https://opendemocracy.net.

Miller, Michael and Margaret Peters. "Restraining the Huddled Masses: Migration Policy and Autocratic Survival." *British Journal of Political Science* 50 no. 2 (2020): 403–433.

Moore, Barrington Jr. *Injustice: The Social Bases of Obedience and Revolt.* White Plains, NY: M.E. Sharpe. 1978.

Moss, Dana. "Repression, Response, and Contained Escalation under 'Liberalized' Authoritarianism in Jordan." *Mobilization: An International Quarterly* 19 no. 3 (2014): 489–514.

Moss, Dana. "The Ties That Bind: Internet Communication Technologies, Networked Authoritarianism, and 'Voice' in the Syrian Diaspora." *Globalizations* 15 no. 2 (2018): 265–282.

Moss, Dana. "Transnational Repression, Diaspora Mobilization, and the Case of the Arab Spring." *Social Problems* 63 no. 4 (2016): 480–498.

Motyl, M., R. Iyer, S. Oishi, S. Trawalter, and B. A. Nosek. "How Ideological Migration Geographically Segregates Groups." *Journal of Experimental Social Psychology* 51 (2014): 1–14.

Munshi, Kavian. "Networks in the Modern Economy: Mexican Migrants in the U.S. Labor Market." *Quarterly Journal of Economics* 118 no. 2 (2003): 549–599.

Mylonas, Harris and Scott Radnitz, eds. *Enemies Within: The Global Politics of Fifth Columns.* New York: Oxford University Press. 2022.

Nackerud, Larry, Alyson Springer, Christopher Larrison, and Alicia Issac. "The End of the Cuban Contradiction in U.S. Refugee Policy." *International Migration Review* 33 no. 1 (1999): 176–192. https://doi.org/10.2307/2547327.

Nyberg-Sørensen, N., N. Van Hear, and P. Engberg-Pedersen. "The Migration-Development Nexus: Evidence and Policy Options." *International Migration* 40 no. 5 (2002): 49–73.

Nyst, C. and N. Monaco. "State-Sponsored Trolling: How Governments Are Deploying Disinformation as Part of Broader Digital Harassment Campaigns." Palo Alto, CA: Institute for the Future. July 19, 2018. http://iftf.org/.

Oppenheimer, F. E. "Governments and Authorities in Exile." *American Journal of International Law* 36 no. 4 (1942): 568–595.

Orjuela, Camilla. "Distant Warriors, Distant Peace Workers? Multiple Diaspora Roles in Sri Lanka's Violent Conflict." *Global Networks* 8 no. 4 (2008): 436–452.

Osaghae, Eghosa. "Exiting from the State in Nigeria." *African Journal of Political Science / Revue Africaine de Science Politique* 4 no. 1 (1999): 83–98.

Østergaard-Nielsen, Eva. "The Democratic Deficit of Diaspora Politics: Turkish Cypriots in Britain and the Cyprus Issue." *Journal of Ethnic and Migration Studies* 29 no. 4 (2003): 683–700.

Østergaard-Nielsen, Eva. "Democratization and Contestation of Transnational Spaces between Moroccan Migrants in Spain and Morocco." In *Politics from Afar: Transnational Diasporas and Networks*, eds. Peter Mandaville and Terrence Lyons. New York: Columbia University Press. 2012.

Østergaard-Nielsen, Eva. "Diasporas in World Politics." In *Non-State Actors in World Politics*, eds. D. Josselin and W. Wallace, 217–235. New York: Palgrave. 2001.

"Overview of Immigrants' Eligibility for SNAP, TANF, Medicaid, and CHIP." U.S. Department of Health and Human Services Office of the Assistant Secretary for Planning and Evaluation. March 26, 2012. https://aspe.hhs.gov/.

Ozdogan, Zeliha. "The Effects of Democratic Regression on Turkish Economy and the Brain Drain." In *Human Rights in Turkey: Assaults on Human Dignity*, eds. Hasan Aydın and Winston Langley, 365–382. Cham: Springer International Publishing. 2021.

Paarlberg, M. "Transnational Militancy: Diaspora Influence over Electoral Activity in Latin America." *Comparative Politics* 49 no. 4 (2017): 541–559.

Parvaz, D. "Expats Join Syrian Revolution from Afar." *Al-Jazeera English*, September 8, 2011. www.aljazeera.com/indepth/features/2011/09/201195123037726408 .html.

Paulauskaitė, E., L. Šeibokaitė, and A. Endriulaitienė. "Big Five Personality Traits Linked with Migratory Intentions in Lithuanian Student Sample." *International Journal of Psychology: A Biopsychosocial Approach* 7 (2010): 41–58.

Pearlman, Wendy. "Narratives of Fear in Syria." *Perspectives on Politics* 14 no. 1 (2016): 21–37.

Pedersen, P. J., M. Pytlikova, and N. Smith. "Selection and Network Effects–Migration Flows into OECD Countries 1990–2000." *European Economic Review* 52 no. 7 (2008): 1160–1186.

Pemstein, Daniel, Kyle L. Marquardt, Eitan Tzelgov, Yi-ting Wang, Juraj Medzihorsky, Joshua Krusell, Farhad Miri, and Johannes von Römer. "The V-Dem Measurement Model: Latent Variable Analysis for Cross-National and Cross-Temporal Expert-Coded Data." V-Dem Working Paper No. 21. 8th ed. University of Gothenburg, Varieties of Democracy Institute. 2023.

Pérez-Armendáriz, C. "Cross-Border Discussions and Political Behavior in Migrant-Sending Countries." *Studies in Comparative International Development* 49 no. 1 (2014): 67–88.

Pérez-Armendáriz, C. and D. Crow. "Do Migrants Remit Democracy? International Migration, Political Beliefs, and Behavior in Mexico." *Comparative Political Studies* 43 no. 1 (2010): 119–148.

Péridy, Nicolas. "Welfare Magnets, Border Effects or Policy Regulations: What Determinants Drive Migration Flows into the EU." *Global Economy Journal* 6 no. 4 (2006): 1–35.

"Personal Remittances, Received (% of GDP)." World Bank. 2014.

Peters, Margaret and Michael Miller. "Emigration and Political Contestation." *International Studies Quarterly* 66 no. 1 (2022).

Pfaff, Steven. "The Limits of Coercive Surveillance: Social and Penal Control in the German Democratic Republic." *Punishment & Society* 3 no. 3 (2001): 381–407.

Pfaff, Steven and H. Kim. "Exit-voice Dynamics in Collective Action: An Analysis of Emigration and Protest in the East German Revolution." *American Journal of Sociology* 109 no. 2 (2003): 401–444.

Pfutze, T. "Does Migration Promote Democratization? Evidence from the Mexican Transition." *Journal of Comparative Economics* 40 no. 2 (2012): 159–175.

Pop-Eleches, G. and J. A. Tucker. *Communism's Shadow: Historical Legacies and Contemporary Political Attitudes*. Princeton: Princeton University Press. 2017.

Poprawe, Marie. "On the Relationship between Corruption and Migration: Empirical Evidence from a Gravity Model of Migration." *Public Choice* 163 no. 3/4 (2015): 337–354.

Portes, Alejandro. "The Debates and Significance of Immigrant Transnationalism." *Global Networks* 1 no. 3 (2001): 181–193.

Portes, Alejandro and M. Zhou. "The New Second Generation: Segmented Assimilation and Its Variants." *The Annals of the American Academy of Political and Social Science* 530 no. 1 (1993): 74–96.

Portes, Alejandro, L. E. Guarnizo and P. Landolt. "The Study of Transnationalism: Pitfalls and Promises of an Mergent Research Field." *Ethnic and Racial Studies* 22 no. 2 (1999): 217–237.

Przeworski, A. and F. Limongi. "Modernization: Theories and Facts." *World Politics* 49 (1997): 155–183.

Pugliese, Anita and Julie Ray. "Nearly 900 Million Worldwide Wanted to Migrate in 2021." *Gallup*. January 24, 2023. https://news.gallup.com/.

Quinsaat, Sharon M. *Insurgent Communities: How Protests Create a Filipino Diaspora*. Chicago: University of Chicago Press. 2024.

Rauch, J. E. "Diasporas and Development: Theory, Evidence, and Programmatic Implications." Department of Economics, University of California at San Diego. 2003.

Rauch, J. E. and V. Trindade. "Ethnic Chinese Networks in International Trade." *Review of Economics and Statistics* 84 no. 1 (2002): 116–130.

"Remarks by President Biden on the United Efforts of the Free World to Support the People of Ukraine." *White House*. March 26, 2022. www.whitehouse.gov/.

Remhof, Stefan, Marjaana Gunkel, and Christopher Schlaegel. "Goodbye Germany! The Influence of Personality and Cognitive Factors on the Intention to Work Abroad." *International Journal of Human Resource Management* 25 no. 16 (2014): 2319–2343.

Reny, Tyler and Justin Gest. "Viewers Like You: The Effect of Elite Co-identity Reinforcement on US Immigration Attitudes." *Politics, Groups, and Identities* 12 no. 5 (2023): 969–985.

"Report of the Independent International Commission of Inquiry on the Syrian Arab Republic." United Nations Human Rights Council. August 9, 2018. https://documents-dds-ny.un.org/.

"Return Migration: A New Perspective," OECD Directorate for Employment, Labour and Social Affairs, Employment, Labour and Social Affairs Committee, September 17, 2008. https://one.oecd.org/document/DELSA/ELSA/MI(2008)6/en/pdf.

Rice-Oxley, Mark and Jennifer Rankin. "Europe's South and East Worry More about Emigration than Immigration – Poll." *The Guardian.* March 31, 2019. https://theguardian.com/world/2019/apr/01/europe-south-and-east-worry-more-about-emigration-than-immigration-poll.

Robinson, P. "The White Russian Army in Exile, 1920–1941." PhD thesis, University of Oxford. 1999.

Rodden, J. A. *Why Cities Lose: The Deep Roots of the Urban-rural Political Divide.* New York: Basic Books. 2019.

Ross, Michael. "Will Oil Drown the Arab Spring." *Foreign Affairs* 90 no. 5 (2001): 2–7.

Rovny, J. "Circumstantial Liberals: Czech Germans in Interwar Czechoslovakia." *HAL Open Science.* 2020. https://sciencespo.hal.science/hal-02459013v1/document.

Roy, D. "Egyptian Emigrant Labor: Domestic Consequences." *Middle Eastern Studies* 27 no. 4 (1991): 551–582.

"Russians Founded More than 300 Companies in Serbia Since the Beginning of the War in Ukraine." *Maj Novsitad.* April 2, 2022. www.mojnovisad.com/.

"Russians Have Emigrated in Huge Numbers Since the War in Ukraine." *The Economist.* August 23, 2023.

Sainsbury, D. *Welfare States and Immigrant Rights: The Politics of Inclusion and Exclusion.* Oxford: Oxford University Press. 2012.

Salehyan, Idean. *Rebels without Borders: Transnational Insurgencies in World Politics.* Ithaca, NY: Cornell University Press. 2009.

Sava, Justina Alexandra. "Main Reasons Why Young People Decide to Leave Romania in 2019." Statista Research Department. 2019. https://statista.com/statistics/1103824/reasons-to-leave-romania/.

Saxenian, Annalee. *Silicon Valley's New Immigrant Entrepreneurs.* San Francisco: Public Policy Institute of California. 1999.

Schachar, A. "The Race for Talent: Highly Skilled Migrants and Competitive Immigration Regimes." *New York University Law Review* 81 (2006): 148–206.

Scott-Railton, J., B. Abdulrazzak, A. Hulcoop, M. Brooks, and K. Kleemola. "Group5: Syria and the Iranian Connection." Toronto: The Citizen Lab, Munk School of Global Affairs, University of Toronto. 2016.

"Serbia's Incumbent President Vucic Set to Win Second Term." *Reuters.* April 3, 2022. https://reuters.com/.

Shain, Y. *Marketing the American Creed Abroad: Diasporas in the US and Their Homelands.* New York: Cambridge University Press. 1999.

Shain, Y. "The Role of Diasporas in Conflict Perpetuation and Resolution." *SAIS Review* 22 no. 2 (2002): 115–144.

Shain, Y. and Ravinatha P. Aryasinha. "Spoilers or Catalysts? The Role of Diasporas in Peace Processes." In *Challenges to Peacebuilding: Managing Spoilers During Conflict Resolution*, eds. Edward Newman and Oliver Richmond, 105–133. Tokyo: United Nations University Press. 2006.

Shain, Y. and A. Barth. "Diasporas and International Relations Theory." *International Organization* 57 no. 3 (2003): 449–479.

Sheffer, Gabriel. *Diaspora Politics: At Home Abroad*. New York: Cambridge University Press. 2003.

Shehata, Samer S. "In Egypt, Democrats vs. Liberals." *The New York Times*. July 2, 2013. https://.nytimes.com/2013/07/03/opinion/in-egypt-democrats-vs-liberals.html.

Silventoinen, K., N. Hammar, E. Hedlund, M. Koskenvuo, T. Rönnemaa, and J. Kaprio. "Selective International Migration by Social Position, Health Behaviour and Personality." *European Journal of Public Health* 18 no. 2 (2008): 150–155.

Siu-lun, Wong. "Emigration and Stability in Hong Kong." *Asian Survey* 32 no. 10 (1992): 918–933.

Sjaastad, Larry. "The Costs and Returns on Human Migration." *Journal of Political Economy* 70 no. 5 (1962): 80–93.

Skeldon, Ronald. "Emigration and the Future of Hong Kong." *Pacific Affairs* 63 no. 4 (1990): 500–523.

Skytt, Lasse. *Orbánland: Why Viktor Orbán's Hungary Matters*. Williamstown, MA: New Europe Books. 2021.

Smith, Hazel and Paul Stares. *Diasporas in Conflict: Peace-Makers or Peace-Wreckers?* New York: United Nations University Press. 2007.

Smith, Michael and Luis Guarnizo. *Transnationalism from Below*. New Brunswick: Transaction. 1998.

Sökefeld, Martin. "Mobilizing in Transnational Space." *Global Networks* 6 no. 3 (2006): 265–284.

Somin, I. *Free to Move: Foot Voting, Migration, and Political Freedom*. New York: Oxford University Press. 2020.

Spadacene, Dominic. "Orban Has Begun Taking Steps to Preserve His Power." *EURACTIV*. May 5, 2021. https://euractiv.com/.

Spillembergo, Antonio. "Democracy and Foreign Education." *American Economic Review* 99 no. 1 (2009): 528–543.

Stark, Oded and David Bloom. "The New Economics of Labor Migration." *American Economic Review* 75 no. 2 (1985): 173–178.

"Statement Issued by Syrian Organizations Working in the Fields of Documentation, Accountability and Transitional Justice in Support of the Work of the International, Impartial and Independent Mechanism (IIIM)." Syria Justice & Accountability Centre. 2018. https://stj-sy.org/uploads/pdf_files/IIIM%20Statement%20Final_%20Signed.pdf.

Stefanos, Amal. "Eritrea's 'Diaspora Tax' Is Funding Violence and Oppression." *Al Jazeera*. February 20, 2023. https://aljazeera.com.

Stepan, Alfred and Juan J. Linz. "Democratization Theory and the 'Arab Spring'." *Journal of Democracy* 24 no. 2 (2013): 15–30.

Stojanovic, Milica. "Russian Flights Tickets to Serbia, Turkey, Sell Out After Mobilization." *BalkanInsight*. September 21, 2022. https://balkaninsight.com/.

Stokke, Espen and Eric Wieselhaus-Brahm. "Syrian Diaspora Mobilization: Vertical Coordination, Patronage Relations, and the Challenges of Fragmentation in the Pursuit of Transitional Justice." *Ethnic and Racial Studies* 42 no. 11 (2019): 1930–1949.

"Syrian Malware, the Ever Evolving Threat." Kaspersky Lab Global Research and Analysis Team. 2014. https://media.kasperskycontenthub.com/wp-con tent/uploads/sites/43/2018/03/08074802/KL_report_syrian_malware.pdf.

Szulecki, Kacper, Davide Bertelli, Marta Bivand Erdal, Anatolie Coșciug, Angelina Kussy, Gabriella Mikiewicz, and Corina Tulbure. "To Vote or Not To Vote? Migrant Electoral (Dis)engagement in an Enlarged Europe." *Migration Studies* 9 no. 3 (2021): 989–1010.

Tabar, P. "'Political Remittances': The Case of Lebanese Expatriates Voting in National Elections." *Journal of Intercultural Studies* 35 no. 4 (2014): 442–460.

Tapparova, Lilia. "Putin Is Doing Something Almost Nobody Is Noticing." *The New York Times.* September 23, 2024. https://nytimes.com/.

Tarrow, Sidney. *The New Transnational Activism.* New York: Cambridge University Press. 2005.

Taylor, J. E. "Undocumented Mexico-U.S. Migration and the Returns to Households in Rural Mexico." *American Journal of Agricultural Economics* 69 no. 3 (1987): 616–638.

Tertytchnaya, K., C. De Vries, H. Solaz, and D. Doyle. "When the Money Stops: Fluctuations in Financial Remittances and Incumbent Approval in Central Eastern Europe, the Caucasus and Central Asia." *American Political Science Review* 112 no. 4 (2018): 758–774.

Thielemann, E. "The Effectiveness of Governments' Attempts to Control Unwanted Migration." In *Immigration and the Transformation of Europe,* eds. C. A. Parsons and T. M. Smeeding, 442–472. Cambridge: Cambridge University Press. 2008.

Troianovski, Anton. "Putin Assails Russians Who Back the West, Signaling More Repression." *New York Times.* March 16, 2022. https://nytimes.com/.

Troianovski, Anton. "Spurred by Putin, Russians Turn on One Another Over the War." *New York Times.* April 10, 2022. https://nytimes.com/.

Tsourapas, Gerasimos. "Why do States Develop Multi-tier Emigrant Policies? Evidence from Egypt." *Journal of Ethnic and Migration Studies,* preprint (2015).

Tufekci, Z. *Twitter and Tear Gas: The Power and Fragility of Networked Protest.* New Haven, CT: Yale University Press. 2017.

Udesky, Laurie and Jack Leeming. "Exclusive: A Nature Analysis Signals the Beginnings of a US Science Brain Drain," *Nature,* April 22, 2025. Accessed via: https://nature.com/articles/d41586-025-01216-7.

van Buuren, Stef and Karin Groothuis-Oudshoorn. "Mice: Multivariate Imputation by Chained Equations in R." *Journal of Statistical Software* 45 no. 3 (2011): 1–67.

van Dalen, Hendrik P. and Kène Henkens. "Emigration Intentions: Mere Words or True Plans? Explaining International Migration Intentions and Behavior." Social Science Research Network. 2008.

Van Der Velde, M. and T. Van Naerssen. *Mobility and Migration Choices: Threshold to Crossing Borders.* London: Routledge. 2015.

Van Hear, Nicholas. *New Diasporas: The Mass Exodus, Dispersal and Regrouping of Migrant Communities.* London: UCL Press. 1998.

Van Hear, Nicholas. "Sustaining Societies Under Strain: Remittances as a Form of Transnational Exchange in Sri Lanka and Ghana." In *New Approaches to Migration? Transnational Communities and the Transformation of Home*, eds. Nadje al-Ali and Khalid Koser, 202–223. London: Routledge. 2002.

Van Hear, Nicholas and R. Cohen. "Diasporas in Conflict: Distance, Contiguity and Spheres of Engagement." *Oxford Development Studies* 45 no. 2 (2017): 171–184.

Vandor, Peter. "Are Voluntary International Migrants Self-selected for Entrepreneurship? An Analysis of Entrepreneurial Personality Traits." *Journal of World Business* 56 no. 2 (2021): 101142.

Vasovic, Aleksandar. "A Mini Russia Emerges in Serbia as Thousands Flee War." *Reuters*. September 10, 2024. https://reuters.com/.

Vertovec, Steven. "Trends and Impacts of Migrant Transnationalism." Centre on Migration, Policy and Society WP-04-03, Working Paper No. 3, University of Oxford. 2004.

Wahba, Jackline. "Return Migration and Economic Development." In *International Handbook on Migration and Economic Development*, ed. Robert E. B. Lucas, 327–349. Edward Elgar Publishing. 2014.

Wahba, Jackline. "The Economics of Return Migration." In *Handbook of Return Migration*, eds. Russell King and Katie Kuschminder, 24–37. Elgar Handbooks in Migration Series. Northampton: Edward Elgar Publishing. 2022.

Waldinger, Roger and David Fitzgerald. "Transnationalism in Question." *American Journal of Sociology* 109 no. 5 (2004): 1177–1195.

Wang, Quan-Jing, Gen-Fu Feng, Hai-Jie Wang, and Chun-Ping Chang. "The Impacts of Democracy on Innovation: Revisited Evidence." *Technovation* 108 (2021): 102333.

Wang, Vivian and Joy Dong. "Hong Kong Is Holding Elections. It Wants Them to Look Real." *New York Times*. September 24, 2021. https://nytimes.com/.

Ware, H. "Demography, Migration and Conflict in the Pacific." *Journal of Peace Research* 42 no. 4 (2005): 435–454.

Warin, Thierry and Pavel Svaton. "European Migration: Welfare Migration or Economic Migration." *Global Economy Journal* 8 no. 3 (2008): 1–30.

Wayland, Sarah. "Ethnonationalist Networks and Transnational Opportunities: The Sri Lankan Tamil Diaspora." *Review of International Studies* 30 no. 3 (2004): 405–426.

"'We Will Find You': A Global Look at How Governments Repress Nationals Abroad." Human Rights Watch. February 22, 2024. https://hrw.org/.

Weber, Max. *Economy and Society*, eds. Guenther Roth and Claus Wittich. Berkeley: University of California Press, 1968.

Wellman, Elizabeth Iams, Nathan W. Allen, and Benjamin Nyblade. "The Extraterritorial Voting Rights and Restrictions Dataset (1950–2020)." *Comparative Political Studies* 56 no. 6 (2023): 897–929.

White, A. and I. Grabowska. "Social Remittances and Social Change in Central and Eastern Europe: Embedding Migration in the Study of Society." *Central and Eastern European Migration Review* 8 no. 1 (2019): 33–50.

Winters, P., A. D. Janvry, and E. Sadoulet. "Family and Community Networks in Mexico-U.S. Migration." *Journal of Human Resources* 36 no. 1 (2001): 159–184.

Witze, Alexandra. "75% of US Scientists Who Answered Nature Poll Consider Leaving." *Nature*, March 27, 2025. https://nature.com/articles/d41586-025-00938-y.

Woodruff, C. and R. Zenteno. "Remittances and Microenterprises in Mexico." UCSD, Graduate School of International Relations and Pacific Studies Working Paper. 2021.

"World Population Prospects 2019." United Nations Department of Economic and Social Affairs Population Division. 2019. https://population.un.org/wpp/Publications/Files/WPP2019_Highlights.pdf.

Wright, M., M. Levy and J. Citrin. "Public Attitudes Toward Immigration Policy Across the Legal/Illegal Divide: The Role of Categorical and Attribute-Based Decision-Making." *Political Behavior* 38 (2016): 229–253.

Wrobel, Sharon. "War Spurs Brain Drain, Outflow of Israeli High-tech Employees, Report Finds," *The Times of Israel*, April 7, 2025. Accessed via: https://timesofisrael.com/war-spurs-brain-drain-outflow-of-israeli-high-tech-employees-report-finds/.

Yang, Dean and Claudia Martinez. "Home Areas: Evidence from the Philippines." In *International Migration, Remittances, and the Brain Drain*, eds. Çaglar Özden and Maurice W. Schiff, 81–122. Washington, DC, Basingstoke, and New York: The World Bank and Palgrave Macmillan. 2006.

Yiu, Cheng Yut. "State Media Calls on Hong Kong to Compensate for Tide of Emigration." *Radio Free Asia*. August 30, 2021. https://rfa.org/english/news/china/emigrate-08302021135106.html.

Ziblatt, Daniel. *Conservative Parties and the Birth of Democracy*. Cambridge: Cambridge University Press. 2017.

Index

240 *Index*

Printed by Integrated Books International,
United States of America